Lesbian and Gay Parenting

Also by Yvette Taylor

WORKING-CLASS LESBIAN LIFE: Classed Outsiders

Lesbian and Gay Parenting

Securing Social and Educational Capital

Yvette Taylor
Newcastle University, UK

First published 2009 by
PALGRAVE MACMILLAN

Palgrave Macmillan in the UK is an imprint of Macmillan Publishers Limited, registered in England, company number 785998, of Houndmills, Basingstoke, Hampshire RG21 6XS.

Palgrave Macmillan in the US is a division of St Martin's Press LLC, 175 Fifth Avenue, New York, NY 10010.

Palgrave Macmillan is the global academic imprint of the above companies and has companies and representatives throughout the world.

Palgrave® and Macmillan® are registered trademarks in the United States, the United Kingdom, Europe and other countries.

ISBN-13: 978–0–230–20272–6 hardback

This book is printed on paper suitable for recycling and made from fully managed and sustained forest sources. Logging, pulping and manufacturing processes are expected to conform to the environmental regulations of the country of origin.

A catalogue record for this book is available from the British Library.

Library of Congress Cataloging-in-Publication Data
Taylor, Yvette, 1978–
    Lesbian and gay parenting : securing social and educational capital / Yvette Taylor.
        p.   cm.
    Includes bibliographical references and index.
    ISBN 978–0–230–20272–6 (alk. paper)
    1. Gay parents.   2. Lesbian mothers.   3. Parenting—Social aspects.
    4. Children of gay parents.   I. Title.
    HQ75.27.T39 2009
    306.874086'64—dc22   2009013644

10   9   8   7   6   5   4   3   2   1
18   17   16   15   14   13   12   11   10   09

Printed and bound in Great Britain by
CPI Antony Rowe, Chippenham and Eastbourne

Contents

Acknowledgements

There are many people to thank here. First, thanks to those who participated in this project and made this book possible. This research was funded by The British Academy '*What Would the Parents Say? Gay Parents and Social Capital*' (2006–2008) and I thank them for their contribution.

Thanks to those who listened to changing thoughts and who were good and patient enough to read drafts: to Steph Lawler for her succinct advice on word-counting and manuscript length; hopefully, this piece is not 'still too long!'. To Jacqui Gabb who commented on very initial, straying ideas and who was good enough to offer encouragement and guidance. To Diane Richardson, and to Mark Casey and Cathrine Degnen for their readings and support throughout. Thanks to colleagues in Geography, Politics and Sociology at Newcastle University who have offered friendship over the years and special thanks to Michelle Addison who worked with me on the ESRC project '*From the Coal Face to the Car Park?: Intersections of Class and Gender in the North East*' (2007–2009). Thanks to Sally Hines for all the laughs at Newcastle – and beyond.

Introduction

This book explores intersections between class and sexuality in lesbians'
and gay men's experiences of parenting and the everyday practices and
pathways navigated therein, from initial routes into parenting and
household divisions of labour, to location preferences, schooling choice
and community supports. In a context of legal changes such as the
UK Civil Partnership Act (2004) and the 1996 US Defence of Marriage Act (DOMA), it seeks to situate parents as both sexual and classed
subjects, interrogating the relevance, transmission and accumulation
of class and sexual (dis)advantages. This research is situated between
unconnected and competing positions; frequently lesbian and gay families are positioned at the vanguard of transformations in intimacy
while often still empirically absent in such declarations: they are misplaced in this dual over-emphasis (as agents of social change) and
sidelining (under-investigated when compared to the research on heterosexual families). Although a now growing field, much current work
on lesbian and gay kinship still overlooks the significance of socio-
economic status (Weston, 1991; Bernstein and Reimann, 2001; Sullivan,
2001). Even where there has been attention to gendered dynamics
and constraints, class, as a crucial component of parental 'choice' and
experience, has been neglected (Gabb, 2004, 2005; Ryan-Flood, 2005;
Lindsay et al., 2006).

Based on US research, Agigian (2004) is somewhat unique in exploring
the intersection between sexuality, race and class in lesbian insemination, yet there remains much to be explored beyond the specificities
of routes into parenting. Agigian utilises a rather limited notion of
class, applying this solely to financial exclusion – this book seeks to
extend Agigian's analysis of class, functioning in and beyond routes to
parenthood, into continued interactions with social and educational
providers, across everyday parental terrain. Gabb (2001) and Dunne
(1997, 1998), for example, have explored the everyday practices of
lesbian mothers, including involvement in schooling, community networks, employment and leisure – however, I suggest these everyday
practices are very much classed (Taylor, 2007), posing the question
of just whose 'everyday' we are concerned with? In addressing the
significance of class to contemporary lesbian and gay parented families, this book hopes to illuminate how family practices, choices

and institutional (dis)engagements are mediated and shaped by classed dimensions.

The 'families of choice' literature continues to have widespread salience, framing much of the research on lesbian and gay parenting (Stacey, 2006). In their influential work, Weeks et al. (2001) explore experiences of self-invention and well-being amongst 'non-heterosexual' families (see also Weston, 1991; Dunne, 1997). Deploying the notion of 'social capital' they highlight strategies of networking and community building and the generation of self-consciously created communities whereby locally embedded constructions of capital compound familial resources. However, the overt optimism of their account glosses over potential exclusion and here I seek to inflect the discussion of choice with the constraints imposed by differing access to social capital.

As such, this research explores a range of topics, including routes to parenthood, geographies of inclusion and exclusion and the educational system. It seeks to bridge the gap between studies on the reproduction of class privileges in heterosexual families (Ball, 2003; Devine, 2004) against quite different, often un-classed, notions of social capital in lesbian and gay families. The theoretical opposition – and merging – of different uses of 'social capital' (Bourdieu, 1984; Weeks et al., 2001) is used to advance class conceptualisations and intersections, exploring too the ways that (middle) classed capitals sometimes do not pay off, as a result of occupying non-normative sexualities. In exploring the ways that class and sexuality frame possibilities and parameters, I ask if middle-class lesbian and gay parents seek to protect their children via greater choice over their educational and social environment: are they able to secure educational advantage in a context where their sexualities are formally marginalised and grounds for educational disaffection? Can such practices be said to constitute an effort to protect and replicate class privilege or simply 'make up' for a loss of educational and societal affirmation? Are working-class parents 'doubly disadvantaged' in such negotiations?

Stacey and Biblarz's (2001) classic article '(How) Does The Sexual Orientation of Parents Matter?' challenges the notion that children of lesbian and gay parents are at a higher risk for a variety of negative outcomes (e.g., educational failure), calling for a more sociologically informed critique, as opposed to endless psychological measures framed by a defensiveness, even necessity, in proving 'normal', 'safe' parenting. 'Diversity' is positively asserted, where the difference of lesbian and gay parents is politically, strategically declared *and* contested, as 'normal' outcomes and achievements are still questioned and measured. Stacey and Biblarz do, rather quickly, note that the degree of effort needed to negotiate such judgements in varied legal, medical and welfare contexts often means that only the most privileged groups are able to secure their rights. But the question remains as to when, to paraphrase, 'differences become deficits' – and the classed constructions and consequences of this in terms of parenting experiences and sexual citizenship more generally. In seeking to answer such questions, this book details the experiences and views of 60 white parents (46 lesbian mothers and 14 gay dads) from working-class and middle-class background across a range of localities in the United Kingdom, ranging in age from 18 to 63.

This first chapter 'The Straight and Narrow?' introduces key debates, disputes and cultural discourses around conceptualisations of 'the family', particularly in relation to the sidelining of lesbian and gay families, against the ongoing promotion of heterosexual, two-parented 'nuclear' families. It considers who has the 'choice to choose' beyond the straight and narrow, inflecting the 'families of choice' literature with a discussion of the significance of class in relation to the 'difference' of lesbian and gay parented families. Arguments about parental 'sameness' and 'difference' rarely consider the difference class makes in accessing, claiming and gaining a respectable 'ordinary' (homonormative) status. Claims upon and desires for 'ordinariness' feature in academic and everyday discourses, sometime circulated in unexpected places (Richardson, 2005).

For example, in the special 'Family Issue' (13 June 2007) of *Diva*, a UK lesbian lifestyle magazine, readers would perhaps be pressed to identify any difference between gay and straight families as the 'ordinary', 'same' signifiers of family life are displayed and discussed. Nonetheless, these 'ordinary' practices are as classed as they are sexualised; within the pages of the special issue, pointers are given on identifying 'England's most gay friendly school catchment areas' – these 'good' schools, set within 'good' areas, are implicitly classed in the coding of these as 'tolerant', 'resourced' and overall 'educated' spaces. Another classing of such descriptions is in the presumption of parental investment in consuming strategies of finding out the 'right' placement and, importantly, resourcing any relocation required to secure an acceptance. Claims to 'ordinariness' are complex, ever threatened by quite a different normative drive – the desire to prove and position (only) heterosexual families as proper and legitimate. Who can resource and achieve 'ordinariness' and how should these claims be understood?

Consider another example: the playful video *I've got you* by Black, female, gay US rapper, Mélange Lavonne, which represents some of the issues of raising children in LGBT (Lesbian, Gay, Bisexual, Transgender) households. The images and accompanying song depict the normal activities of childhood and parenting and we witness the not so unusual footage of children in play parks, held lovingly, if notably, between two mums. The song describes anticipated discrimination, to be dealt with and buffered by preparedness (such as education, which sets a 'good foundation'), maturity and financial investment. While an 'ordinariness' is undermined *and* mobilised throughout, responding to anticipated negative responses constructed through sexual, class and racial inequalities, there seems to be a tension in voicing defences and 'attacks' without re-invoking normative notions of what – or who – constitutes good or bad parents. This is heard in the call for some parents to rethink their parenting skills, placed in the context of crime, drug taking and parental disinterest, summarised in the defiant declaration that 'I'm not saying I might be a better parent than you, what I'm saying is that I *am* a better parent than you'. Again such claims, even if subversively and defiantly made, may also deploy and re-inscribe distinctions of value, worth and respectability. Of course, such examples also highlight increased visibility and presence, set against a more hostile, discriminatory and doubtful climate, witnessed in continued newspaper headlines such as 'Fathers are out of the picture as lesbians get IVF' (*Times*, 13 July 2006); '"Fathers not needed" as IVF for lesbians is approved' (*Daily Mail*, 12 July 2006); 'Anglicans back Catholics in gay adoption row' (*The Guardian*, 24 January 2007). The 'straight and narrow' version continues to circulate, where deviance is still projected onto – and responded in – lesbian and gay parenting narratives and experiences, even in the context of social, cultural and legal change.

Chapter 2 'Gay Parents, Games Lessons and Gambling with the Future' focuses upon the concept of social capital, combining a Bourdieusian notion of capital as specifically *classed*, alongside that developed by Weeks et al. (2001) in studying lesbian and gay 'families of choice'. An absence in charting new familial constructs and choices is the processes facilitating and inhibiting choice, in *materialising* connections: 'choice' does not exist as a free floating abstraction but rather is often a mobilisation and manifestation of classed resources. If social networks are at the base of new elective affinities, then it is important to establish what groups are affirmed through or denied such agentic capacities. Herein lies a contrast between the social capital positioned at the heart of lesbian and gay transformations in intimacy and quite different, classed and gendered notions of social capital, which centre the constraints in generating such a resource. Moreover, the different ways that differently classed, gendered and sexualised subjects generate, deploy and accumulate social capitals through relational links speak to intersectional processes of (de)legitimacy in doing and being family. Not all families, however broadly conceived, are recognised as flexibly and competently adapting to new conditions; instead they are positioned as simply making the wrong, irresponsible choices and connections. The last section in this chapter 'Complexities and complications: Researching class and sexuality' provides a methodological outline of the study and utilises two brief case studies in demonstration of classed and sexual complexity.

Chapter 3 'Ticking All the Wrong Boxes? Gay Parents and the (Im)possibility of Being Right' examines interviewees' routes into parenthood and the confirmations, denials and complications involved in achieving and affirming parental status. While lesbian and gay parents' 'creative' routes into parenting have been evidenced as innovative, even revolutionary, this perhaps sidelines more 'normative' pathways, as well as their disruptions and discontinuities (Weston, 1991; Stacey, 1996; Weeks et al., 2001; Agigian, 2004). The emotional, social and material resources and capitals which interviewees are able to draw upon to consolidate and affirm their sense of family are highlighted. The *choice* of family was not taken up, enacted or experienced equally and choices were often framed by both implicit and explicit classed 'costs' where parents were often materially and morally assessed. Both middle-class and working-class lesbian and gay parents face struggles in their routes into parenting, and in establishing solid, legitimate parental 'credentials' thereafter, ever threatened by, for example, the (un)known status of donors, legal and clinical costs, custody battles and through the general social disapproval in not being deemed 'fit for purpose'. While interviewees reported disagreements with (ex)partners, clinicians, social workers and medics, middle-class status could often, but not always, partially buffer and protect against these, 'ticking (almost) all the boxes' of parental approvals.

Continuing this theme, Chapter 4 'Family Fortunes' uncovers the resources and capitals necessary in 'doing things differently', in private and public settings. While the literature on lesbian and gay parents often centres creativity as facilitating a more equalised division of labour, here both working-class and middle-class interviewees experienced a myriad of limiting – and facilitating – factors in allowing and disallowing such practices. The financial and emotional aspects of parenting are investigated, including attention to when things 'go wrong' as well as when things 'go right', exploring the ways that respondents 'do' family in terms of financing parenting, coping with and sharing caring.

Chapter 5 'Mixed Signals at the School Crossing' investigates the relevance of class and sexuality in parental choices and interventions in children's education. From accessing the 'right' school to having no choice but the 'wrong' school, from the fostering and creation of suitable networks and knowledges to the limitation, exclusion and drawing back from such practices, both class and sexuality are relevant in the confidences, resources and entitlements, enacted educationally. Both are intertwined in the construction of positive 'difference' and 'added value' where, for middle-class parents, difference is claimed and put to use, educationally and socially. Access to social and economic capital, including the knowledge mobilised and the manoeuvring of finances, affected school choices and experiences.

Chapter 6 'Privileged Locations? Sexuality, Class and Geography' explores the desire for and construction of 'good' parental space, investigating notions of a constructive, enhancing, educational 'mix', following on from discussion in Chapter 5. The negotiation of everyday space is often difficult for lesbian and gay parents across the class spectrum. That said, many middle-class parents articulated a desire for a 'good mix' in their immediate localities and neighbourhoods. The ability to occupy correctly 'mixed' space is a classed process, where a 'mixed' terrain, as opposed to a homogeneous middle-class setting – or an excessively working-class setting – was considered beneficial, even necessary, in accommodating and facilitating belonging, affinity and a sense of affirmation.

Chapter 7 'Just Cause or Impediment? Costs of Civic Acceptance' explores the uptake, negotiation and refusal of civil partnerships, where such legal consolidation may be seen as actively materialising family, making that which was sidelined and under-valued included and recognised. Legislative changes enforce a reconsideration of family, especially for lesbian and gay families who are faced again with naming, creating and challenging, with the weight of success (anticipated by supporters) and the burden of failure (endlessly declared by the less enthused). Such negotiations are indeed complex, as lesbian and gay families seek to survive and thrive, and indeed capitalise on such legislative changes. Herein lies a consequential classed difference between those who can afford to conceptualise such changes as beneficial – particularly in relation to finances, but also in relation to social status, respectability and esteem – and those who cannot: to have a new currency is a mobilisation and mainstreaming of class privilege, as it is of sexual status. Overall then, the purpose is to chart intersections between class and sexuality in lesbians' and gay men's experiences of parenting.

1
The Straight and Narrow?

This chapter introduces key debates, disputes and cultural discourses around conceptualisations of 'the family', particularly in relation to the sidelining and disapproval of lesbian and gay families, against the ongoing promotion of heterosexual, two-parented 'nuclear' families ('Familial re-runs'). To some extent the transformation – and continuation – of such debates involves the marking of familial territory beyond 'the straight and narrow', even as this descriptor still highlights the endorsement of heteronormative, classed configurations of parenting. Many authors propose that 'family' is no longer what it once was, being freed from traditional ties including gendered obligations and biological (im)possibilities. Such 'freedoms' are relatedly conceptualised as offering new choices but also new 'risks', where 'what to do' in relation to familial hopes, formations and responsibilities are no longer straightforward. Instead these are to be negotiated, disrupted and even facilitated, through reproductive technologies, social networks ('families of choice') and legislative changes. Who then has the choice to choose 'brave new families' – and who will be recognised as legitimate agentic subjects, paving new familial paths, reflexively relating in conditions of 'postmodern perplexity'? If once taken-for-granted assumptions are being disputed, they are also, however, being re-confirmed, even as legislative changes providing same-sex rights proliferate internationally ('Different conceptions, same contradictions?').

This chapter considers who has the 'choice to choose', inflecting the 'families of choice' literature with a discussion of the significance of class in relation to the 'difference' of lesbian and gay parented families. Arguments about parental 'sameness' and 'difference' rarely consider the difference class makes in accessing, claiming and gaining a respectable 'ordinary' (homonormative) status. Similarly, the central

1

focus on lesbian and gay parents' routes into parenthood often centres reflexive, creative choices, effacing the classed routes into and experiences of 'alternative' parenting ('The best laid plans...'). This chapter is structured into three sections: 'Familial re-runs'; 'Different conceptions, same contradictions?'; 'The best laid plans...'. Chapter 2 'Gay Parents, Games Lessons and Gambling with the Future' will focus upon the concept of social capital, combining a Bourdieusian notion of capital as specifically *classed*, alongside that developed by Weeks et al. (2001) in studying lesbian and gay 'families of choice'. Where class and sexuality have often been separated, charting their intersection can be both complex and complicated, frequently drawing upon disparate bodies of research and disconnected projects. These initial two chapters hopefully identify gaps and connections, seeking to go beyond the straight and narrow in conceiving class and sexuality as entwined in lesbian and gay parenting experiences.

Familial re-runs

This section explores the continuities and changes in family formations, where the contemporary plurality of families is variously conceived, from pessimistic views which denounce the end of family, to more optimistic views which credit family changes with a positive, even revolutionary potential. In attempting to trouble such dichotomised stances it asks who, in classed and sexual terms, is likely to be positioned as succeeding or failing family conventions *and* changes. I explore the 'individualisation thesis' where individuals are positioned as necessarily reflexive actors, compelled to choose and create in risky, uncertain times. Here, lesbian and gay families are frequently positioned as postmodern pioneers, paving brave new paths through such perplexity. This is queried as positioning certain classed subjects as simply failing to capitalise on beneficial 'reflexive relations'.

Definitions and disruptions

The shape and form of 'the family' continues to be debated internationally in academic and everyday discourses, whether that be in policies which legitimise 'new' family formations through the rights of lesbians and gay men to marry, adopt and access new reproductive technologies, or in measures which supposedly alleviate the gendered burden of combining employment and care (Weston, 1991; Jamieson, 1998; Bernstein and Reimann, 2001; Weeks et al., 2001). Demographic figures provide an administrative gauge on what families are and the ways that they are changing. Such technical facts, however, do not in themselves answer the social issues of family formation, and the socially constructed nature of families beyond biological 'facts' (Edwards et al., 2006). The traditional view that 'blood is thicker than water', that family ties are obvious, inherent, genetic and more binding than friendship ties is contested by many studies which highlight social bases underpinning relationships (Weston, 1991; Nardi, 1999; Pahl, 2002). The Cosby Show family of today must encompass more than simply siblings and cousins.

Yet the family is still variously represented as a unit in crisis, a gloomy portrayal, shoring up the decline of somewhat mythical and romanticised familial ties, as against the rise of individualism, single-hood and 'selfish' childless, career-orientated women. If these accounts are to be believed, it would seem that whole sections of society are turning their backs on 'family values', preferring instead to while away their hours working, reading about celebrities and periodically binge drinking with like-minded deviants. Unpacking the cyclical re-runs in family re-visitations, Gillies (2003) demonstrates the three main perspectives on understanding contemporary personal relationships: those who emphasise the breakdown of family life, offering a pessimistic analysis whereby we seem to be ever-heading towards a state of crisis; those who instead emphasise the increasing diversity and plurality of lifestyles; and a third position which is sceptical of the extent of change, either positively or negatively conceived, and instead emphasises the continuity of family structures, and their ongoing relation to gender, class and sexuality. Here, there is often a more explicit realisation that pessimistic and optimistic notions of familial change and continuation rest upon what is seen as relevant, threatening or enhancing – positions which are inevitably always political. First gear, reverse or neutral, it would seem to depend on whose hand is on the gear stick.

Yet the last more nuanced in-between approach is often effaced in dichotomised ideological stances. Theories around 'the family' include early functionalist accounts that actively sanctioned and promoted 'nuclear' family living, assuming a male 'head of household' and a female caregiver, as socially beneficial: mother, father, tea on the table, dog underneath. What could be better? The 'functioning' 'nuclear' family perhaps always worked more as an ideal, rather than as a reality, obscuring the diversity of 'past' family existence (Adam, 1996; Gillies, 2003, 2006). Jamieson (1998) argues that contemporary theories of current transformations in family life (Giddens, 1992) and intimacy more generally are modelled on a historical narrative structure deploying a threefold periodisation: 'pre-modern', 'modern' and 'post-modern', referring to pre-industrial, industrial and contemporary (post-industrial) periods (Stacey, 1996; Klesse, 2007). Yet, focusing on continuities and specificities across time perhaps offers a more complex understanding of the shifting and continued terrain of family changes, rather than a completed (either optimistic or pessimistic) 'before' and 'after'. It is doubtful that 'the family' woke up one day and, realising that it was now post-industrial, decided upon a complete spring clean of ways of being.

Nonetheless, repeated concerns are aired over which types of relationships can and should be described as family, which are normal, which are out of the ordinary? Which ought to receive social approval, legitimation and state support? (Beck-Gernsheim, 2002). If I use the term, does that make it so? Within such inclusions and exclusions, lesbian and gay parented families often cannot fit seamlessly into the story of a traditional nuclear (heterosexual) family, as a straightforward 'success'. Indeed, they often continue to be viewed as somehow outwith and beyond such dynamics or, more dangerously, as menaces and threats to *the* family, which depends upon and upholds a very straight and narrow definition: 'The plausibility of the contention that gay people pose a threat to "the family"…depends upon a view of family grounded in heterosexist relations, combined with the conviction that gay men and lesbians are incapable of procreation, parenting and establishing kinship ties' (Weston, 1991: 25). It would seem that some things are just too oppositional to sit well together.

Conflict comes from varied corners, and many authors, discussing different international context, have explored the resurgence of Christian right-wing discourses in, for example, the United States and the United Kingdom, where the 'homosexual' is represented as a threat to 'normal' family relations (Smith, 1994; Herman, 1997; Durham, 2000; Naples, 2004, 2007; Stein, 2005; Acosta, 2007). The conjuring up of 'real', 'chosen', 'pretend' families endlessly occurs, from political and media discourses over the repeal of Section 28[1] and the Civil Partnership Act (2004) in the United Kingdom, to the 1996 US Defence of Marriage Act (DOMA), which re-affirms the definition of marriage as between a woman and a man (Hicks, 2005).[2] However, who get constituted as a 'real', 'pretend' or 'failing' also rests upon other, intersecting hierarchies, where 'pious family-values rhetoric' endangers the rights and interests of varied disadvantaged groups including poor single-mothers as well as lesbians and gays (Stacey, 1996).

Nevertheless, there has been a growth of confidence and visibility in the United States, the United Kingdom and beyond, inspiring a claiming of rights even as these have been accompanied by a strong assertion of traditional 'family values'; often victories remain somewhat problematic, both in terms of their legislative framing and substantive effects (Cooper and Herman, 1995; Wilson, 2007). Yet, following such gains, much has been said of the move away from the family as a repressive site, where lesbians and gays seek to escape its injustices, towards an active uptake of family, including its blessings and privileges (Weston, 1991; Stacey, 1996; Bernstein and Reimann, 2001; Sullivan, 2001). Within a brave new world, family can be something to move towards rather than pull away from.

The choice to choose?

The *rules* of the family, as conforming to a traditional nuclear heterosexual ideal, are seen to 'no longer apply', with flexibility and adaption evident as people begin to live in productive tension with new ways of living and working, rather than adhering to the rules and pathways of guiding frameworks and structures (Beck-Gernsheim, 2002; Edwards et al., 2006). As individualised subjects we are positioned as having 'no choice but to choose', to manage our own paths: everything changes and the family is no exception. Perhaps it is because of its closeness that it is easy to overlook the array of variety, compounds and change that is ever on-going, with the potential to re-draw old lines with a slightly less clear hand. For example, medical technology currently provides opportunities to create families beyond heterosexual reproduction, yet access to this is far from straightforward and its existence leads to questions over entitlements, finances and responsibilities, returning us again to notions of (im)proper families: '...should the possibilities of artificial insemination be open only to married women, on the grounds that marriage still offers the best protection to the child's welfare? Or should they be available to anyone who so wishes – including unmarried and homosexual couples or women without a partner – on the grounds that the child's need will be for care and affection, not an official rubber stamp?' (Beck-Gernsheim, 2002: 7). Questioning the ethical and financial boundaries of access and entitlement highlights potential conflicts and controversies in accessing new opportunities, pointing also to the official 'rubber stamp' of state (de)legitimation.

Beck-Gernsheim's (2002) 'individualisation thesis' presents an age of modernity bringing with it new risks and opportunities; actors are viewed as liberated from convention, with increasing self-reflexivity leading to a 'democratisation of personhood' (Skolnick, 1992). Life then becomes a 'building site', a do-it-yourself approach, where normative biographies are displaced by creativities and possibilities, colourful networks and complex genealogies, where the extended family is a tangible reality in most people's lives: 'Do-it-yourself biographies have been given (albeit unintentional) support by welfare states by the provision of minimum incomes for households which do not correspond to those of the traditional family, thus making alternative lifestyles economically possible' (Weeks et al., 2001: 181). In contrast, Gillies (2006) details the role of the welfare state as a disciplining, regulatory force, making some 'choices' simply impossible, begging the question of who is excluded from this picture of change? If people are searching for 'new ways of living' what hopes, and failures, are associated with the search – what subjective and material possibilities and impossibilities are relevant and, ultimately, who gets lost in this sweep of change, in the relegation of what has 'past'?

Conveying an optimistic portrayal of family re-constitutions, Giddens' (1992) notion of the 'pure relationship' depicts relationships as entered into and exited from for their own sake, free of the constraints of obligation and traditional ties. Problematically, he claims that lesbians most typically achieve the 'pure relationship' exemplifying new forms of intimacy. The 'pure relationship' can be terminated at will by any participant at any point and in such circumstances family may be seen to mirror friendship, blurring the lines between the voluntary and the obligatory. However, notions of choice found in the expanding literature are often under-theorised, where choice is positioned solely in terms of individual lifestyle (Wilson, 2007); when choice is foregrounded various impossibilities are sidelined. Further, 'choice' can invoke hostile responses towards poor decision makers – 'if only they made the *right* choices'. Nevertheless, an increasingly common phrase that points to more fluid family compositions is that of 'families of choice', first used by Weston (1991) and continued thereafter in much empirically grounded research on lesbian and gay parenting and kinship (Nardi, 1999; Weeks et al., 2001). That said, Weston also frames choice as a 'bourgeois notion that focuses on the subjective power of an "I" to formulate relationships to people and things, untrammelled by worldly constraints' (1991: 110–111). This alludes to the complexities of resourcing choice via socio-economic positioning, a point central to much feminist research (Jamieson, 1998).

Exploring the experiences of alternative families, using in-depth interviews with 96 self-identified non-heterosexuals in the United Kingdom, Weeks et al. (2001) suggest that doing family arises from a new confidence, embodying a hankering for the family, as well as an ability to now 'do things differently'. But there may well be painful as well as positive instigators of family transformations, with familial rejection necessitating the formation of alternative support structures and classed resources both enabling and curtailing their realisation. And however free we may be to choose our own family, it is unlikely that we were able to choose the family from which we originated; here several authors have cited the endurance of biological family as 'real' family, even for lesbian and gay interviewees (Lewin, 1993; Gabb, 2004). Such cited 'contradictions' make for perplexing reading, apparent in accounts of 'postmodern families', which lesbian and gay parented families are regularly positioned as part of.

Postmodern perplexity

Although charting the continued promotion of *the* family as a sacred ideal – generating attacks on 'unfit mothers' in US and UK welfare policy and media representations (Lawler, 2000; Reese, 2005; Gillies, 2006) – Stacey (1996) argues that these are manifestations of the changes forced by 'postmodern families'. The pull of the 'past' results in a lurch between postmodern uncertainty and nostalgic familiarity. Lesbian and gay parented families are seen to offer a distinctive challenge to and de-centring of the heterosexual nuclear family, serving as a 'lightening rod' for cultural anxieties about family change. In her account 'postmodern families' are both threatening and daring, yet a positive framing of family change is preferred, as offering increased democratisation, equality and choice in intimacy. Stacey (1996) neatly demonstrates the relationship between family politics and the politics of gender, race, sexuality and welfare, and while this would suggest a stronger positioning of the structural and institutional elements (in)validating certain families, the (optimistic and hopeful) move to name families as 'postmodern' perhaps erases such a focus: not all families have experienced 'change' equally and not all changes are recognised and validated.

Significantly, most studies of lesbian motherhood predominantly sample white, middle-class, educated professional women (Hare and Richards, 1993; Lewin, 1993; Wright, 1998; Dalton and Bielby, 2000; Dunne, 2000; Hequembourg, 2004; Ryan-Flood, 2005), where the majority of research on lesbian parents also comes from North America and the United Kingdom. There are benefits in separate explorations of different kinds of lesbian parent families: 'Lesbian are often theorised from their vantage point as the Other, rather than critically examined in terms of their situatedness along other axes of identity, for example as members of national and ethnic collectivities and in terms of socio-economic background and resources' (Ryan-Flood, 2005: 190; see also Almack, 2007).

Theoretically and empirically, then, concepts of diversification and democratisation, embedded in postmodernisation theories, have been interrogated and their respective 'pioneers' revealed as somewhat misguided, if not lost (Wilson, 2007). While gay men and lesbians have been absent from such theories, Klesse argues they are often attributed a strangely privileged position in the ones that include them in the analysis. They are frequently represented as the pioneers of intimate and sexual democratisation, where such absence (empirically) and privileging (theoretically) has resulted in same-sex relations gaining an 'awkward popularity in the literature on... families' (Klesse, 2007: 63). In seeking to avoid 'crude misrepresentation' Klesse advises an urgent engagement in sociological perspectives that '... can capture the complexities and subtleties of the "interlocking system of oppression" around, for example, gender, sexuality, race and class in people's intimate and sexual lives' (Klesse, 2007: 72). Instead, structural inequalities are often downplayed by supposing an economically efficient, autonomous and 'properly' individualised subject. Choice would be all well and good, if only it would realise its postmodern responsibility to be ever available.

Reports of transformations in intimacy may be contrasted with the perpetual dominance of heterosexuality as a disguised and 'neutral' identity and practice, yet one which potentially consolidates gender inequalities and structures 'other' outsider sexualities by their distance from its normative position. Different family formations and practices are still not equally validated and notions of choice and transformation sit uncomfortably with continued forms of de-legitimation, where only specifically classed subjects are recognised as autonomous, responsible actors, as good reflexive choosers.

Reflexive relations

In exploring the experiences of 'marginalised mothers' in the United Kingdom, Gillies (2006) forces a consideration of class changes – and continuations – in light of increasing discourses of individualisation; how do these 'changes' offer new opportunities, or limit possibilities, re-cycling 'old' inequalities in new guises? The applicability of notions of individualised responsible 'risk' takers undertaking new challenges in a post-industrial landscape is queried as reliant upon an agentic middle-class capacity, able to legitimately present and practice 'family': 'There is strikingly little recognition that the individualised, agentic self theorised by the Becks and Giddens and valorised in UK government policies requires access to middle-class economic, cultural, social and emotional capital' (Gillies, 2006: 76). The classing of such (non)individualised subjects is clear when considering who can and cannot present as properly able to partake of new opportunities and excel in the challenges of post-industrial family life.

For Gillies, like many others, such 'changes' represent a continuation – even heightening – of class inequalities, in relation to family constructions and experiences, where 'individualisation' and 'mobility' are overplayed effacing structural inequalities, particularly those of class and gender (Skeggs, 1997; Reese, 2005).

This can be witnessed in contemporary UK and US discourses and policies which have re-focused attention on the *wrong* sort of mothers, who are then positioned as the embodiment of sexual excess and associated with a range of 'failed' outcomes, socially, economically, educationally and politically (Lawler, 2000; Kefalas, 2003; Skeggs, 2004). Such 'bad mothers' are represented as ignorant, a threat to economic progress and a drain on the state; these are not the postmodern pioneers evident in other representations but are instead 'misrepresented, disrespected and scapegoated' firmly located in the 'centre at society's ills' (Gillies, 2006). Choice is all well and good, but for every positive there must be a negative, for every vibrant cowboy riding out into the new frontier there must be somebody who can't afford the horse, somebody who is letting the side down.

In the United Kingdom changing political stances, from Conservatives' 'Back to Basics' to New Labour's 'third way', have resulted in a contradictory 'tolerance' of some diversity, '... expressed through an endorsement of heterosexual marriage as an ideal, within an overall rhetoric of progressive liberalism and acceptance of other family forms' alongside an abhorrence of the 'irresponsible', who cannot be included as conscientious 'diverse' citizens (Gillies, 2003: 12). Those focusing on sexual citizenship have pointed to the increased privatisation of such struggles, fostering a more personal politics where families are again placed as individually responsible. Within the responsibilising politics of 'fitting-in' working-class individuals are often sidelined as the unacceptable margin, expelled from mainstream movements and unable to be recuperated as 'homonormative' subjects (Binnie, 2004; Naples, 2007).

Different conceptions, same contradictions?

This section considers the struggle for sexual citizenship. While parenting is distinct from issues of partnering they are clearly related, not least in the ways that such related policies themselves *materialise* families, offering new possibilities for societal recognition, legal recourse and access to welfare services. Focusing on sexual citizenship as it relates to lesbian and gay parents inevitably leads to a re-visitation of issues of 'sameness'/'difference', which have dominated debates on lesbian and gay parented families, highlighting who gets included, even incorporated into the good citizen/family, and who remains excluded.

Increasingly, commentators are denouncing this tired binary, pointing to the awkward 'in-betweenness' in desiring citizenship, difference and even ordinariness and a degree of belonging. This framing may well be useful in highlighting the tensions, contradictions and intersections between class and sexuality in materialising the family – in confirming or negating inclusions on practical and symbolic levels. Assertions of lesbian and gay 'sameness'/'difference' have perhaps been motivated by a refusal of failure and by a political desire to 'do things differently'. But when it is (im)possible to do things 'differently' and how do these 'differences' get claimed, recognised and legitimised? Where rights are claimed on the basis of respectability, functionality and conventionality a classed binary of the good/bad (sexual) citizen is frequently re-mobilised.

The unalienable rights of the sexual citizen – Life, liberty and the pursuit of happiness (Except if you're working class)

There has been increasing international legal recognition of same-sex relationships with commentaries and controversies born out of the celebration of (monogamous) coupledom extended to same-sex partners, albeit, those who conform to a perceived tolerable and respectable ideal way (Richardson, 2004; Meeks and Stein, 2006). Along with the expected outrage from various evangelical Christian groups, aghast at the appropriation of a sacred convention, there has also been opposition from those who believe that gays and lesbians have no place within an institution (even as a facsimile of an institution), which is seen as reinforcing firmly conservative, heteronormative family values. Questions around the propriety of gays and lesbians engaging in such non-deviant practices have created a number of thought-provoking stances. Within this collage of intellectual debate the issue of class has been somewhat ignored.

Plummer (1995) uses the term 'intimate citizenship' to describe how political claims have been made through the articulation of personal and sexual narratives, shaping new public repertoires around which communities mobilise but it would seem clear that narratives are themselves not immune from either judging or being judged appropriate. Citizenship discourses inevitably 'reveal intricate interconnections of class, race, nationality, gender – and sexuality' (Weeks et al., 2001: 196), and Cahill demonstrates such interconnection in the positioning of poor single-mothers and same-sex couples as overly threatening: 'Since the mid 1990s political and religious conservatives and reactionaries have constructed two seemingly contradictory threats to the American body politic: poor, presumably heterosexual, single mothers who fail to marry, and same-sex couples, presumed to be economically privileged, who seek to marry' (2005: 169).

Also writing about the North American context Phelan (2001), like Naples (2007), argues for an intersectional approach to citizenship, where queering citizenship, then, must mean more than citizenship for queers: 'The persistent intertwinement of gender, race, and sexuality in modern America, and the extensively documented relations between each of these and citizenship and kinship, make clear that citizenship cannot be queered without confronting the structures of gender and race through which it is constructed...' (Phelan in Naples, 2007: 13).

Far from 'queering' citizenship, the fight for equal rights can in fact uphold rather normative frameworks (Richardson, 2004). Sullivan (1995), for example, claims that the mainstreaming and extension of marriage to lesbians and gains would 'normalise' lesbian and gay relations and will thus solve the *all* political concern: 'If nothing else were done at all, and gay marriage were legalized, ninety percent of the political work necessary to achieve gay and lesbian equality would have been achieved. It is ultimately the only reform that truly matters' (quoted in Hull, 2006: 81). Equality and marriage, horse and carriage. In a rather different vein to Sullivan, but still echoing the pull of being 'properly' included in the mainstream, Agigian claims that changing rights to 'marry' '...would solve many legal problems of lesbian AI [assisted insemination] in one fell swoop' (2004: 142). Claims are also (re)made on marriage as a bedrock offering material and emotional stability to its members, judged in the 'best interests' of children. Nonetheless, same-sex marriage may offer the most appeal, acceptance and assets to those already closest to the mainstream. What is good for the goose may not be of help to the marginalised gander.

Practicalities and promises

The invisibility of same-sex couples within the context of means tested benefits was historically something of an in-joke: while indignation could be expressed about bureaucratic discrimination, at the same time it was quite good to 'get one back' on the system by being exempt from dual income means testing. For once there was an economic benefit to be had, and a moment of smugness. The inclusion of same-sex couples in means testing negates this exemption, forcing benefit claimants to 'come out' on paper. Civil partnerships include the duty to provide reasonable maintenance for a civil partner, the duty to provide for children and assessment for child support purposes. 'Only fair', some cry, 'if they want equality then they have to take the heterosexual rough with the smooth', but the removal of this differentiation has different implications for different people. These negotiations are not novel or new, they pre-date varied sexual citizenship legislation and will be around long after this has developed and mutated. What is different and novel is the ways that legislation has served to foreground same-sex relationships within the context of straight ones, to compare and contrast and by doing so subject them to a more rigorous scrutiny, classed or otherwise.

There are practical benefits to be accrued in increasing legal entitlements, offering a material and symbolic validation of partnering and parenting. In the US context the 1049 protections and benefits extended to married couples under federal law is commonly cited as a reason for same-sex marriage: 'Since more than one thousand benefits accrue to couples through marriage, the economic benefits are sizeable. Same-sex marriage would diminish the cost of legal paperwork that lesbians and gay men must complete to protect themselves and their children (Chambers, 2001, in Naples, 2004: 680). Endorsing civil partnerships and same-sex marriages via anticipated benefits surely diminishes when these remain minimal or non-existent, as Weston suggests: 'The value of domestic partnership lessens dramatically when nobody in the corporation receives a pension or health benefits' (1991: xix). Of course, value can be measured beyond monetary terms alone but others remain sceptical about steadfastly aligning economic benefits with such inclusions, undoubtedly affecting perceptions and ability to 'belong' more generally.

Moving the debate on the meanings of same-sex marriage from the theoretical to the empirical level, Shipman and Smart (2007) explore the reasons why same-sex couples in the United Kingdom have commitment ceremonies and what meanings such ceremonies might have in legitimating same-sex relationships in the eyes of their (heterosexual) families and in wider society. Hull (2006) also notes that in the raging controversies and widespread media coverage in the United States and beyond, the voices of ordinary same-sex couples are sometimes difficult to hear. As such, Hull interrogates the ways individuals interact with and utilise the law, claiming that the pursuit of same-sex inclusion offers a profound threat to legal institutions and to society more generally where meanings and boundaries are 'up for grabs'. Institutional possibilities – and constraints – are important in everyday negotiations and Hull forces a consideration of the 'practicalities' and 'promises' in doing and being family, as sanctioned in changing legal contexts (see also Lewin, 1998).

Drawing upon Bourdieu's notions of symbolic power held by and conferred through the legal system, Hull makes a case for the importance of a symbolic sense of inclusion, through recognition and affirmation: 'Law is the quintessential form of the symbolic power of naming that creates the things named, and creates social groups in particular' (Bourdieu, 1987, in Hull, 2006: 116). What Hull (2006) has sidelined, however, is the connected Bourdieusian sentiment that only those with recognised social, economic and cultural capitals can achieve standing as legitimate subjects, in effect, a 'symbolic capital'. It is not enough to recognise the power and significance of the law in itself but rather, holding true to Hull's (2006) desired attention to real life effects, the question arises as to who may still be disqualified in inclusive moments: what resources are required to engage and be recognised?

Legal recognition was desired by Hull's interviewees, given legal and financial benefits and the symbolic recognition of 'full equality', of being socially 'normal' (see Lewin, 1998). The 'ordinariness' of such ceremonies sits alongside another normative notion, that of the 'right thing to do' and the right time to do this, intersecting with classed and gendered (im)mobilities. Hull's respondents situated themselves in 'life stages', where personal life trajectories were measured in traditions, in realisations, in imaginings and in projected futures. Same-sex marriages were often seen as a consolidation of 'ordinary' trajectories, as making 'good sense', given achievements in educational, employment and familial realms. Empirical accounts, such as Hull's (2006) and Shipman and Smart's (2007), highlight the intersection of the symbolic, material and cultural dimensions of official endorsements in partnering and parenting. These deserve further scrutiny where '[t]he making of citizens has become privatised as never before, subcontracted to families without means to make a go of it' (Meeks and Stein, 2006; Phelan in Naples, 2007: 10).

Official endorsements

Developments in sexual citizenship only extend to *certain* citizens and may in fact cement exclusions, renewing and heightening boundaries of (un)acceptability between the 'dangerous queer' and the 'good homosexual', who preferably resides in a 'gay nuclear family', living a 'homonormative' lifestyle (Duggan, 2002). Such distinctions press at whether citizenship struggles inevitably constitute an impossible bid for respectability or a realistic claim on being and becoming 'normal'. Writing before the introduction of the UK Civil Partnership, Weeks et al. (2001) note that none of their respondents wanted to 'mirror' heterosexual coupledom, or establish a new norm of couple commitment that created new divisions within the non-heterosexual world. However, often regardless of such articulated desires, social forces can conspire to re-draw and re-establish punitive distinctions of worth, decency and respectability, simultaneously incorporating homonormative subjects and expelling others (Berlant, 1997). If one size is to fit all, and that size is 'the happy couple' then it could be difficult times ahead for those who can't or won't fit in.

Perhaps challenging notions of a sweeping 'homonormativity', lesbian and gay movements may at once involve both assimilation and transformation, oscillating between a 'moment of transgression' and a 'moment of citizenship' (Weeks, 1995). Many see the dualism between assimilation and transformation as a false one, setting up a weighty expectation of revolutionary potential as against stagnant failure (Meeks and Stein, 2006; O'Brien, 2007). There are tensions and complexities in establishing ways of belonging within heteronormative frameworks and such tensions displace the binary of assimilation/transformation stances and the notion of 'model' and 'paradigm' which they imply (Weston, 1991; Ahmed, 2004). Lesbians and gay men continue to be positioned as threats to the sanctity of the heterosexual order and must complexly situate their citizenship struggles within this positioning (Bernstein and Reimann, 2001). Such a fraught negotiation involves striving to become part of mainstream *and* self-positioning as different. Where real life intentions of same-sex couples have been highlighted marriage is seen as dynamic and changing, exceeding a simple positioning as assimilatory (Meeks and Stein, 2006). Within this, there are justifiable and pragmatic reasons why lesbians and gay men invoke 'ordinariness', claiming to be 'the family next door'.

In invoking radical *and* assimilatory stances lesbian and gay parents are seen to 'have their cake and eat it'; Clarke (2001a,b) reasons that such a strategy involves both satisfied appetites and room for more. Like Weeks et al. (2001), Clarke is attentive to the socio-historical circumstances allowing for and necessitating such a critique. Researchers in lesbian and gay studies are now not writing in the context of silence and invisibility, where critical stances may well be possible only because

'…a literature in lesbian and gay parenting already exists (that can be bought in defence of parents)' (2001: 38). Nonetheless, although useful and indeed necessary at times (if strategically so), normalising discourses can only ever be responsive to a mainstreaming agenda. Normalising discourses are ever reliant on 'measuring up', in proving ordinariness, which then re-invokes problematic binaries around good and bad citizens: 'Normalising lesbian and gay parenting regularly results in the silencing of difference and diversity among lesbian and gay parents, especially those parents who fall short of the image of acceptable middle class whiteness that is often projected in an effort to achieve (mainstream) acceptability' (Gamson, 1998, in Clarke, 2001b: 40).

Measuring up? Being ordinary

In focusing on the mundane everyday aspects of family life, lesbian and gay parented families may make themselves recognisable as similar to heterosexual families (Gabb, 2004; Hequembourg, 2004), which then dissipates the anticipated *wrong* kind of difference linked with the unknown, dangerous, other 'gay lifestyle': 'The "ordinariness" strategy… propounds that lesbian and gay parents help their children with their homework, do the dishes, go shopping, make packed lunches, argue about their children's bed time – all recognisable components of normal family life' (Clarke, 2001: 5). The establishment of common familial ground, where gays are typically positioned as only sexual, may well force the straight viewer into seeing commonalities, recognising too the 'normal' symbols of home and everyday practices that carry kinship connotations (Weston, 1991). It would seem that it is the 'dullness' of life which creates communalities and builds good, straight bridges. The grey light overshadows the pink and bathes all good parents in its glow.

However, in contrast, Dunne emphasises the radical potential of lesbian parenting, 'celebrating differences rather than defensively denying them' and ends with a pronounced 'dare to be different' (2001: 7). Again, the difficulty in negotiating sameness/difference in relation to parenting practices and expectations is further complicated by Gabb's (2001) analysis that, unlike Dunne's (1997) and Weeks et al.'s (2001) respondents, her interviewees were concerned with their 'ordinariness'. Lesbian mothers spoke of just being 'ordinary' like hetero families, and spoke of difference as something 'real' (radical, politicised) lesbians do (see also Almack, 2007). Gabb's research into lesbian parented families suggests that 'doing things differently' is not experienced on a wholesale basis: 'In fact nearly all of my respondents queried whether this type of family was more "community myth" than reality' (2001: 318). This raises questions about the worth in centring radical potentiality, absent from 'real life' scenarios, as something only for the truly 'real' or 'radical'. Yet, even with the desire to be 'like other families' lesbian and gay parented families are likely to experience moments when they are made to feel different – different by design, deliberation or discrimination.

Sullivan (1995) argues that most gays want to be 'normal' and those who do not are giving the 'virtually normal' cohorts a bad name. Yet this normality may only be available to 'but for' lesbians; those who resemble their idealised, white middle-class heterosexual counterparts *but for* the sex of their partner (Agigian, 2004). In contrast, Bernstein and Reimann (2001) not only make visible working-class and other disadvantaged groups but credit them with a transformative capacity: 'Queers of color, low-income LGBTs, resistance to dyadic coupled bliss, preference for nonmonogamy, same-sex couples wanting children, lesbians not wanting children – all confound heteronormativity, contest the hegemonic family ideal, and complicate lesbian and gay politics' (2001: 5). 'Queer' is differently placed as misguided or transformative and as differently available to and enacted by variously classed, racialised, gendered and sexualised subjects.

The privileging of certain forms of family and the securing of material and emotional capitals for some often de-legitimises others, a familiar process adapted to 'new' citizenship moments: 'If gay people begin to pursue marriage, joint adoptions, and custody rights to the exclusion of seeking kinship status for some categories of friendship, it seems likely that gay families will develop in ways largely congruent with socio-economic and power relations in larger society' (Weston, 1991: 209). Differences do matter and points of contrast exist not only between gay and straight families but also within and amongst gay parents, often obscured by the 'looking-glass' language of sameness and difference (Weston, 1991). From the queer to the 'ordinary' there is a need to avoid positing lesbian and gay families as an alternative ideal *or* as an acceptable 'norm' (Carrington, 1999; Ahmed, 2004). A focus on the possibilities and impossibilities which (dis)allow transgression prevents a reading and reduction of lesbian and gay parented families as transformative or assimilative for '"transgression" must be psychically, emotionally, materially, socially possible' (Ahmed, 2004: 153). Here, assimilation and transgression are not choices available to individuals, easily practiced and achieved; rather they are complexly inhabited and refused, structured and reproduced. There are multiple contradictions within similar and different conceptions, witnessed too in pathways into parenting.

The best laid plans...

This section focuses on lesbian and gay individuals' opportunities to parent as well as their disparate access to reproductive technologies and medical approval, which are often uneasily negotiated. Even the best laid plans can come apart in the myriad of legal and financial constraints and while some researchers have emphasised creative capacities generated here, such 'self-fashioning' and 'reflexive deliberation' tell a gendered, classed and sexualised tale. Discourses of resistance and self-invention in contemporary stories of intimacy are often linked with new reproductive technologies as a form of family making available to lesbians and gay men. Yet the controversies aroused here demonstrate the gap between creating, even extending families and choices, as against criticisms of 'selling-out' to nuclear family norms or, conversely, making a mockery of such 'proper', socially legitimated, families. While such technologies exist on the marketplace their (unequal) availability raises questions about the commodification of bodies and their component, reproductive parts and the continued dichotomy between supposedly real, authentic families, heterosexually created versus 'fake' and 'bought' families, selfishly indulged in. Practices such as adoption also complicate and clarify the biological and social nature of families. Lesbians' and gay men's access to such services underscores continued linkages between the family and the marketplace, a relation which is often disguised and naturalised in conventional heterosexual family formations.

The family challenge

Stacey (1996) optimistically presents 'brave new families', where familial possibilities are unhinged from fixed, biological categories and taken-for-granted routes, proliferating beyond the automatic and the expected, to include the creative, the fought for and the still disputed. The 'panoply of options' (Weston, 1991) in becoming a parent include foster care, adoption, co-parenting, alternative insemination and heterosex (Agigian, 2004). If lesbians decide to attempt pregnancy, the process may involve accessing fertility treatment or finding a man to donate sperm, whether that be in casual networks or through clinics (see *Gender and Society*, 2000, vol. 14, no. 1; *Sexualities*, 2005, vol. 8, no. 2; Donovan, 2000).

Weeks et al. (2001) speak of the opening up of the possibilities for parenting, including changes in where and when people 'come out' and the communities that they have access to: 'One of the important factors that can influence people's stories is their access to community knowledges, which can supply both an alternative (more positive) construction of non-heterosexualities and the resources to support non-heterosexual parenting' (Weeks et al., 2001: 161). Parenting stories are categorised in three ways, consisting of stories of impossibilities, stories of opportunities, stories of choice; it is the stories of choice and opportunities which are given precedence over and above impossibilities, pointing towards reflexive confidences and familial reclamations, foregrounded in the experiences of those who openly choose to conceive as gay (Lewin, 1993; Benkov, 1994; Nardi, 1999).

Like others, Weeks et al. (2001) also point to the increasing number of gay men opting for parenting (Hicks and McDermott, 1999; Dunne, 1999; Stacey, 2006). Gay men in particular have been positioned as free from kinship, defined instead by sexual prowess, capital accumulation and consumption (Weston, 1991). This association is also commented upon by Agigian (2004) who suggests that adult manhood is now marked by a flight from families defined instead by the norms of radical individualism. In contrast, Stacey (2006) charts gay men's struggle for access to 'the means of production'. Based on interviews with gay men in Los Angeles, Stacey maps out interviewees' routes to parenting categorising these from 'predestined progenitors, parent-seeking-partner, refuseniks, situational parents and non-parents'. Despite connotations between gay male culture and commercial self-indulgence, there were very few 'refuseniks' in her study. Nonetheless, Stacey points to the divisive processes by which gay men may, or may not, access the means of production, where most pursued parenthood through adoption, which is marked by 'profound racial and sexual asymmetry' (Stacey, 2006: 32). While pathways to parenting are expansive and varied, there are connected structural (im)possibilities in the formation and recognition of 'brave new families'.

For example, Bock (2000) details the 'ruckus' in US condemnation of single-mothers, where single middle-class mothers claim that they are 'different' and not tied in with the rest of the 'single-parent scandal'. Exploring the experiences of single-mothers by choice (SMCs), accounts indicate that they feel *entitled* to enter solo motherhood because they possess four essential attributes: age, responsibility, emotional maturity and fiscal capacity. Their 'going it alone' narrative may be viewed as fundamentally middle-classed, whereby such parents are able to place themselves at the top of the parenting hierarchy. Such mothers, it is claimed, are more readily accepted because they do not place an economic burden on society, although their single status potentially still disrupts heteronormativity: 'Middle-class status [in the perceptions of

SMCs], compensates for the stigma of illegitimacy; this represents a huge (and important) gulf between these children and the welfare-dependent children of teen mothers' (Hertz and Ferguson, 1997, in Bock, 2000: 73). SMCs engage in justifications as an active and real part of their everyday lives. Such justifications are rooted in the 'vocabulary of motive', seeking to explain in culturally acceptable ways, while de-legitimising others in advancing their own morally and economically acceptable routes.

Again based on US research, Hequembourg (2004) explores the differences among lesbian mothers based on their trajectories to motherhood (see Hare and Richards, 1993), addressing the unique difficulties they face as they negotiate their roles and relationship within their families and the extra layer of problems experienced in interactions with institutions (e.g. legal, educational). One resilience strategy included 'normalization tactics', where mothers emphasised ordinariness ('garden variety mom') even as there were inevitable tensions in 'marginal-mainstream identities' (Hequembourg and Farrell, 1999). Nonetheless, the emphasis on ordinariness enabled mothers to create and sustain a sense of family in the context of social and legal discrimination, where reflections and intentions were compelled and queried.

It didn't 'just happen': Reflection, intention and deliberation

Many commentators on lesbian and gay parenting have pointed towards the high degree of reflexivity and intentionality with which they construct and plan families, with biological constraints compelling a profound re-thinking of families (Agigian, 2004; Clarke and Kitzinger, 2005; Lindsay et al., 2006): 'the decision to parent is by necessity a more deliberative and less socially scripted process' (Dalton and Bielby: 2000: 59). Well-considered decisions amongst lesbians and gay men are often made over extended periods of time (Wilson, 2007), where deliberations and choice have been fostered by the explosion of 'expertise' on pink parenting (Weston, 1991; Weeks et al., 2001). The lack of role models for lesbian and gay parents is also seen to foster and necessitate an ability to creatively differ as new knowledges are produced and accessed: 'The availability of different knowledges in the form of literature aimed at non-heterosexual parents, therefore, can be invaluable in the reflexive process, and the ever increasing number of books on the subject reflects this demand and, of course, helps generate it' (Weeks et al., 2001: 170).

Pathways to parenting are viewed as necessarily 'reflexive', yet also uncertain, and potentially 'interrupted' at various points by various institutions (Weston, 1991; Dunne, 1997; Hequembourg, 2004). In making claims to familial territory (potential) parents may have to prove their worth to professionals, or find themselves in conflict and dis-repute with medical and social regulators. In becoming a parent, gay people may strategically, or otherwise, emphasise that they 'really want' children (Stacey, 1996) contrasting their desires with that which can 'automatically' or 'easily' be achieved. While this perhaps redeems or establishes their own credentials, it may well serve to reinforce a binary between the reflexive, properly planned parenting and the 'easy' unthought, 'just happened' kind, where discourses of 'bad' unplanned parenting are re-visited (Gillies, 2006). Beck-Gernsheim (2002) speaks of 'family planners', carefully thinking through all aspects of having children. Here life plans are constantly being revised but an implied negative effect of this, a reverse side of 'choice', is the lack of a (valued) life plan, leading to disapproval as 'naïve' or 'irrational', where life is unplanned and 'just' unfolds.

The optimism present in foregrounding active 'family planning' must be set within the climate of risk, suspicion and cost, faced more by some than others – of having to 'prove' parenting credentials and indeed to have 'actively planned' to avoid real conflict, rather for the pleasure in the plans alone (Clarke, 2001a,b, 2002). Since lesbians may not have the privilege of the 'automatic', the heterosexual route to parenthood, they may have to give more thought to what to tell their child and how such information might affect them (Agigian, 2004). But this effaces les-bian and gay parents who have had children via heterosexual relations and who may or may not consider this 'easily' 'automatic'. Much has been written about the struggles in deliberate planning; this struggle and urgency is echoed by Weston that '... planning and deliberation increase the chances that children will not be forcibly wrested from their parents at a later date' (1991: 192). But must such planning and deliberation be practised, endorsed and established as a sign of active, respectable par-enting, which can only ever be available to certain classed actors with the requisite knowledges and resources?

Lewin's (1993) respondents, for example, spoke of routes to lesbian motherhood in such contemplative ways, inspiring a 'coming out' and a move towards self-actualised subjecthood. Divorce from previous het-erosexual partners was spoken of as a passage to adulthood, as indicating independence and individuality, where respondents related becoming a 'full person' and no longer only taking care of kids and husbands. Yet Lewin (1993) draws data from lots of very affluent interviewees, where respondents spoke of embarking on parenthood, at the right time, in the right place, with the right person who reflected their desire for 'stability'. Ideas of 'being ready' for parenthood, as linked to age, financial and relational 'stability', potentially reinforce the good, planned choice against the mistaken 'just happened', gliding over the factors making deliberate 'family planning' possible (Bock, 2000; Hequembourg, 2004). In Lewin's (1993) research, respondents spoke of financial resources as enabling, but also obliging, them to have children as a way of sharing their resources. Agigian (2004) relates this to class, shaping assessments of potentiality and lesbian mothers' sense of when they are ready to mother, as linked to what they can give emotionally and materially: 'Closely intertwined with other decision-making factors are prospective mothers' assessments of their financial situations and their ability to manage motherhood on their own. Subjective judgements of what constitutes a sufficient income or an adequate standard of living vary considerably, as does the extent to which mothers engage in concrete financial planning' (Agigian, 2004: 59). It seems that notions of 'reflexivity' cannot be separated from the materiality grounding plans and choices.

The required reflexivity in routes into parenting – and thereafter – is evident in lesbians' negotiation of assisted insemination and the role of biological/social fatherhood (a process perhaps becoming more difficult in the context of legislative changes re-emphasising the importance of fatherhood). Some of Stacey's (1996) respondents spoke of 'going straight', desiring the ease of having 'built-in' loved ones, while others envisioned parenting only in the context of heterosexual relations. Others resorted to heterosex quite instrumentally, doing so outwith the medical context, perhaps bearing more, or different, risks: 'In pursuit of sperm, some lesbians have resorted quite instrumentally to heterosexual intercourse, but most prefer alternative insemination strategies, locating known or anonymous donors through personal networks or through private physicians or sperm banks' (Stacey, 1996: 111). Stories of choices tell of creation and deliberation and even the necessity of 'doing things differently' but they also potentially reveal limitations within choices, where such technical facts are only the starting point in materialising parenting.

Getting off on a technicality

In the United Kingdom the Human Fertilisation and Embryology Act (1990) made it possible for lesbians and gay men to access fertility treatments in private clinics (Wilson, 2007). While a review in 2003 entertained extending access to National Health Service (NHS) fertility services to lesbian and gay men, it remains the case that individual doctors must grant permission for NHS elective treatment. As such,

access potentially remains '...subject to scrutiny and possible prejudice' (Wilson, 2007: 51). Further, the removal of anonymity under the
Human Fertilisation and Embryology Authority (HFEA) (Disclosure of
Donor Information) regulations may be understood as an attempt to
underscore the bio/social necessity of male intervention and to clarify –
or complicate – legal and financial responsibilities in every situation
(Jones, 2005). While in the United Kingdom sperm has been viewed primarily as a valuable therapy for infertility, in the United States sperm is
viewed as a commodity and valued as a product (Ertman, 2003; Barney,
2005). In both cases the 'basic steps' of parenting may constitute a maze
of expensive, time-consuming steps.

Institutions continue to shape and regulate choices about routes to
parenting, where lesbian and gay parents have to prove themselves to
various health and social welfare professionals (Donovan, 2000). Weston
(1991) speaks of her respondents as fighting back, where their combative strategies highlight their vulnerability and endurance in having
to keep fighting. But for some more than others, this 'fight' is all too
familiar and ever-present, where the level of medical and legal intrusion
cannot be buffeted by a 'model minority' status (Boggis, 2000; Dalton,
2001): 'Both the monetary cost and the requirement to become a "model
minority" creates disparate access for queers who wish to become parents, depending on race/ethnicity and class' (Bernstein and Reimann,
2001: 10).

As lesbians and gays negotiate these social and medical terrains,
Agigian (2004) proposes that they are actively transforming it and being
transformed in turn, a 'transformation' which she links to intersections
of class and sexuality. In highlighting the relevance of class, Agigian
lists the costs of family, a bit like a shopping list, and argues that
'Market forces and class privilege often trump "moral" prohibitions and
protocols. Lesbians with cash more easily find a way to bypass legal,
physician, or insurance company proscriptions and inseminate under
private medical supervision, while non-wealthy lesbians must shoulder
the legal and medical, and therefore the psychological, insecurity of self-
insemination' (Agigian, 2004: 94–95). Technology is morally and materially driven (Rapp, 2000; Beck-Gernsheim, 2002), where 'Lesbians of the
liquid classes are much more likely to have the resources to "do" family
in all its forms, including undertaking AI', even as lesbians and gay men
do have families whatever resources they have (Agigian, 2004: 98).

Rather than using clinics, self-insemination and friendship arrangements can represent a 'low tech', less expensive option where
community co-operation can heal rifts of gender, class and racial

divides, or less optimistically, can continue such inequalities. Accessing reproductive technology or informal arrangements through lesbian and gay networks, friends and connections requires time, energy and sophisticated consumption skills (Hogben and Coupland, 2000), which serve to support and *legitimise* middle-class parenting. The consequential difference is a classed one, re-creating boundaries of sameness/difference beyond sexuality, where similarities amongst low-income women, whether they are lesbian or heterosexual, may be drawn out (Agigian, 2004). Moral and material dilemmas construct choices and chances in accessing and assessing different routes into parenthood and parenting experiences thereafter, where different burdens are experienced or deflected (see also Hequembourg, 2004). This can be witnessed amongst Weston's interviewees, where 'Some cited lack of money and dead-end jobs as reasons to postpone childrearing, while others with low incomes and no prospects for upward mobility responded "if not now, when?" ... Others felt that having "one or two strikes against you" (race or class oppression) was sufficient, without asking children to bear the added stigma of a gay or lesbian parent' (1991: 167).

In exploring the 'economics of lesbian insemination', Agigian focuses on the commercialisation and class-based stratification of lesbian AI and the contradictory (alienating/liberating) potential of buying from sperm banks. Commercialisation is chief among the issues that feminists have taken up in relation to procreative technologies while Agigian (2004) notes that commodification is ever present and seeks neither to pathologise or romanticise it. Indeed, women's procreative capacities and sexualities have long been the object of exchange, where heterosexual baby-making is also 'tainted' by economics (Dunne, 1997). In light of such critique it may well be impossible to distinguish between the 'real' and the 'pretend' or assisted route into parenthood but these divisions nonetheless permeate decisions and distinctions in lesbian and gay families.

Mix or match: Making it 'real'

Unlike the interviewees of Gabb (2004) and Lewin (1993), Weston's sample frequently defined family in opposition to biological ties, with many interviewees also feeling that elements of choice rather than inevitability contributed to the maintenance of blood ties; there were familial selections and rejections, to be created rather than compelled. Edits were made to family trees, where the rhetoric of 'mix n match' was also used. Demonstrating such selections, the use of a known or unknown donor can be used to negotiate distance and proximity where soliciting sperm from male relatives may bolster claims on kids and thus 'buttress their tenuous legal, symbolic, and social claims for shared parental status over their "turkey baster babies"' (Stacey, 1996: 112). Lesbian parents may well be compellingly concerned with the role of the father, situated within a changing political context necessitating the ability to prove the 'right' type of contractual relations. Seizing upon biology to make 'real' claims, however, shores up the instability of these categories (as well as foregrounding them).

Exploring advertisements in the US gay press placed by lesbians and gay men to find reproductive partners, Hobgen and Coupland discuss the ways that identities are constructed and desires managed when bio-data functions in a CV-Building capacity where individual 'goods' '...can be seen in the choice of nomenclature and the catalogue of qualities and attributes (e.g. physical characteristics, age, personality, and interests) through which the individual identifies and packages him/herself as desirable' (2000: 463). An important reminder is issued on the supposed 'incompatibility' of homosexuality and parenting, where the desired and projected identities of 'intelligent', 'professional', 'solvent', 'well-established', may be understood as manifestations of – and negotiations within – the prevailing reproductive lexicon.

In the US sperm is a commodity to be sorted and classified according to hierarchical categories of social and physical dominance where genes have social categories already built into them (Haimes and Weiner, 2000; Franklin and McKinnon, 2001; Thompson, 2001; Jones, 2005). There are many factors in choosing a donor from the willingness of the donor to be known, to health, racial and cultural factors and affinities, where 'good genes' are read from race, education, sexual orientation, strength, height and so on. In investing in 'ubersperm' consumers are seen to be managing risk and ensuring more for their investment (Schmidt and Moore in Agigian, 2004: 99). Central to finding 'good sperm' is the desire to ensure a good 'match' with physical and intellectual resonances, which reinforce classed and racial distinctions, where the semen '"worth paying for" is the semen of the socio-economic elite' (Agigian, 2004: 102; see also Barney, 2005).

Another side to the desired 'good match' is the need to 'pass' as family precisely by 'looking like a family' (Jones, 2005). The desirability of 'looking like a family' is itself sanctioned by the UK Human Fertilisation and Embryology Act Code of Practice (2004, para 3.19) and, as such, is hard to subvert. Such negotiations by lesbian mothers may take on a strategic importance, consolidating legal ties in the context of vulnerability, where lesbians must necessarily engage with these processes: 'This is not because lesbians are particularly interested in practicing human engineering. Rather, it seems more related to the culture of consumerism that most liquid classes in the United States are more or less comfortable with' (Agigian, 2004: 123). Ultimately, Agigian views the buying of sperm as offering a chance at agency, albeit to the few who can afford such 'subversive commerce'. When sperm is given an 'exchange value', this opens up choice (for some) and forces a consideration of the types of exchanges that can take place between professionals, clients and consumers. Here, Agigian situates such exchanges as part of an intersectional dilemma requiring intersectional solutions where 'the lesbian AI mother, like most of us, is both proprietary and property, variously located in the grids of class exploitation. Finally, she is both appropriate and inappropriate, accumulating a variety of statuses through various identities and acts' (Agigian, 2004: 110).

In exploring discourses of fatherhood among lesbian parents in Sweden and Ireland, Ryan-Flood (2005) suggests a similarly complex web of subversion and re-inscription. Swedish lesbian parents generally expressed a strong preference for a known donor who would play an active part in parenting, whereas Irish parents usually chose an unknown donor. Rather than positioning interviewees as inevitably 'selling-out' to notions of normality in establishing their own 'homonormative' status, Ryan-Flood details the significance of social context where interviewees may be understood to be mobilising resources, even 'putting a floor on circumstances' in the context of judgement and hostility (Skeggs, 1997): 'The ways in which lesbian parents in the two countries reinvent and reinscribe prevailing discourses of the family according to their own situatedness as social and cultural actors highlights the significance of context to understanding of lesbian parent experiences, possibilities and constraints' (Ryan-Flood, 2005: 190). In the negotiation of pathways to parenting, the diversity and complexity of heteronormativity and *its* ability to reinforce itself should be considered alongside notions of privilege in the construction of homonormativities (Duggan, 2002). Rather than positioning parents as potential sell-outs or queer transformers (Ahmed, 2004), Ryan-Flood suggests that the interest – and complication – lies in considering the negotiation of prevailing discourses of parenthood.

Such a 'complex choreography' is suggested by Cussins (1998), where tactical, strategic and necessarily struggles for family can work to produce new norms, where comparisons of sameness/difference are again re-visited: 'Difference is only accommodated to the extent that "the other" becomes "the same" ... the acceptability of lesbians and gay men may be predicated upon their reproduction of dominant behaviours, values and culture...As some lesbians and gay men gain admittance into the status quo, familial ideology may be strengthened and others may be further marginalized' (in Jones, 2005: 233). As some lesbians are, often uneasily, included, others continue to face material and moral exclusions, where points of difference and division manifest around class, constructing (il)legitimate parental pathways and positions, sustained by classed claims and resources (Bock, 2000; Agigian, 2004).

Conclusion

The legal, political and social changes which have taken place with regard to lesbian and gay parented families have done more than to just shine the spotlight on something that is most definitely not new. They have focused attention once again onto the dynamics of gay and lesbian parenting within the context of a society which, while it may tolerate and pay lip service to ideas diversity, often remains very uneasy about the idea of same-sex parents. The concept of the family, however fluidly that may be defined, continues to be both a cornerstone of societal value and a yardstick against which concepts such as 'normativity', 'worth' and 'properness' can be measured and judgements made. The complexity of family relations has long been acknowledged, but when issues such as class and sexuality are mixed in, these already murky waters can become opaque.

As can be seen, choice and all the implications thereof can be characterised as one of the dominant dialogues within the debates around the modern family in general and gay and lesbian families in particular. Although the trope of 'the family' is one of the longest standing within sociological discussion, it is, as has been seen, an ever changing one. The demands placed on it by the emergence of queer families and gay-bys is matched only by the demands that it itself places onto those who wish to claim and appropriate family and family values, within a new imagining of those concepts. Although it may now be easier for lesbian and gay parents to lay claim to the rights of family, or at least acknowledgement of family status, this is far from an automatic right, and to ignore the profound effect that class, social capital, long-term prejudice and economic factors have on this conferral of rights would be wounding to those who struggle on a daily basis not only to be citizens but also parents within a society that would deny them both.

2
Gay Parents, Games Lessons and Gambling with the Future

This chapter seeks to highlight the gap between studies on the reproduction of class privileges in heterosexual families (Ball, 2003; Devine, 2004) against quite different, often unclassed, notions of social capital in lesbian and gay families; combining a Bourdieusian notion of social capital with that of Weeks et al. (2001). Weeks et al. (2001) explore experiences of self-invention and well-being in 'non-heterosexual' families. They deploy the notion of social capital to highlight strategies of networking and community building whereby locally embedded constructions of capital compound familial resources. The ability to relocate to 'friendly', 'diverse' spaces with 'sympathetic' schools and supportive social networks is nonetheless affected by material inequalities. The overt optimism of Weeks et al.'s account glosses over potential exclusion and the classed shaping of inclusions.

An absence in charting new familial constructs and choices – and the compounding of social capital through diverse networks – is the processes facilitating and inhibiting choice, in *materialising* connections: 'choice' does not exist as a free floating notion but rather is often a mobilisation and manifestation of resources. If social networks are at the base of new elective affinities, then it is important to establish what groups are affirmed through or denied such agentic capacities. Herein lies a contrast between the social capital positioned at the heart of lesbian and gay transformations in intimacy and quite different, classed and gendered, notions of social capital, which centre the constraints in generating such a resource.

Bourdieu's model of *classed* capitals, and their intersecting social, economic and cultural components, is outlined, where many have drawn upon this framework to illustrate the multifaceted aspects of class formations, reproductions and distinctions. While class analyses increasingly combine the material, subjective and spatial aspects of class, they also focus on the mutual constitution of gender, sexuality and class ('Classed reproductions and intersections'). Here, classed 'reproductions' and 'intersections' will be explored in relation to lesbian and gay parenting experiences, and the consolidation of the 'right' kinds of networks ('Capitals and connections: Which group do you belong to?'). Rather than viewing networks as purely facilitative and enabling, a Bourdieusian perspective focuses attention on the different types of 'networks' where some may permit movement and mobility, through 'bridging ties'. Here instrumental gains are sought and provided in 'getting ahead', as opposed to the 'bonding ties' in more working-class networks, which enable everyday survival in 'getting by' in the immediate social space (Gillies, 2006).

Yet the consideration of class and sexuality complicates such a formulation, where points of sameness and difference within and between classed and sexual communities may complicate bonds and bridges; the ability to capitalise on networks, friendships and supports may at once be fractured by inhabiting positions in-between classed 'advantage' and sexual 'disadvantage'. The theoretical gap between Weeks et al.'s (2001) notions of social capital and a classed notion of intersecting capitals is also a real life one, embodied in everyday parental practices and distinctions, affected also by gendered inequalities ('Mummy and mummy still can afford the babysitter: Divisions and distinctions').

This chapter combines often separated bodies of literature aiming to inflect the discussion of choice with the constraints imposed by differing access to social and economic capital. It extends the use of class as exclusively financial resources to a more nuanced understanding of class as an everyday embodied and social practice, witnessed in notions of 'good' and 'bad' parenting. These occur in experiences of and negotiations with the educational system ('Prospective locations: Realisations, residences and relocations') and in geographies of inclusion and exclusion ('The spaces in-between: Difference, diversity and distinction'). While much literature has revealed parenting as a classed practice, the heterosexuality of interviewees within many empirical studies is rarely made explicit. Conversely, research on lesbian and gay experiences of neighbourhood, community and schooling has rarely featured class in their scope, where the evident optimism of accounts of multiple 'social capitals' locally deployed by 'families of choice' sidelines limitations.

The combination of two often disconnected bodies of work potentially reveals much about intersectional (dis)advantages in the context of family life and parental practices, situated here in the spheres of community networking, educational negotiations and the uptake of space. Although Devine examines members of the middle-class mainstream, unpacking how they retain their power and privileges, other researchers have explored other less 'mainstream' families, who may be compelled *and* creatively inspired to 'do things differently', rather than repeat normative practices (Weeks et al., 2001). An important question when considering family practices and strategies in the negotiation of (dis)advantage is, how do sexuality and gender fit in to (de)stabilise class inequalities? What of (un)successful reproductions across time and place and the slippages between having and failing to transfer middle-class privileges? Are lesbian and gay parents able to sustain their advantages or does societal prejudice make this impossible? This chapter aims to consider the replication, mediation and negation of classed capitals – where lesbian and gay parents are often viewed as 'gambling' with children's futures, failing to resource them socially and educationally (through the provision of games lesson or other healthy pursuits), can capitals ever easily be secured?

Classed reproductions and intersections

In the United Kingdom class has been a previous forerunner in sociological debate now displaced by increasing attention to other social divisions. Even defining class becomes difficult in a climate of supposed 'classlessness', where class inequalities are thought of as increasingly 'complex', shifting or non-existent. Class dynamics within the United States are similarly disappeared by the (stronger) rhetoric of 'equal opportunity' and 'classlessness', even with rich, ethnographic accounts of the continued effect of social class in the United States (Zweig, 2000; Bettie, 2003; Kefalas, 2003; Lareau, 2003; Reese, 2005). Although class has fallen off the sociological agenda it is making a comeback, albeit in a different form from earlier economist writings and ungendered analyses. While women's disadvantaged labour positions have been subsumed in class analysis, lesbians have been further ignored, or presumed to be too confusing for comment (Penelope, 1994; Raffo, 1997; Valentine et al., 2003). Yet many feminist researchers have highlighted the intersection of class and gender, where a certain class of women may well be benefiting from the movement of capital into new forms of work (Walby, 1997; Walkerdine et al., 2001). Such changes are suggestive of a more complex notion of class, albeit one which can still be articulated.

In bringing class back onto the agenda, many researchers have deployed Bourdieu's model of classed capitals, demonstrating not only the transformation of class inequality relevant to 'new' cultural sites, but also the perseverance of 'old' economic imbalances. Feminist authors have done so in reshaping re-engagements, providing a theoretical framework for new understandings of class distinctions and reproductions, where class is viewed as dynamic and nuanced, infiltrating and shaping various social spheres and experiences (Adkins and Skeggs, 2004; Gillies, 2006). Bourdieu's theories are concerned with the material and cultural reproduction of social life, specifically the ways that social relations are maintained, reproduced and replicated. Provided is a theoretical framework which conceptualises class as a matter of both the structural and the subjective. Moreover, it also lends itself to the incorporation of other social inequalities such as gender and sexuality (Adkins and Skeggs, 2004). Taking notions of class beyond economist 'class on paper' models, individuals' position in social space are viewed as complexly constructed, defined not only in relation to modes of production but also in terms of social relationships in general, where social class is characterised by social practices and activities, combining 'choice' and structure.

A broad range of divisions construct class, including divisions of culture, education, occupation and forms of social choice in everyday life, all combining to determine individual positions within social space. The social world is structured by the differential distribution of capital as people strive to maximise their capital, where 'getting ahead' seemingly just makes good sense, as an accumulation of advantage. Such processes nonetheless reproduce disadvantages where one form of capital can be transformed into another. For example, economic capital can be converted into cultural capital (e.g. giving children private schooling) while cultural capital can be readily translated into social capital (e.g. contacts and networks formed with other parents with children at private school). The persistence of inequality in relation to the family has been related to differences in social capital, where '... society is witnessing neither the explosion nor the transformation of social capital, but rather its consistent deployment in the reproduction of privilege and inequality' (Evans, 2006: 18).

Social capital is bound up with other central (economic and cultural) resources, or capitals, which determine individuals' status as well as their likely trajectory, their subjective and material movements, through space. Although social capital derives from family and other social relationships, its type and content is shaped by the material, cultural and symbolic status of the individual and family concerned. Such a model

allows for a situation of lesbian and gay parents as also classed subjects, positioned on varied axes of (dis)advantage, rather than generating
social capitals solely through lesbian and gay communities and networks. Everyone may have access to social capital, but for some more
than others the 'pay offs' are greater, the resources are higher and the
ways of doing and accumulating these are also valued more. It is not
just a matter of being 'in place' of accessing the right network and forms
of social supports, rather there is a more complicated story about the
journey into such 'spaces' and their respective classed accumulation and
transference thereafter.

Reflecting the convertible mature of capitals, Skeggs suggests that
'Class positions are not just relative forms in social space, they are institutionalized positions: the cultural capital of the middle classes can offer
substantial rewards in the labour market' (1997: 10). Gender and class
provide the relations in which capitals come to be organised and valued; 'they become gendered through being lived, through circulation,
just as they become classed, raced and sexed: they become simultaneously processed' (Skeggs, 1997: 9). Femininity and masculinity can be
used as resources where whiteness, maleness and heterosexuality are
more valued; such formulations also raise questions about the valued
or 'valueless' forms of femininity and masculinity in relation to gay
and lesbian parental positions. In her *Formations* research, Skeggs (1997)
shows how working-class women invested in heterosexual femininity
as a way of 'putting a floor on their economic circumstances', affecting their negotiations and resistances in everyday interactions. In this
case, attention to appearance was invested in as a kind of physical, bodily capital, a creative solution to 'blocked chances', offering profits in
some arenas (the institutions of heterosexuality and marriage). However,
because femininity is of restricted value, its use was to halt any more
losses, failing to yield high returns in the labour market or education
system.

This analysis is useful in considering how differently placed lesbian
and gay parents can halt potential losses to resources, where heterosexual femininity and masculinity have seemingly been rejected; how
then is value established, accumulated or simply held in slippery circumstances? With the exception of Skeggs' (1997) work, feminist adaptions
of Bourdieu's model have tended to neglect sexuality, suggesting a need
for a framework which can hold sexuality and class together, as material and institutional, structural and subjective (see Adkins and Skeggs,
2004). Intimacy theorists have also not dealt with the classed aspects

of social capital where class, gender and sexuality can intersect to fracture or cement embeddedness in social networks, with gains, losses and (im)mobilities (Gillies, 2006).

In considering material movements and a subjective 'sense of place', Bourdieu emphasises that individual movement is not random and free but circumvented by the forces that structure social space. These forces include both objective mechanisms such as qualifications, money and so on, and the subjective, embodied, disposition (habitus) of an individual (Bourdieu, 1984). Habitus is a way of describing the embodiment of social structure and history in individuals, consisting of lasting dispositions, created and reformulated within the individual (Johnson and Lawler, 2005). It is generative of distinctive social practices, which result from social conditioning related to one's position in social space. Indeed, class manifests in an everyday sense of place: 'The sense of one's place, as a sense of what one can or cannot "permit oneself", implies a tacit acceptance of one's place, a sense of limits ("that's not for the likes of us", etc.) or, which amounts to the same thing, a sense of distances, to be marked and kept, respected or expected' (Bourdieu, 1985: 728). Reay has noted that 'power and self-determination over one's space and place is a major advantage in the negotiation of contemporary society' (2000: 153), where the privileged and dominant may move as 'fish in water' (Bourdieu, 1990).

Dispositions are embedded although adapted and modified by ongoing experiences where, for example, the habitus acquired in the family underlines the structuring of school experiences, and the habitus transformed by schooling in turn structures subsequent experiences. Habitus is a generative system of dispositions which function as a 'matrix of perceptions, appreciations, and actions' (Bourdieu, 1977: 83). The reproduction and resilience of this 'second nature' means that the practice is reproductive rather than transformative. For Reay (1995), habitus provides a tool to explore the social inequalities in everyday social life, highlighting how the dominated and privileged interact in everyday situations, activated in relation to the 'field' (e.g. education). It may well be hard to envisage what this all means for the everyday practices of parenting, yet the confidence, knowingness even entitlement conveyed here can be applied to everyday institutional and interpersonal negotiations experienced by differently classed lesbian and gay parents. This leads to the question of what happens if the habitus does not 'fit' in the social world, but rather is constructed in conflict, where the spaces of class, sexual and parental identity and negotiation (home, local neighbourhood and school) are sites of conflict?

Such questions prompt consideration of the intersecting nature of social divisions; while 'intersection' is now a common trope in discussions of social dynamics and identities (Anthias, 2001, 2002; Brah and Phoenix, 2004), in the case of class and sexuality these intersections are often gestured towards without being fully interrogated or fleshed out (Skeggs, 1997; Berger, 2004; Taylor; 2007; Acker, 2008; Schilt, 2008).[1] This forces an awareness of the social divisions that are thought of as new, still relevant, even cutting edge, as against those that are seen as simply old and settled (Richardson et al., 2006). In reconsidering intersectionality and contemporary feminist politics Yuval-Davis (2006) poses the above question in a different way, asking which social divisions matter: what is useful, additional, or simply too weighty? The debate can range from exhausted addition to fragmentation and back again where the easy 'buzzword' status of 'intersectionality' (Davis, 2008) may serve to sideline continued interrogation of inequalities in the sweep of what we 'already know'.

Rather than portraying intersectionality as a list to be constructed and completed, whereby inequalities are rated and ranked, others have pointed instead to ongoing complexity and multiplicity, as intersectional processes and binds, so that race, gender and class '... cannot be tagged onto each other mechanically for, as concrete social relations they are enmeshed in each other and the particular intersections involved produce specific effects' (Anthias and Yuval-Davis, 1983: 62). Instead, the 'situated accomplishments' of identities are spoken of as intersecting social structure and agency, producing clashes and contingencies and ongoing (dis)identifications (Anthias, 2002). In this model, the focus and burden on the disadvantaged to come clean, to reveal themselves and make their position on the intersectional axes known is potentially displaced by considering how privileged positions are done and undone and how powerful identities are inhabited, maybe even uninhabited (Butler, 1990; Valentine, 2007). However, the focus on multiple and shifting dis-identifications still requires attention to the ways that identities become salient in specific contexts and, for the purposes of this research, in particular parental contexts.

Capitals and connections: Which group do you belong to?

Rather differently from Bourdieu's classed model, Weeks et al. (2001) analyse the ways that access to 'social capital' enables emotional and material well-being, fostering mutually supportive 'networks' in everyday lives. Using the idea of a 'network society' (Beck, 1992; Castells,

1996, 1997, 1998; Urry, 2000) they see lesbian and gay families of choice as examples of 'network families'. While the lack of cultural guidelines is viewed as freeing, offering more opportunity to differently 'create', this positioning risks placing others as without agency, choice, as 'stuck' and unable to capitalise on such networks for emotional and material assistance (Weeks et al., 2001; Agigian, 2004). In contrast to the theorisation of capitals as classed, gendered and sexualised, there is little sense of the intersecting elements (dis)allowing accumulation and transference.

Many studies have detailed the importance of networks and friendships in dealing with experiences of insecurity (Nardi, 1992, 1999; Pahl, 2002), when 'old communities' of fate and necessity are seen to be in decline, transformed by 'elective affinities' (Beck-Gernsheim, 1998). Such an evolving friendship ethic, although circumscribed by a host of 'differences', is seen to be shaped in response to the prevailing heterosexual assumption. In living 'connected lives' lesbians and gay men are seen to ' ... shape new ways of understanding their relationships, and acquire the new skills necessary to affirm the validity of different ways of life' (Weeks et al., 2001: 58). If friendship is indeed the key to understanding non-heterosexual ways of life (Nardi, 1999) then the classed, gendered and sexual context and choices behind these deserve further analysis (Gillies, 2006; Taylor, 2007).[2]

Weeks et al. (2001) see friendship as facilitative of 'life experiments', rather than as a mere 'crutch', yet Gillies (2006) interrogates the value of different friendships and suggests that middle-class participants were more likely to view friends as instrumental buffers against 'risk', offering, for example, access to classed knowledges and resources such as the 'good school' and the potential employer. What then of the intersection between gender, class and sexuality in lesbians' and gay men's friendships, where social supports may act as instrumental buffers? Weeks et al. (2001) hint at the relevance of material inequality, noting that unequal access to social capital in lesbian and gay families has been overlooked (Wan, 1995; Weeks, 1996). Points of sameness and difference, including parental as well as class status, inform lesbian and gay friendships and networks (Lewin, 1993; Taylor, 2007). Here ideas of togetherness are challenged if not eclipsed in attention to the ties made and broken through social status, ethnicity, geography (Weston, 1991; Gabb, 2004; Taylor, 2007). After all, it is hard to hang out with other, to cross boundaries and be a social adventurer if you have to do it all in one pub.

While viewing 'social capital' as generative – rather than as disappearing in communal decline and familial breakdown – the notion of 'social capital' deployed by Weeks et al. (2001) is unclear. Gillies comments that such a theoretical absence is in fact common amongst research on intimacy, even as 'capitals' are empirically evidenced: 'Although few intimacy theorists explicitly address the theoretical concept of social capital, their research points to a regeneration of social connectedness rather than a breakdown' (Gillies, 2003: 17). In a methodological and theoretical departure Gillies (2003, 2006) has pointed to the individual-ising rhetoric of 'choice', via social capital, and the limits of choice in family and friendships.

Rather than evidencing 'networks' based on families of choice, Lewin (1993) notes that 'culture building' amongst her lesbian mother respon-dents is more of a continuity of kinship systems also available to heterosexual single-mothers. Lewin found that respondents did not typically substitute friends for family, and there was no expectation of friends acting 'as family' (see Gabb, 2004). The similarities rather than distinct differences between lesbian mothers and single hetero-sexual mothers may be noted – particularly around the absence of a father and their shared, often insecure material circumstances and low social esteem – potentially impacting upon the generation of social cap-ital. However, the significance of financial resources alone is disputed, where embeddedness in support systems and resulting 'social capitals' is instead highlighted: 'Despite wide variations in the income on which mothers and children actually live, women's evaluations of its adequacy has more to do with the support systems than with the amount of money they actually have in hand each month' (Lewin, 1993: 60). If mothers have support, situated mostly in biological families then, in this analysis, they are more likely to perceive circumstances as manage-able regardless of income. While writing in different geographical and historical contexts, both Lewin (1993) and Weeks et al. (2001), in their contrasting perspectives, perhaps fall short in unpacking the intersect-ing dynamics of gender, class and sexuality in creating networks and systems of support.

The interest in social networks, communities and kinship systems has been revived by social capital theorists, departing from Bourdieu's framework, in attempts '...to measure the value of social connected-ness' (Gillies, 2003: 4).[3] Various attempts to measure the social capital available to children in their families are made, charting outcomes such as educational success which rest upon narrow and normative notions of 'success' and 'failure' (Evans, 2006; Gillies, 2006). In studies focusing mostly upon heterosexual families, class-differentiated configurations of support have been identified as highly gendered, with mothers creating and maintaining networks (Reay, 2004; Gillies, 2006). Working-class women do indeed form 'networks', with emotional and social if not material 'returns', where concerns may centre on issues of time, money, locality, schooling and kin (see also Bagnell, Longhurst and Savage, 2003). Social capital is accumulated even as it does not 'pay off' in monetary terms; instead, it functions as a way of making 'ends meet' where resilience in and reliance on tight-knit communities is often stretched to limits: '... working-class parents were more likely to describe a core network of highly reciprocal, supportive relationships supplemented by connections to more peripheral contacts. Middle-class parents, in comparison, discussed their attachment to a more dispersed and less bonded social group, with few obligations or responsibilities beyond socialising' (Gillies and Edwards, 2006, in Gillies, 2006: 72). For some parents, pulling together happens more than just at sports day.

Gillies' (2006) account constitutes a thorough account of social capital as classed, arguing that the social capital held by the socially disadvantaged enables survival ('getting-by') but offers little opportunity for increasing prosperity ('getting-on'). Social capital is also a highly gendered resource, organised and maintained by mothers rather than fathers. Like Weeks et al. (2001), Gillies (2006) also wants to avoid analysis that foregrounds individualised rejection and despondency; both potentially speak to ongoing inequalities – and of agency not readily acknowledged. The different accounts of the significance of social capital, as it is seen to intersect with – or stand apart from – other capitals and resources, bring into focus the divisions and distinctions between theoretical models and empirical demonstrations. Sexuality, class and gender variously intersect in these models, sometimes as implicit absences and sometimes as foregrounded concerns. The 'critical differentials' are somewhat effaced in the gap in between.

Mummy and mummy still can't afford the babysitter: Divisions and distinctions

Stories of lesbian parent families perhaps consolidate an (imaginary) ideal, obscuring the presence of less 'progressive' practices beneath the weight of a 'community narrative' (Gabb, 2004: 174). This leads Gabb (2004, 2005) to question what gets written into and out of accounts on lesbian and gay parenting, the 'critical differentials', in the understandable struggle to present as competent, progressive, different, even better. Gabb's research presents a different picture from Weston (1991) and Weeks et al. (2001), being similar to earlier comparative research

between lesbian and heterosexual mothers (Lewin, 1993), modestly situated as one voice amongst many, rather than a more rigorous, truthful
account. Such a reserved positioning still demands attention to stories
of constraint, alongside 'choice', and tales of division and rejection,
alongside elective affinities and equalities. But, like others Gabb does
not deeply 'class' her own analysis, while still concluding that 'Irrespective of class and/or social status, nearly all the families asserted that their
childcare and parental roles derived from pragmatic concerns, including
"making (financial) ends meet" ' (Gabb, 2004: 173).

The significance of childcare, parental roles and responsibilities, not to
mention the financing of these, are identified as deeply gendered. Some
researchers have noted the lack of attention paid to changes in fathering in the context of labour market restructuring, where the erosion of
masculine, manual jobs may change the ways that men parent. Brannen
and Nilsen (2006) conducted research with 31 men (presumed to be heterosexual) of three family generations from 12 families in the United
Kingdom, exploring change and continuity among fathers and sons.
The analysis in this research draws out intersections of class and gender
with respect to structural and cultural changes evident in each generation. A typology of fathering is developed: the 'work-focused fathers'
identity is primarily shaped by work ethic and rather low involvement
with their children, a representation evident across classed cohorts. The
'Family man', evident in the two older generations, placed value on
breadwinning capacities and on 'being there' in the home, participat-
ing to some extent in childcare. The 'hands on' fathers, evident in those
occupying lower-class positions, were all heavily involved in childcare
whilst partners took up the role of breadwinner. What Brannen and
Nilsen (2006) are able to show is change in the ways individuals talk
about fathering, as a shift from 'breadwinner' fatherhood to a more
active involvement in the upbringing of children. Although this study
examines issues of gender and class in the construction of fathering
and intergenerational changes and continuities, questions arise about
inclusion of sexuality in conceptualising fatherhood.

This is partly addressed by Stacey (2006) in ethnographic research
with gay men in Los Angeles. Her sample included 50 self-identified
gay men, 16 of whom were single at the time of the study, 31 were in
couple partnership and some were in open relationships. Stacey notes
the juxtaposition of Los Angeles, positioned as a place of sexual excess
and consumer culture, while situated at the 'vanguard of gay fatherhood'. Gay cruising seems to open up a world of opportunity for social
mobility, melting away social barriers, where grass-roots organisations

are abundant (e.g. 'PopLuckClub'). These create social networks for gay (potential) parents and provide information about surrogacy and adoption, resonating with Weeks et al.'s (2001) notion of network building. However, it would appear that social inequalities exist here, downplayed by the championing of cruising as a means of climbing the social ladder.

In one case study, we are encouraged to celebrate the monogamous relationship between an affluent, white, Jewish, Ivy-League-educated individual and an Afro-Brazilian, impoverished, Catholic, 'undereducated' individual raised by a single-mother. The former provides funding so that his partner can become educated and socialised in the practices of middle-class America. In doing so, they stand a better chance of fulfilling their hopes and dreams of fathering children which, in the end of this fairy tale, they are able to do through two expensive surrogacy procedures. 'Ozzie' (the working-class partner) now stays at home with the children as Ozzie and Harry do not believe in childcare. This tale where love conquers the evils of social inequalities has a bitter side. The couple were able to generate enough economic and social capital between them to participate in the heternormative structures which legitimised them both as 'suitable' for fatherhood.

Dunne (1999) also explores gay fatherhood and the dimensions of difference at play based on an international project involving interviews with gay fathers mostly from the United Kingdom, but also from New Zealand, Canada and the United States. A reassertion of previous findings is made (Dunne, 1997); same-sex intimacies have greater scope to critique conventional gender scripts and refashion them to better meet their egalitarian ideals (see Short, 2007). Yet the transformation and 'undoing' of gender may be affected by material and emotional resources (Sullivan, 2004), queried by Carrington (1999) who found that lesbian and gay couples were not particularly egalitarian. Carrington's (1999) ethnographic study involved interviews with fifty-two 'lesbigay' households in the San Francisco Bay Area, in which he found that those couples with more money were much more likely to consider themselves family, regardless of the longevity of their relationships: 'The ability to achieve familyhood is differentially distributed and the stark reality is that the affluent more easily, and more frequently, achieve the status for themselves' (Carrington, 1999, in Agigian, 2004: 97).

Unlike Dunne's (1997) respondents whose lesbian status 'allowed' for the non-existence of fathers in their immediate families and households, many heterosexual women in Gillies' (2006) study maintained contact with male ex-partners framing this in terms of their children's 'best interests'. In making ends meet and parenting on a low income interviewees' caring and employment decisions were often structured by investment in and involvement of a male partner. Gillies' research uncovers the persistence of gender inequalities in shaping parenting, where fathers could be recognised as 'good' even while physically distant from the practice of childrearing – in sharp contrast to notions of 'good mothering'. Again, there is an apparent disconnection between the bodies of research focused on heterosexual families and those exploring lesbian and gay families, with the distinctions between these complicated by the apparent crossovers in, for example, the significance of class and gender inequalities.

As gender shapes parenting discourses and practices so too does class (Walkerdine and Lucey, 1989; Duncan, 1995; Lawler, 2000). The common assumption of mothering as a classless practice is queried when motherhood can be seen as '...central to contemporary individualised and codified representations of class, with disadvantaged mothers depicted as ignorant, promiscuous, uncaring, irresponsible and most significantly, undeserving' (Gillies, 2006: 19). US authors have also empirically evidenced the classing of motherhood, in relation to welfare, educational and employment realms (Kefalas, 2003; Reese, 2005) where working-class mothering practices are also '...held up as the antithesis of good parenting, largely through their association with poor outcomes for children' (Gillies, 2006: 2). As the face of 'bad' motherhood appears to be changing, it is also mis-recognised and distorted through the usual categories of division and distinction. As such, Agigian aims to attend to the interconnections between sexuality, class and race in the experience of lesbian motherhood: 'As with each of these oppositions [other/mother/lesbian], it is rarely so simple, since neither lesbian nor mother is a completed identity. Each is significantly transformed by co-axes of class, race, ethnicity, (dis)ability, and a host of other marked identity classifications in particular national and cultural contexts' (Agigian, 2004: 110). Agigian's application of intersectionality could also potentially speak to the relative axes of (dis)advantage inhabited by differently classed gay fathers.

Becoming a mother can provide scope to resolve stigma, for certain (classed) women, while being a father is rarely imbued with such social, political and even personal significance. Lewin's respondents spoke of mothering as a natural choice, foregrounded on gender essentialism, rather than a political one: '...to the extent that wanting to be a mother is a profoundly natural desire, and is perceived as having nothing to do with cultural or political choices, then achieving motherhood implies movement into a more natural or normal status than a

lesbian can ordinarily hope to experience otherwise' (Lewin, 1993: 74).
A lesbian who becomes a biological mother can enjoy a new societal
acceptance that renders lesbian identity less salient (Stein, 1997; Naples,
2004), although this is likely to be a classed process, where working-class
mothers are rarely esteemed through motherhood and their attempts to
become respectable much denied (Skeggs, 1997; Gillies, 2006). While
Lewin (1993) makes clear the similarities between non/heterosexual
mothers, class as a factor in the redemption of 'good mothers' and
the condemnation of 'bad mothers' is somewhat sidelined. Alongside
classed and sexualised representations of parenthood exists a concern
for the child as a receptor of familial capitals, to be invested in and
resourced – and 'proper' parenting measured through.

Prospective locations: Realisations, residences and relocations

Several authors have commented on the 'intensification' of parenting where proliferating discourses in popular culture, social policy and
expert practice increasingly promulgate, even enforce, what it is to be
good, attentive parents: here the child is placed at the centre of the
family, commanding timetabling (Phoenix et al., 1991; Lawler, 2000;
Furedi, 2002; Vincent, 2002). This is evidenced in Devine's (2004)
research which compares the accumulation and transference of class
advantages in UK and US families, named as white and middle-class
(parents are also ostensibly heterosexual). Middle-class parents are seen
as strategic actors where parental choices are determined by evaluations of the costs and benefits of different courses of action; they
have a knowingness and judgement about the right things to do to
secure social, economic, cultural privilege and to ensure their children's educational and occupational success (Bourdieu, 1984). The
minutiae of middle-class parenting practices are founded on an active
manipulation of social capital to ensure advantage is passed down
through the generations, even if this is increasingly complex and
uneasy.

Lareau's (2003) detailed ethnography of race, class, gender in US
family life explores the creation of the 'cultivated child', arguing that
approaches to childrearing are deeply classed in terms of values and
practices. In Lareau's research, middle-class parents engage in 'concerted
cultivation' in timetabling organised, 'worthwhile' activities, increasing their children's social networks. The facilitation of useful networks
enables the creation of individualised, reflexive, middle-class subjects
who exploit opportunities and feel an entitlement about their value and

place in the world. Such orientating practices, generating a middle-class 'habitus', ensure a fit and easy alignment with institutional fields. Such a notion of social capital, unlike Weeks et al. (2001), relatively benign one, enforces a consideration of the divisions and distinctions in lesbian and gay parented families as they engage in everyday family practices. In considering how parents utilised their social networks to their child's advantage (see also Byrne, 2006), a comparison may be made with Weeks et al.'s (2001) research. Rather than inculcating values from one generation to another, Weeks et al. (2001) spoke of their respondents 'doing things differently', creatively reworking rather than reproducing normative familial frames. But is the 'gold standard' of parenting still firmly heterosexual, with lesbian and gay parenting always measured against this?

In both Lareau's (2003) and Devine's (2004) research interviewees spoke of their high expectations for children's academic success: it was assumed they would do well at school and this was reflected in their everyday lives, projected on into imagined futures. Middle-class hetero-sexual families also spoke of living in 'nice' localities, where decisions about schooling involved appraisals and imaginings of future expecta-tions, also affirmed and enacted in sought interactions with the 'right' pupils and parents (the great 'like minded'). Rather differently, Gillies (2006) carefully frames working-class mothers' choices and actions as part of dialectical relation, pointing to agency, all too often denied, oper-ated within the limitations of poverty and stigma. It makes perfect sense for working-class (heterosexual) parents to ground their choices in the immediacy of 'here' and 'now', where 'the future' imagined by middle-class parents cannot be envisaged. Working-class mothers also invest in their children's futures, advising a 'knuckling down', to ensure survival in school as an 'average' pupil, hoping to 'fit in' and become an adult with a 'decent job', rather than an exceptional one. The sense of place, and the varied negotiations and navigations through parental territo-ries, enforces a consideration of the mobilisation of capitals, effecting what is desired, what is seen as different, normative, failing or good enough. For some parents 'choice' of educational location may be an impossibility, while for others sexuality may be a consequential factor in considerations of (dis)comfort and (dis)location (Weston, 1991; Weeks et al., 2001).

Byrne (2006) conducted 35 interviews with white, middle-class moth-ers living in two areas of south London and discussed their roles as mothers, choice of schooling and after-school activities. In sending chil-dren to the 'right' school Ofsted reports, school league tables, word of mouth and the school's general reputation in the local area were fundamental factors in the decision-making process. These activities can be understood as 'performative of race, class and gender', positioning white, middle-class motherhood as the normative model. Conscious decisions were often made based on class and race where ('filtered') friends were not 'too similar' or 'too different' from one's own positioning, thereby adding a value in connection. Unfiltered friendships were fraught with classed tensions from choice of school to style of parenting and form of discipline. Relations, locations and sites (e.g. the playgroup, antenatal classes, baby clinics) of friendship formation were often divided and required resources including space, time and transport.

'Diversity' within locale is often valued by middle-class consumers/ parents as a commodity which can be used to expand their child's understandings, where the 'other' as is 'knowable' and consumable, and the benefits of knowingness accrue to the child. In accounts of the choice of schooling and residence, middle-class locations with a benefitable sprinkling of 'others' can be tolerated as enhancing, as against those with too many 'others', where the difference becomes too much as excessive and dangerous, an 'undesired difference' (Goffman, 1973; Lindsay et al., 2006). In Byrne's study, middle-class mothers were often concerned with the acquisition of the 'right' social and cultural capitals. A school that was 'too black', 'too white', 'too working class' could not expose their children to a 'balanced mix' of different backgrounds or the 'right' capitals and instead would serve to threaten 'desired stability': 'Openness to difference and multiculturalism fitted into general liberal desires for freedom, creativity, and friendliness, as long as ... there was not too much difference' (1008). Classed distances – and proximities – were negotiated in ways that ultimately served to distinguish and resource middle-class subjects.

The production of class and racial inequalities within schools are clearly visible: what can be added to Byrne's research is the consideration of sexuality in terms of what is considered a 'good mix' and in anticipated school failures, interactions and social capital formations. The classed boundaries of (un)acceptability can be expanded – or indeed contracted – by a focus of the relevance of class and sexuality in the constructions of (un)desirable 'difference'. Sexuality intersects with class, race and gender in school 'choices', affecting the desired diversity championed by the middle classes. What would be considered the 'right' mix, or an excessive drain, in this context? The conscious decision to raise children in 'diverse' settings may vary for differently classed heterosexual and gay parents, highlighting when and where difference matters; what is beneficial, allowable or simply too much?

Researching lesbian parented families in Australia, Lindsay et al. (2006) note that class and ethnic diversity in local communities impacts upon school experience, with a 'good mix' signifying a cosmopolitan acceptance, while 'excessively' working-class areas are viewed as less accommodating to 'difference': 'Those families who live in a generally open minded, inner city suburb that is both cosmopolitan and diverse had a better chance of having positive experiences within the school setting... Working-class suburbs and middle and upper-middle class suburbs dominated by people from white Anglo backgrounds seemed less accommodating than inner city suburbs that are dominated by the educated middle-class' (Lindsay et al., 2006: 1065). Diversity, in this example, is coded as liberal middle-class knowingness, spatialised in the specific 'cosmopolitan' terrain of the inner city. Bodies and values coalesce in the construction of boundaries of (un)acceptability, where lesbian parents' concerns for an 'accommodating' school may also be seen as a manifestation of classed – and sexual – desires and constraints.

Points of institutional accommodation are illustrated in *Involved, Invisible, Ignored*, where Kosciw and Diaz (2008) examine the experiences of children who have been verbally and physically abused within US schools as a result of having gay or lesbian parents. While arguing that parents and pupils are often made to feel invisible (Wallis and VanEvery, 2000), they interestingly warn against the consequences of such invisibility as a potential loss of investment, resources and capitals which LGBT parents could bring with more active engagements: '... The LGBT parents we surveyed are more likely than other parents to be actively engaged in the life of their child's school – more likely to volunteer, to attend parent-teacher conferences or back-to-school nights and to contact the school about their child's academic performance or school experience. Such findings suggest that LGBT parents are, as a group, potential assets for any school community, engaged and concerned about the quality of their children's education and the school of which they are part' (vii). As 'potential assets' these parents are to be welcomed but the inclusion of others *without* the requisite classed resources and capabilities is, however, rather unclear (Gillies, 2006).

In discussing the ways that lesbian parents and their children negotiate school, Lindsay et al. (2006) are keen to emphasise the harsh consequences of exclusion, beyond and including educational failure: 'We are not simply talking about progressive families not quite fitting into a conservative context but more fundamental issues of parents and children feeling respected and safe rather than feeling ashamed, excluded, stigmatized, discriminated against or bullied' (1065). The negotiation and tension of home–school boundaries is very acute for differently placed lesbian and gay parents, where involvement in school is a sign of 'good parenting'.

Such negotiations are made all the more complicated for lesbian and gay parents in that their children are often already positioned as somehow disadvantaged and failing, lacking 'proper' gender role models (Cahill, 2005; Clarke and Kitzinger, 2005). Well-rehearsed arguments regarding lesbians and gays as bad parents sit alongside competing arguments claiming that they compare favourably (for reviews of this literature, see Tasker and Golombok, 1997, and Hequembourg, 2004). Still, claims of the 'best interests' and the ability to guarantee this are also fraught by formations and mediations of class, where the 'diversity' of class cannot be reclaimed as the 'diversity' of sexuality may be. Equally important is the significance of class in educational negotiations; where sexual status may enforce a home/school boundary, and a reluctance to 'come out' and engage, so too might class, where school space is often felt as extremely uncomfortable for working-class parents and pupils alike (Evans, 2006; Gillies, 2006).

Parents have disparate access to institutions that support, regulate or condemn their families, forcing varied (in)visibilities and mis-fits (Bourdieu, 1984; Bernstein and Reimann, 2001). Lindsay et al. (2006) use Goffman's notion of discredited identity, where lesbian parents' 'difference' is undesired in specific contexts/places. They link this to levels of insider/outsider occupation, mediated by more comfortable 'diverse' spaces/bodies, and the performance work and anxiety generated in negotiating and possibly 'coming out' in institutional contexts. Given such fraught negotiations, middle-class gay and lesbian parents may be unable to 'capitalise' upon privilege in a straightforward way (Devine, 2004; Byrne, 2006; Gillies, 2006) and working-class parents may be neither included as diverse assets (Kosciw and Diaz, 2008) nor able to articulate their 'entitlement' to educational inclusions.

Mercier and Harold's (2003) research on lesbian parents in the US mid-west reported on strategies used to minimise anticipated bullying including (1) selecting schools known for openness and multiculturalism; (2) establishing direct contact with teachers and administrators; and (3) maintaining self-imposed invisibility. Strategies are viewed as dependent upon, for example, routes into parenthood, the age of children, the extent of community visibility and the presence of other lesbian parents and/or lesbian teachers (see Weston, 1991; Weeks et al., 2001). Other factors discussed included the 'resilience' of children, although the ways that differently classed parents talked about and situated such 'resilience' and resistance were not analysed (Evan, 2006; Gillies, 2006). Overall, then, the world of family life appears rather different depending on the immediate social context inhabited and created by the family. Lindsay et al. (2006) query the homogeneous family 'type' typically presented in research on lesbian families with little attention given to the different social context inhabited by these (see also Gabb, 2004). The idea that social divisions interact in complex ways with the doing and experience of family is present, while class is implicit rather than explicit, in the notion of 'social context' articulated. Sexuality, gender and class have an impact on the understanding of and ability to access on everyday space, beyond and including the school playground (Moran, 2000; Perlesz and McNair, 2004; Taylor, 2007).

The spaces in-between: Difference, diversity and distinction

Frequently, lesbian and gay parented families fall off the map of human geographies, just as they fall into the cracks of social sciences more generally. They are habitually absent from attention to 'typical' (heterosexual) family and typical lesbian and gay spaces (Browne et al., 2007), uneasily positioned between dichotomous terrains. Research on the spatial strategies and investments of lesbians and gay men has tended to focus on commercialised scene space, while differently demarcated, mapped and occupied parental space reinforces this 'in-between' status, as neither here nor there. This is challenged in framing lesbian and gay presence as 'everywhere' (Gabb, 2004, 2005).

That said, such a presence still focuses on city space with many studies of lesbian and gay life conducted in cosmopolitan, progressive urban areas (e.g. New York City, San Francisco in the United States and London, Brighton, Manchester in the United Kingdom. See Lewin, 1993; Browne et al., 2007). While Weston (1995) has demonstrated the significance of accessing community and support structures in getting to 'a big city', this arguably collapses the (in)visibilities and (im)possibilites between and among urban and rural terrains (Bell and Valentine, 1995; Binnie and Valentine, 1999). Clearly, locality is important in the creation of diversity – and distinction. The continual struggle to find a stable, 'ordinary' sense of home, place and identity, as against a queer transgressive global mobility, is highlighted by Binnie (2004). He investigates the distinctions between 'cosmopolitan', 'sophisticated' centres and 'provincial', 'unsophisticated' towns, providing a corrective to previous studies of a (singular) 'coming out geography', centred around commercialised urban scene spaces.

In 'opening the map' the wider terrain of combined sexual, classed and parental geographies can be charted, where a Bourdieusian model of capitals and movements through space can usefully be combined with queer theories of spatiality (Lovell, 2000). Such a focus draws attention to the ways that certain bodies, appearances and identities are rendered unentitled to occupy heteronormative space, the mediation of which is also a classed process (Bourdieu, 1984; Skeggs, 1999, 2001). It also refocuses attention on the historical movement into spaces and position, on the fact that individuals, in this case lesbian and gay parents, do not arrive completely dis-located from space but rather inhabit and rework space on the basis of 'past' dispositions, knowingness and capitals. Classed (dis)comforts and resources seem significant to the uptake of, inclusion into and exclusion from space, whether that be commercialised queer space, everyday home space or institutional space (schools, welfare services, etc.). Lesbians and gay men may indeed be everywhere rather in special, queer enclaves, yet the ability to reconcile, inhabit and spatialise sexual and parental identities may also vary according to classed capitals (Ahmed, 2004).

Speaking of the 'search for home' as individuals negotiate the hazards of everyday life, Weeks et al. (2001) claim that access to community generates emotional well-being, providing a form of 'social capital'. Yet this may not be the starting point for such generation but may well be a continuation, or transformation, of other (classed) capitals, whereby locally embedded constructions of capital compound familial resources (Bourdieu, 1984). Weeks et al. identify the ability to 're-skill' in community knowledges as affected by socio-economic resources, gender and ethnic positioning, as well as the other variables that 'open and foreclose possibilities': 'Though access to community knowledges may be limited by such factors as gender, geography, ethnicity, socio-economic resources and physical access issues, their existence has been responsible for the growing confidence of non-heterosexuals not only to live openly non-heterosexual lives, but to do so with a sense of pride rather than an apology' (Weeks et al., 2001: 182). They note the limits and exclusions of these, while stressing increased possibilities (for some).

Strategic movements and locations amongst lesbians and gay men, residing in and constructing communities that support diversity have been widely evidenced (see Weston, 1991; Stacey, 1996; Short, 2007). Relocations offer a potential comfort and ease, an ability to 'fit' in, or indeed 'stand out', communally disrupting the heterosexualisation of public spaces (Valentine, 1996). Agentic capacity – even transformative abilities – are often foregrounded here, where respondents are credited with sophisticated spatial strategies in negotiating 'safe' space. Yet spatialised (dis)comforts and the sense of being 'out of place' continue, where one cannot access, locate or embody a positive 'diversity', a 'good mix', where social capitals generate and multiply (Byrne, 2006; Taylor, 2007, 2009).

Examining the identity strategies deployed by gay men across different spaces, times and places, Brekhaus (2003) takes the focus upon gay identity out of city spaces and into the suburbs. Aspects of the everyday, the ordinary, the invisible and the mundane are centred. However, the 'ordinariness' or 'extraordinariness' of interviewees' desires to be average 'Joe fags' may be pondered – just how 'ordinary' are the suburbs and its inhabitants? Interviewees often mixed aspects of their unmarked characteristics, such as their whiteness, masculinity (and middle-classness), with their marked status of being gay, to create a more diffused, balanced self, contrasting this with the extreme outliers, or gay 'lifestylers', situated in commercialised scene space. While the 'ordinary' unseen spaces of the suburbs are made visible, a greater exploration is needed of the materiality constructing movements and strategies across place, where esteem accrues to the mobile, reflexive, chooser often marked with a transformative potential in the ability to change space (Ahmed, 2004; Byrne, 2006). What then are the limitations and opportunities for differently classed lesbian and gay parents in everyday spaces and scenarios?

There are many contradictions in navigating heteronormative spaces and institutions, where privileges may be mobilised to mediate misplacement. This may always be an uneasy negotiation: ' ... the care work of lesbian parents may involve 'having' to live in close proximity to heterosexual cultures (in the negotiation with schools, other mothers, local communities), whilst not being able to inhabit the heterosexual ideal. The gap between the script and the body, including the bodily form of 'the family', may involve discomfort and hence may 'rework' the script. The reworking is not inevitable, as it is dependent or contingent on other social factors (especially class) and it does not necessarily involve conscious political acts' (Ahmed, 2004: 152). While attentive to the structuring of social space as heterosexual, materialised in institutions which presume and promote heterosexuality, Ahmed's account considers the mediation and challenge in such spaces, where it would be too simple to declare an automatic disadvantage or displacement, in light of class advantages also embodied, materialised and capitalised upon.

The everyday reality of (not) 'coming out' in everyday contexts, simultaneously 'outs' and disappears gay parents, where they must wind their way through multiple institutional contexts, interacting with other parents, teachers and doctors (Lewin, 1993). For some then 'the closet' is sometimes the safest place, securing well-being and even survival. Yet even as this strategy makes sense, it can never really be achieved and requires constant negotiation: 'Because sexuality brings people into relationships its implications can never be contained within the parameters of identity or some ideally privatised sphere' (Weston, 1991: 67). As Gabb (2004) has discussed, lesbian mothers cannot easily control where or when they are 'outed' because children often did this to them in, for example, the school or the supermarket, meaning that parents' relation to risk is often hard to manage.

The choice to 'come out' is often about what is at risk, and what can/not be recognised between those doing and those witnessing disclosures, where classed positioning also involves a mis-recognition, a negation of esteem and value, impacting upon access and ease within space (Bourdieu, 1984; Skeggs, 1997; Gillies, 2006). Classed and sexual mis-readings complicate acts of visibility where '...visibility is not simply an act performed by queers but the result of complex interactions and exercises of power between queers and their interlocutors' (Bernstein and Reimann, 2001: 10). Yet, in appreciation of the complexities of coming out, including how (in)visibilities and viabilities intersect with other social divisions, it is possible to think of middle-class lesbian and gay parents as exercising more power and choice in some contexts. Ahmed also points to differing classed strategies and abilities and the (dis)comforts in 'fitting in': 'Some working-class lesbian parents, for example, might not be able to afford being placed outside the kinship networks within local neighbourhoods: being recognised as "like any other family" might not simply be strategic, but necessary for survival. Other working-class lesbian parents might not wish to be "like other families": what might feel necessary for some, could be impossible for others' (Ahmed, 2004: 153). Necessities and impossibilities suggest both the complexities and complications in exploring interconnections between class and sexuality in the re-production of (dis)advantage. Class and sexuality are mutually constituted and intertwined, rather than separate, known and fixed; it is such an intersection which has been methodologically challenging as well as empirically apparent.

Complexities and complications: Researching class and sexuality

This research draws upon 60 in-depth interviews with white lesbian ($n = 46$) and gay ($n = 14$) parents in the United Kingdom, from middle-class and working-class backgrounds. My sample included parents with partners, parents in variously combined households, 'step-families' and single mums and dads, ranging from 18 to 63 years old. For brevity, this section will be condensed, given that a more thorough methodological account has been produced elsewhere (see Taylor, 2009).

Class is indeed complex; many have felt, known and theorised this complexity, even as class analysis is derided as simplistic, confusing and no longer relevant. In seeking to speak to both working-class and middle-class parents, I wanted to explore the inter-relatedness as well as the inequality between these lived in categories. I wanted to explore the difference of class, as a lived in, structuring experience, reproduced and ruptured in relation to sexuality. Interrogating middle-classness is difficult given its 'neutral' status, where my comparisons and contrasts at times felt similarly difficult, even disturbing. I wanted to be respectful to interviewees' lives. And attentive to inequalities painfully experienced and grappled with.

In conducting this research, I have wrestled again with my own frustrations, which is not to foreground these but to make them explicit, so that the knowledge which I construct and produce here can be situated (this frame of frustrations is not, however, my sole or primary reference point either theoretically or methodologically). Such frustrations frequently posed an interrogation of personal and professional positionings vis-à-vis interviewees (Almack, 2007), particularly in relation to sexuality, gender, class and parental status (see Taylor, 2009). I do not have children, which potentially disrupts an alignment of 'sameness' based on sexuality (see Weston, 1991; Lewin, 1993). In problematising 'insider status' there may be a range of significant factors that structure the differences between researcher/researched and the production of knowledge therein.

As researcher I have been challenged by the apparent desire for 'sameness', understood as access to the same privileges and entitlements of heterosexual parenthood and to the same processes of legitimisation. Privileges, resources and entitled expectations were frequently mobilised, for example, in the securing of a 'good' school, in telling 'good' parental tales and in generally presenting as good subjects and citizens, manifest also in desires to undertake civil partnerships. The necessity to act, present and tell the self in such ways is a difficult thing to do when parenting 'credentials' are fraught and challenged in everyday encounters; once secure positions are seemingly disappeared. But the classed difference here may be in their resurrection and reappearance. It may well be painful to present, and be queried, as the 'proper' parent. But the knowingness, even naturalness of such proper presentations, and the materialisation of these across social spaces, did secure advantages for middle-class parents.

Where discussion of sameness/difference has been situated between heterosexual parents and their non-heterosexual counterparts, a consequential *classed* difference appears in the ways that middle-class interviewees could be rescued in terms of 'just' doing things that 'make good sense', using the resources that they had and seeking to accumulate more. Rarely, if ever, are working-class parents able to easily align with such classed sentiments of 'good sense'. Nor are they able to mobilise material resources to secure and legitimise their parenting, whether that be in negotiations with social and educational providers or in movements away from – or towards – specific locations, school and communities.

Below, I draw upon a case study of two interviewees' lives, deliberately avoiding a polarised picture of working-class and middle-class interviewees (such stark contrasts are, however, evident in the data). The differences that I present are also the ones which I have been forced to reconsider and readdress in light of accounts of the complexity of middle-class lives. Feminists have recently asked what the best methodological approaches are to cast light upon connected categories (such as working-class, middle-class) as they are lived out, inhabited and re-produced. Both Valentine (2007) and McCall (2005) highlight the use of the case study approach, which seeks to take an individual's experience and then extrapolate to the broader social location embodied by an individual. This is an approach I will use in discussing the intersection of class, gender and sexuality. The reader may judge if the intersectional efforts are mired in confusion, where intersectionality stalls and breaks down, or if the coming together of different axes of difference and inequality illuminates the mutually constituted lived-in experience of class, gender and sexuality.

Consider these two interviewees' experiences and accounts of being a lesbian mother and a gay dad: Abi (36) and Geoff (44). Their different stories cast light upon the varying privileges and disadvantages, intersecting classed, sexual and gendered (im)possibilities. These stories may be perceived as oppositional and indeed there are times when this seems the most plausible tale, a drastic difference and an evident inequality in routes into parenting and of family life more generally, buffered by or isolated from social supports and networks. Yet accounts are inevitably rendered more complicated, in the messy inhabitation, contestation and replication of social categories, forcing attention to the 'differences that matter' across time. Class, gender and sexuality are mutually and co-constructed here, where social ropes elevating status may be taken-for-granted, necessary and disappeared at different times.

In using these two interviewees as case studies I wish to highlight the tangled webs navigated by Abi and Geoff; while I see the worth in considering the location embodied by these interviewees I am also conscious that these two interviewees don't stand for all the complexities and complications in lesbian and gay parental experiences. Again, their accounts don't emerge, disembodied 'from nowhere', to be summarised in print. Of course, Abi and Geoff embody a history, present (and anticipated future) with journeys before and beyond parental pathways and practices. Such paths exemplify transitions and tensions across time, intersecting class, gender and sexuality.

Differences and distinctions are captured in the readable 'success' of Abi who identified as middle-class, with postgraduate qualifications and a professional career, as against the 'struggle' of Geoff who was unemployed and had experienced periods of homelessness as a result of 'coming out' and exiting the heterosexual family unit. Not only do Abi's and Geoff's material locations differ, but also their routes into parenting and their 'coming out' narratives differ; where one is a story mostly of ease and acceptance, the other tells of secrecy and the living of a 'double life' for many years. For Geoff, the category 'gay dad' was claimed and contested throughout the interview, seemingly fractured by not being 'real' enough (a real man, a real father and a real gay man), not being 'out' long enough, not knowing the 'right' contacts and communities, and not quite fitting in generally.

This sense of being out of place had, unfortunately, been all too realistic given a period of homelessness, following an episode of mental and physical breakdown. Geoff's sense of reaching 'breaking point' was told through the initial denial of access to his two sons, as well as through material hardships. Abi's emotional stress was perhaps no less painful or fraught on a personal level as she struggled to finance assisted insemination over a eighteen-month period. Her involvement in everyday childcare arrangements and schooling experiences differed from Geoff's ongoing exclusion here, although, for Abi there were difficulties in establishing parental credentials to educational providers and in balancing work/care commitments with her partner and co-parent. Privileges and disadvantages reappeared and disappeared in the negotiation of familial and institutional spheres.

Commonalities in Geoff's and Abi's accounts exist in the retelling of mobility, in terms of an upward mobility for Abi from what she described as a 'lower middle-class' upbringing to a financially secure

'middle-class' existence. Conversely, Geoff described a 'descent' in material terms and in familial and societal esteem, moving from a middle-
class heterosexual family where he was the main breadwinner to a
current single, unemployed status. The lack of employment was also
explained in terms of 'getting better', demonstrating his expectation of
also 'getting on' (again), contrasting perhaps from a long-term sense
of fixity and despair. The pondering of how much these individuals
have moved, what they have lost or gained in their travels, seems somewhat of a blunt calculation, failing to capture the disturbing upheavals
and everyday efforts in 'getting by'. It seems clear that Abi and Geoff
came from differently (middle)classed backgrounds; for Abi this inspired
a desire to live differently beyond the 'lower middle-class' dynamics
she described her childhood through, where a desperate 'hanging on'
to privilege has been replaced with a financial certainty. In contrast,
Geoff described the relative ease in previous years and of expected – and
fulfilled – educational and employment gains.

While Abi determinedly rejected classed-specific 'conformity', Geoff's
prior everyday existence through such dynamics meant there was a lot
to lose in 'coming out' and rejecting this. Yet having more does not necessarily mean more potential loss and neither Geoff nor Abi is likely to
describe themselves as entirely 'without'. Geoff's 'fall from grace' tells of
personal, family – and societal – gendered and classed disappointments
in him 'failing' to be the traditional family provider. But Geoff's continued reluctance to re-establish contact with his sons and his ex-wife
potentially mirrors a typical tale of 'absent' fatherhood, where the necessary 'escape' from family life was articulated as something he just
had to do – for himself. Abi's upward mobility, to a different strata of
middle-classness, also tells of her refusal of 'fit in' to normative gendered
roles, a struggle she 'wins' in attaining a more 'cosmopolitan' (liberal,
diverse, middle-class) city lifestyle. Abi has gained formal, legal recognition of her civil partnership, while Geoff has had and lost a more valued
recognition. Survival, strategies and struggles exist in Abi's and Geoff's
accounts, problematising (middle)class and sexual reproductions. There
are reversals and refusals within their accounts, which speak of privileges
lost *and* gained, similar to the broader interview sample.

Interviewees differently experienced and related classed experiences
and identifications. For some, positioning in class terms was a 'story to
tell', with a coherent, if disrupted, narrative of upward mobility, moving away from that which had been constraining – whether this was
articulated as a movement away from working-class or middle-class positionings. Others pointed to the variety and instability within what could

be considered 'middle class' where sexuality meant standing somewhat outside the edges of the box. Standing on the edge of other classed – and sexualised – positions was, however, all too 'obvious' for others and went, not as a commentary on individualised mis-placements, but rather as something that 'just is'. Having something to tell, whether that be a story of not fitting in, of moving up or down in terms of social esti-mation and materially, may be contrasted with a matter-of-fact sense of things being how they are, necessitating a 'getting on' with it, where there is 'no story' (McDermott, 2004). As Byrne has argued, discourses of class and gender are '. . . implicated in these different renderings of the self' (2006: 45).

Jacqui has a 'story to tell' regarding her class mobility, moving away from a 'disadvantaged' background, in pursuit of educational achieve-ments. Interestingly, this gain is also expressed as a potential loss, signified by the 'pretensions' standing against a materiality which can still be evidenced:

> I would say I'm working-class with middle-class pretensions (laugh-ter). I'm definitely working-class. In my family, it was never said that we could go to university or we could do anything like that, you know, you've stopped school, you finish school at 16 and you went out and got a job, that's it. (Jacqui)

Others also reflected on the possibilities of upward mobility, reflect-ing on their own changing educational and employment opportunities. Differently, Steph spoke of deliberately moving away from a 'boring and very conventional' suburban middle-class upbringing. In highlighting the variety of middle-classness, from tedious tradition to a tolerant lib-eralism, some interviewees spoke of being a bit 'outside the box' of middle-class standards and signifiers, although these were often still invoked as well as rejected. This is evident in Ann's account of being a 'bit unconventional' but being a 'Guardian reader' nonetheless. Ann's stepping out of the mainstream is directly related to her coming out, claiming a new sense of self.

The variety of class led Lorna to ponder on the mixture of sentiments, loyalties and politics constructing her own sense of class, where her objective employment and educational positioning as a middle-class professional contrasts with a sense of unity in being in the Socialist Workers Party for many years. Lorna asked if I wanted a '5000 word essay on the subject' (I did not), again highlighting the story to tell here, where the conclusion is that she most definitely wants her child to be middle-class: 'I'd say I was middle-class because I aspire for him to be as good a person as he can be.' The moral and material weight of class resulted in an avoidance for some who, aware of all its encompassing nature, desired to stand outside, to get away. Rachel considered class to include 'belief system' as well as 'how you're going to pitch yourself socially' meaning that 'The further into it I sort of go, the more I would actually want to jump out of the system completely.'

In contrast, the sense of 'no story' to tell was apparent in working-class respondents' sense of the 'obviousness' of their class position, where there seemed nothing else to say. It wasn't that these accounts were any less complex but their expression simultaneously co-existed with their sidelining, rather than reflexive foregrounding.

> I would put myself in working-class, just I don't know, just your basic I'm just, I'm not like an upper-class, you know. I wouldn't class myself as being middle-class either. I don't know as low as you can get, no I don't know. I've never classed myself as anything, you know. I've never really thought about it really. Oh lower-class. (Jody)

Jody negotiates the extremes of class, eventually placing herself as 'lower-class', while Karen was very definite, highlighting her position at the 'bottom' of the class spectrum as a result of financial circumstance:

> I would say the bottom of the bottom, I mean when I was very young there was the five of us lived in a one bedroom flat... We didn't have any money, we didn't have anything, everything was always hand-me-downs and it was *not* a good quality of life... and I think the thing of seeing yourself a little bit further down had already set in my mind and that's why I lived sort of the way I do to better myself for me and my baby. (Karen)

Karen tells of obviously knowing and feeling her class position and of the desire to do better. Parental desires and possibilities were often articulated as another manifestation of class, apparent in both Stacy's and Clare's accounts of accessing rights, services and networks, 'trading on privilege', even as Stacy still centres self-determination:

> Yeah, I think, let's be honest, I'm probably from a middle-class background. I think if you go on what my parents are, I would say that my dad is probably upper middle-class. He used to have a very well paid job, but I don't think that that does determine class, I think you

determine your own socio economic group or whatever. I think probably I must be middle-class, in that, you know, the job I do, the type of house I've got, the aspirations I have for my children that sort of thing. I think it's much easier to be, this is going to sound awful, a middle-class lesbian with children, than it would be to perhaps be a working-class lesbian with children, because I just think it's just terrible stereotypes, but I think, within my social circle anyway, because of the kind of people I mix with, they probably are quite accepting of the fact that I'm a lesbian, you know, so I think that has helped really. (Stacy)

Clare speaks of negotiating various clinicians, nonetheless feeling capable of claiming rights with her partner as well-informed, articulate subjects. They have the knowingness, resources and confidences to move in and claim space:

We're scary, you know? Yeah, we are both articulate and we've come from countries where we are used to having our rights and we know how to find out information for ourselves. The health visitors don't like us, they are afraid of us. We just look like the sort of people who could get really annoyed and make complaints and be a nuisance. And I know that's resource-based, but not everyone has that and that's just really unfair that we trade on that privilege. (Clare)

While class positionings and privileges were felt in moments of parental negotiation and intervention, respondents' broader social networks, families and friendship groups also provided a classed gauge where who they were in class terms was made (in)visible in who was – or was not – around them; 'We don't really have acquaintances of any other class so it is difficult for us to comment on whether or not it matters' (Cathrine). Nigel tells of coming to realise that 'classes can mix', the experience of which begins to challenge and erode his own assumptions and 'pretensions'. While Nigel has revised his opinion, Peter notes his 'luck' in being able to move exclusively in 'fairly cultured and liberal circles' amongst individuals with 'very liberal middle-class values'.

Children were also understood as inhabiting classed positions, where Dana spoke of 'brining him [son] down to earth', noting the difference between her own comprehensive and her son's private education, as well as the difference between this personalised contrast, standing against the homogeneous and heredity nature of private schooling in general. As well as educational distinction, others sought cultural distinction for their children, introducing them to 'music', 'art' and a wide range of social and academic pursuits (Ball, 2003; Lareau, 2003; Devine, 2004). This strategy sat alongside another version of parenting where children would learn the 'value of money' rather than taking things for granted and would not be 'spoiled' (Michelle). Notably, Nina told of the difference between her own and her son's background in terms of him *not knowing* about certain things, such as the unemployment queue, even as she is cautious not to class herself above her neighbours, noting that she will always live on a council estate:

> I was made so proud because my younger son...I said 'I've got to go down the post office' I had to go and get stamps. He said 'Are you going to get your money' and I said 'what are you on about Ryan?' and he went, 'Are you going to get your money down the post office like Daniel's mother does?' and I went 'Does Daniel's mother get her money down the post office?' 'Every week' and I was like 'Ok I think she's on the dole'. I explained that Daniel's mother was on the dole and he went 'what's the dole?' and I tried to explain to him and he still didn't get it. I was really proud, because he's never seen that that's a way of life. That makes me sound like a snob sometimes when I sit down and think about it because when I was younger and I was single, well I wasn't a single parent but when I was younger, when I was like 20 I was on the dole but I couldn't contemplate it now and I don't want my children to realise that that's their fall back. You know, they haven't got a clue what it is and I'm quite happy with that. (Nina)

Nina tells of pride and movement of not going back to a place where she had been. The sense of difference and distinction could be felt at different points in time and in different places, negotiated between (ex)partners and households. The 'value of money' is a lesson learned in contrasting parental backgrounds, where Kathy's children also learn respective class differences:

> Jill's mum and dad will bung them £60 to go on their holidays, where mum and dad send them £5 for their birthday...And I'm just saying, I've had to explain, '...my mum cleans toilets, Grandma is a PA to a Company Secretary who's got shares'. (Kathy)

Class and sexuality intersect in interviewees' material and subjective positionings, apparent in naming and doing family across everyday social spheres. The stories which interviewees tell of their lives are classed: where some self-position as agentic subjects, actively transforming their lives in 'coming out' and claiming space, others speak of the uneasy shifts in class positioning, slippages and rejections, of stepping outside the system. The ability to name, practice and resource such a side-step, a different way of being, often relied upon reserves of capitals, mobilised in occupying and securing familial territory. Where some can outline their distance from normative categorisation and practices, feeling a positive sense of difference, others sought to position firmly with the 'ordinary'; 'difference' *and* 'sameness' could be claimed and rejected strategically, still reliant upon and reinforcing a sense of the 'other', as profoundly classed. Others still are hesitant to tell their story, feeling that there is no story; this book seeks to interrogate what this means in relation to parental positionings and (dis)engagements across social arenas. The complexities and complications which interviewees tell in relating their family circumstances, routes into parenting, finances and everyday interactions are therefore highlighted in subsequent chapters.

3
Ticking All the Wrong Boxes? Gay Parents and the (Im)possibility of Being Right

This chapter explores interviewees' routes into parenthood and the confirmations, denials and complications involved in achieving and affirming parental status. While lesbian and gay parents' 'creative' routes into parenting have been evidenced as innovative, even revolutionary, this perhaps sidelines more 'normative' pathways, as well as their disruptions and discontinuities (Weston, 1991; Stacey, 1996; Weeks et al., 2001; Agigian, 2004). Many interviewees (36) had children in previous heterosexual relationships and spoke of the 'inevitability' of this (heterosexual) route (Evans, 2006; Gillies, 2006), as well as ongoing complications in negotiating and refusing this inevitability. Here, possibilities and predictabilities intersected with classed transitions; what interviewees imagined for themselves and what others imagined for them, still, compellingly constructed around heteronormativity. Yet middle-class interviewees articulated their 'coming out' experiences as enactments of determination and confident self-actualisations, breaking with the past. Working-class interviewees, in general, spoke of the inevitability of 'messy' routes and were unlikely to position themselves as autonomous, reflexively aware actors, defining themselves against institutional, familial and even 'community' expectations. Notably, those who had children by alternative means (such as assisted insemination or adoption) were mostly from middle-class backgrounds. All still had to gauge, perform and even resist the constitution of 'respectable' routes into parenthood, often as a defence but sometimes as a (classed) offence where more privileged interviewees positioned themselves against the 'poor' parenting of others – in order to redeem themselves.

In this chapter, the emotional, social and material resources and capitals which interviewees are able to draw upon to consolidate and affirm their sense of family will be highlighted. The *choice* of family was not taken up, enacted or experienced equally and choices were often framed by both implicit and explicit classed 'costs' where parents were often materially and morally assessed. Both middle-class and working-class lesbian and gay parents face struggles in their routes into parenting, and in establishing solid, legitimate parental 'credentials' thereafter, ever threatened by, for example, the known status of donors, legal and clinical costs, custody battles and through the general social disapproval in not being deemed 'fit for purpose' (Cooper and Herman, 1995; Barney, 2005). Medical and welfare services frequently complicate and clarify the biological and social nature of families, where lesbians and gay men's access to such services underscores the classed and sexualised boundaries of (un)acceptability. While interviewees reported disagreements with ex-partners, clinicians, social workers and medics, middle-class status could often, but not always, partially buffer and protect against these, 'ticking (almost) all the boxes' of parental approvals. In a world of judgements and appropriate standards, the middle-class standard may be something worth clinging onto, a glimmer of respectability in a potentially shady landscape.

The first section 'In for the long haul? Family and extended obligations' explores interviewees' experiences of 'doing things differently', where difference was asserted, even as 'tradition' was also embraced and emphasised. The two things are in no way mutually exclusive and this is highlighted by the narratives which encompass both change and continuity within a familial context. This moves onto a discussion of possibilities and perceptions in doing family 'In the best interests of the child? Possibilities and perceptions'; where interviewees are often positioned as compromising the 'best interests' of children many sought to secure their own best interests in establishing themselves as otherwise normal, ordinary parents (Clarke, 2001). To claim this, however, does not always make it so and 'Fit for purpose' explores the professional mediation of parental capacity, via social workers and clinicians. More broadly, 'Respectable routes? Parental pathways and positionings' unearths the construction of (im)proper pathways to parenting, arguing that working-class and middle-class interviewees told their journeys and transitions in quite different ways, where 'respectability' versus 'inevitability' was variously negotiated. Finally, the last section 'Like the letters on countdown? "Picking" children' investigates the material and emotional costs of accessing sperm, whether through clinics or more informally, raising questions about the worth of family as desired biological and social traits are sought, with the need to 'look like' a family profoundly felt (Jones, 2005). Acceptable likenesses and 'resemblances', whether that be in doing things differently or in establishing an 'ordinariness', are often as classed as they are sexualised and here working-class and middle-class parents found that they rarely could tick all the boxes.

In for the long haul? Family and extended obligations

Several interviewees spoke of their families 'not fitting' (heteronormative) conventions, where choices were made with and against such a mis-fit. Yet the situation and discussion of this 'mis-fit' as counter-hegemonic, as offering a different way of life embodied in family members' active creation, planning and choices was only articulated by middle-class interviewees. Edward, for example, had lived in a heterosexual relationship for 14 years and had entered into a 'child rearing project' as a co-parent. Despite their subsequent split Edward was 'in for the long haul', amicably working out shared childcare responsibilities throughout the years. Like Edward, others spoke of their families as being spatially dispersed and composed of multiple layers and reconstitutions, extended in many directions, where new relatives were renamed and bought into family formations ('They now call Emma's mum and dad, "aunty" and "uncle"', Susan). Sam also speaks of the benefits of a large extended family and ongoing involvements, despite the physical – and emotional – distance between different members. The family as displayed here is one of great fluidity and movement, not fixed and stable but reflecting the ever-changing patterns of relationships. This change and mutation is echoed in the changing use of language and descriptions, words being found for combinations of relationships, individuals and histories which had no previous existence. The fluidity of choice was interconnected with a sense of 'not-fitting', positively embraced and actualised in (re)naming family.

Others also articulated notions of an extended family, at times refusing the connections of blood alone, including friends as family and illustrating their different approaches to family formations. As stated, middle-class interviewees were more likely to explicitly name such practices as a positive difference, rather than a necessary strategy in 'getting-by', where this was generally unnamed as a kind of difference in and of itself (Gillies, 2006). Paula articulates a sense of having two kinds of family, blood family and strong 'social networks', while Sarah at once names and separates extended and traditional family, where it would sometimes be 'difficult to distinguish' between the two. This is not about being stuck without family, grasping at whatever support comes her way, but rather works as a choice, where she can move relatively seamlessly between the two groups.

Differently, Sally more firmly rejects the foregrounding of the biological. She is bringing up her young son as a single-parent, following the death of her partner, John-Paul's birth mother. Sally also has an adult daughter and son, co-parented with a different ex-partner and she has combined names across generations and households, making these connections obvious in her young son's hyphenated name. Here she suggests that social connections may be less selfish, in their less automatic, given state, than blood 'rights':

> I'm not one of these people that think blood means family. Family is, people dedicated to each other really…Friends and my daughter…But in my eyes blood doesn't specifically mean family because of, I suppose the commitment and because of the bias that 'I'll do what I want to my family' as in the blood family, the presumptions and also those presumptions under law and everything. Lots of abuse has gone on between husband and wife and children because of the right of blood and that puts a negative bias on it. Um, and sometimes the biggest commitments where people make to each other is through non-blood relationships…I think there's a bigger commitment in a less selfish way through another way of commitment…I also have my twin sister who is gay and her daughter isn't biologically hers but I see her totally as my niece and my parents see her totally as their grandchild, there's no such thing as blood being thicker than water, all that rubbish. (Sally)

While refuting the basis of 'blood' as the starting and finishing point, it is still evident in some accounts, bleeding into articulations and experiences. Kevin co-parents two children with an ex-partner, Jo (14) and Daniel (10), one of whom is his biological child (Jo). In doing things 'differently' he still highlights the value in 'two sets of parents co-parenting two children', at once combining 'difference' and 'traditions', forcing an interesting consideration of the subversion and reinforcement of familial norms.

Peter spoke of the possibilities of creating an 'urban family', undetermined by biological ties, flowing instead from spatial proximity and shared values. He had a daughter in a previous heterosexual relationship, living in a communal household, where parenting was shared. His account is suggestive of the importance of place and space in materialising family and in doing things differently, in being able to live together with – and then apart from – friends and family. Distance and proximity materialise familial (im)possibilities, highlighting too Peter's classed mobility. The terms that Peter uses suggest a degree of knowingness, a community currency, history and politics in claiming a positive difference (Weeks et al., 2001). Interestingly, his lunch time conversation with his friend, a single-mother, invokes their similarities including the ways that children function as a point of contact, even as Peter's experience in a commune would seem, at face value, very different:

> ...we were talking about this notion of 'urban family' and I don't know if it's a sociological notion or not. But we were just using it in the sense that it's not necessarily blood relatives, it's the people who end up being significant in your life and who get involved. Because, she's a single Mum, particularly people who get involved with your kid and their childcare. So for me, family, off the top of my head would be... It would be Chloe, who's my ex sister-in-law and her son Ben who's, we've never quite figured out if I'm really his uncle or not because... Oh, it's a long story but Chloe and I married a brother and sister, a long time ago. We all shared a house hoping to do this hippy commune, bringing up our kids together. Of course, that didn't work at all. And so I divorced the sister, she divorced the brother, and Chloe and I ended up still sharing the house platonically until just four years ago, down in London... They're all family basically. And Derek, who's my ex, and we started going out when Cassie was two and even after we split up, after about six years, he was always still picking her up from school a couple of days a week, and when she goes back to London, he's her favourite person. So he's definitely family... And essentially, it feels like a collection of freaks who are not necessarily, (laughter), they're not necessarily gay or straight, but they're just a bunch of quite interesting, bohemian people who have all become part of this extended, urban family, particularly centred in London. (Peter)

Within Peter's account it is easy to see the currency and validity of 'families of choice', but it is also possible to exercise constraint in the celebration and highlighting of this alone, given that it may be spatially – and materially – specific ('centred in London'), combing the efforts of a 'like-minded' and well-resourced collective. What may appear a fluid and enchanting familial 'mess' would probably not be so idyllic or charming without the resources to support it. It is not difficult to rebrand such an arrangement as chaotic and deviant, simply by placing it within the context of a council estate as opposed to a commune.

Lisa and her partner, Clare, echoed the idea of family as spatially located, if constrained (given their contested citizenship status), involving 'the people present in this room' as a practical descriptor. Kathy also spoke of significant others in different areas, who were nonetheless viewed of as family; she has childcare responsibilities for children that she cared for four years after her friend and colleague gave them up, and views them still as 'part of the package' of family. Nonetheless, most interviewees viewed their family in relatively 'closed' terms, as a 'tight knit unit' (Carrie) where immediate family consisted of the close few, in some cases described solely as themselves and their children ('Me and my daughter, that's pretty much it', Karen). Some spoke of the loss, rather than extension, of family post break-ups, where family 'just vanished' (Geoff) and others just 'popped up now and again' (Diane). Rather than seamless reconstitutions, the breaking down and building up of families often seen refusals as well as acceptances, where 'doing things differently' was variously experienced unlikely, in the case of poor single-mothers, to be socially viewed as an empowered or legitimate choice. This leads to the question of when a difference is recognised as legitimate, even revolutionary and when is it rendered a deficit? The material and subjective intersect here where options and choices are also partially a spatial consideration, reflected in the literature on the importance of space and place in 'doing things differently' and in notions of increasingly mobile and fragmented lives (Weeks et al., 2001; Beck-Gernsheim, 2002). Yet the familial 'vanishing' acts and 'closed units' spoken of here suggest a fixity and finality to families where the long haul issues cannot be conceptualised purely as enactments of ever-extended choices in more fluid spaces. The social and the biological also figure in possibilities and perceptions of 'difference', where accounts show the ongoing relevance of 'tradition' and 'nature', even in the reworking of these (Lewin, 1993; Gabb, 2004).

In the best interests of the child? Possibilities and perceptions

A frequently discussed theme was the issue of changing possibilities, afforded by reproductive technologies, and 'advancing' perceptions. Optimistic accounts hold such developments up as part of a revolution in family possibilities, albeit an unfinished one (Weeks et al., 2001). However, this revolutionary process perhaps masks a more complex, less linear tale, whereby victories are secured and celebrated only for some, the more functional and 'respectable gay' (Boggis, 2001). Andrew, who donated sperm to a lesbian couple and who is minimally involved as a father, speaks about challenging parenting as the 'sole preserve of heterosexuals'. But he does so within a framework of functioning respectability, while simultaneously seeking to undermine safe stereotypes. Being caught between comedic cliché and reliable role models, there is the idea that things will eventually change, where lesbian and gay parents will not be marked out by difference but rather by their strikingly similar normality:

> I feel that society does not have so much of a problem with single, non-threatening, almost asexual gay males such as those we see portrayed in Jack on Will and Grace or Sean on Coronation Street. But to have a sexually active couple who love each other the same way as a heterosexual couple do, and stable enough for the issue of child-rearing to be raised, challenges safe stereotypes of gay men as either effeminate, ineffectual, inept comedians and best friends of single women, or otherwise sexual deviants who are too busy engaging in deviant sexual practices to even contemplate fathering children. It impinges on everything the heterosexist community argue is the sole preserve of heterosexual parenting: stability, love, and balance. Maybe one day, when the public has got used to seeing gay characters accepted into heterosexual society in the media and popular culture generally, and when there are more functional and respectable gay role-models that are outside of gay stereotypes then acceptance will be more becoming. (Andrew)

Andrew's comments demonstrate the almost inescapability of the good homosexual/bad queer binary as threats, fears, safety and normality are at once invoked and dispelled in positioning on the right side of the homosexual fence (Duggan, 2002; Richardson, 2004); the 'gay stereotype' may be seen to be differently deployed ranging from social outcast to mainstreamed citizen. The construction of gay men as particularly sexual, removed from parenting, is evident here, refused in the equation of gay-man-as-parent (Stacey, 2006), which Andrew may do even as he is minimally involved in care responsibilities.

Andrew goes on to position the problem of intolerance as a working-class issue, where good society ('... the liberal, middle-class intelligentsia') is being 'kept back' (Moran, 2000), until the time that things have 'moved on'. Perhaps curiously, Andrew states that lesbian and gay parents should refrain from procreation, conceptualising this as 'selfishly fulfilling their own biological needs and sometimes even the desire for a fashion accessory...' Presumably, Andrew positions himself against those fashion victims, emphasising that his arrangement was *'really* wanted', and again, subjective desires perhaps exist separate from everyday practicalities and involvements in this uneasy compare and contrast account. Interestingly, Jess also separates and combines 'conformist' ideas in queer and straight society, similarly blurring and reiterating boundaries of acceptability, where 'There's less restraints to be a conformist lesbian and so the conformist idea of having kids is more accepted.' Both Jess and Andrew seemingly wrestle with the contradictions in dis-investing in 'queer' and 'straight' possibilities and perceptions. Moving from an acceptable family unit which 'ticked all the boxes' into something 'unconventional', Ann speaks of 'life laundering' as challenging and somewhat negating her middle-class status, socially and economically. The straight 'conformist' version of parenting may be seen to rely upon specifically classed and sexual constructions, where interviewees navigate various pathways through this compelling structure.

Many interviewees spoke of the pressure to stay in heterosexual relationships for the 'best interests of the child', although most had rejected this, while often still feeling the weight of its pressure. Janice, for example, echoed many women's accounts of the gendered scripting of 'wife and mother' where '... you juggle things, and you tend to put everyone else first really and inertia takes over as well'. Maureen states that getting married and having children was seen to be the 'thing to do', a sentiment negotiated in Karen's experience, having got married when she was 19 and feeling the pressure to 'just stay married' to live '... what other people perceived to be a normal life':

His parents wanted us to be together and stuff like that and that was why all the pressure. His mum rang me up after we split up and she said 'Look, can't you just stay with him for the baby's sake, just to try and keep the family going'. But I knew it wasn't the right thing to do. I said 'I'd rather have Erin grow up in two separate happy households than grow up in a household knowing that her mam is miserable and we're not getting on'. You know, I wanted to, she comes first at the end of the day and I wanted her to grow up knowing that we are both happy living separate lives... (Karen)

Karen turns the possible accusation around into a defence, noting that she is indeed concerned with securing her daughter's best interests, reframing her own possibilities and perceptions. That said, the pressure to make the best of a bad heterosexual and two-parent job is evident in many of the narratives and the difficulty in rejecting these options is clearly apparent. It is one thing to be a single-parent; to be a single gay or lesbian parent may, for some, be a step too far.

Despite social pressures, judgements and demands, interviewees often spoke of their desires to parent in terms of 'nature' and 'always knowing', inevitably following a period of 'getting broody'. Others equated their desires and decisions with biological capacities and restrictions, compelling a necessity to act, when time could 'run out'. Stacy spoke of 'always knowing' she would have children, a confidence only temporarily shaken when 'coming out', while Tracy foregrounded her long-standing maternal desires, fearing that these may be undermined by her lesbian status. Her 'natural' adoration of children meant that her desires were of no surprise to others, and her hesitancy was dismissed in light of this. Physical capabilities and innate desires ('Lisa has always wanted a family, like she knows she's going to continue breathing through the day', Clare) were highlighted alongside emotional desires and the 'right timing' of both, which, as conveyed by middle-class respondents, rested upon material, educational and employment, markers (Weston, 1991; Lewin, 1993).

In lesbian relationships desires to have children came with the negotiation of who would carry the child, often involving financial and health concerns. The practicalities of pregnancy were shared by Lisa and partner in 'taking turns':

And then also, financially. You were working, and at that point we were in a sort of transition and it was through your work that we were moving and so that was also helpful. So I did the first one! (Lisa)

While Lisa and Clare speak of 'taking turns', both being 'in for the long haul', they also note the financial factors in their decisions, apparent in Sandra's account of the practical decisions around working, giving birth and caring, where both parents could be part-time workers and part-time mothers, suiting their own best interests. Kathy's partner, Jill, had carried their children as she was the one who was working and could get maternity leave, while Kathy was in poor health ('So there was emotional and practical reasons for who did what when'). This represents another 'classing' of gay parenting, where practicalities and finances figure heavily in possibilities and pathways (Agigian, 2004).

Interviewees had to deal with various reactions from family and friends, managing the variation from positive to negative responses, which changed over time. For Carol, though, the 'physical manifestation' of her lesbian status, a child conceived through IVF, was enough to remove her from her family, and she went with one elated wave. The 'need for a father' was commonly recited to lesbian mothers and here Gemma notes the 'support' offered by a male friend, while seeking to establish her family as 'complete' and 'enough'. The comparison which she shores up in her 'defence' may be understood as particularly classed, where the fatherless children in the 'deprived' area are seemingly invisible in the construction of needs; fathers are perhaps not needed by those who are already without, in more ways than one:

> It's hard for kids of lesbians to not get constantly exposed to that kind of 'There must be a father'. You know, even some of our best heterosexual friends still kind of are very odd about that ... he said 'Do you want me to talk to her about anything?' and I said 'Oh, that's a nice offer, what do you mean?' and he said 'Well, you know, as a father, would you like me to talk to her?' ... There are loads of people that think that children have to have fathers which, considering where we live where large numbers of children don't have fathers, I think that's fascinating. (Gemma)

Such notions commonly invoke what is in the 'best interests of the child' and what children simply need and this is indeed a difficult claim to negotiate across social class, even as it remains predominantly working-class mothers who are known and positioned through their 'failure' in this respect (Lawler, 2000; Gillies, 2006). Many spoke of the importance of getting their families 'on board', undertaking long conversations to have parenting possibilities recognised. This seemed a profoundly middle-class narrative where things were to be negotiated, resourced and planned, rather than 'just happening'. Such endeavours operated beyond immediate family, encompassing friends, where knowledges and supports could be offered. Joc speaks of the importance of acceptance, having discussed this with friends and other lesbian mothers in an online forum. Sandra had also discussed the 'right time to tell' of her pregnancy, fearing the false raising of hopes, rather than outright rejection. Yet potential supports were often complicated and several interviewees spoke of 'hearts melting', where the child whose very existence was the subject of much dispute then became 'adored', even as awkward tensions remained:

> My mother was funny when I told her I was pregnant the reaction I got, em 'cause she started crying and said 'Oh, what am I gonna tell the neighbours, you've had a transplant' (laughs). But then once he was born she just absolutely adored him and was just one of six grandchildren that she had and she's just really always really adored him. (Dana)

The parents of Sarah's partner were 'horrified' and also feared 'what the neighbours would say', nonetheless driving down the motorway at the critical moment to see their granddaughter. It would seem that this change of heart continues in their ongoing disappointments, stony silences and gradual 'warming up'. Even the 'best plans' can come undone in the lack of support, where all the planning in the world doesn't necessarily secure 'privileged' parenting.

Parental reactions often invoked a binary between 'real' biological children and adopted children, which were seen as more or less acceptable. Sharon and Shirley had chosen to adopt a child, which Sharon father couldn't understand. He actively sought to change their minds, updating them with the latest information and legislation on reproductive technologies to secure 'real' biological children supposedly in everyone's best interests. Highlighting the expectation and power of the 'natural' and 'biological', Angie expressed a belief that people are more concerned with and negative about her route into parenting, via adoption, than with her lesbian status. The desire for 'likeness' and familial similarity was often so strong that the remotest hopes – and even impossibilities – of this were often clung to:

> My mum was like, 'Oh, that's quite good, that's like "Buy One Get One Free"'. With my mum, that was it, she was quite excited, and then she did the, 'Ah, well, you know, we do have twins in the family' – didn't get the whole nothing to do with me genetics bit . . . She was like, 'Oh, so we've got twins in the family as well. And Jill's got twins in her family'. (Kathy)

Kathy humorously relates practical explanations, where things are not 'obvious':

> My mum was a bit like . . . 'Oh right, it's another of those weird things you're going to do.' And Jill's mum's was a bit like, 'Well, I've heard it

all now. No man's ever going to want you if you get pregnant'. And
it was like, 'Uh huh'. They were just holding out the hope that eventually she'd grow out of a silly phase...I just said, 'Oh, you know I
used to inseminate...', and she was like, 'Was that when you put
the sperm in the marmite jar' and I was like, 'Yes.' I said, 'We're
going to a clinic, there's no marmite involved but that's what we're
doing.' And she [mother] was like, 'Oh, all right.'...And we thought
that the insemination process, we'll just keep reminding them when
we go, so we had this all - we had this whole package drawn up
about how we were dealing with each family and I had my sisters
prompting my mother to ask what was happening about the savings and stuff. Because my sisters, I get on with both, I've got three
sisters and two of them were very actively involved in promoting
my parents...So we had that...so we had different layers of people
knowing bits and pieces that they needed to know to be helpful and
supportive. (Kathy)

While Kathy's family found this all very confusing, if not disturbing,
she also had a core group of friends to provide support against this,
a 'whole package drawn up', as did Sarah, enacting a rehearsed and
resourced 'life plan'. However, talking 'at great length' via prompts and
reminders illustrates the ways that some families are not simply known
but have to be recalled, rehearsed and literally related, where life plans
may be questioned regardless of the consideration in their construction.
Nonetheless, Sarah tells of going through '...this journey with our best
friends at the same time' where they were 'all for it' and mutually supportive of one another's plans. In the context of varying 'best interests' it
was hard for both working and middle-class interviewees to secure, legitimise and 'retrieve' parenting pathways, as conveyed in continued social
pressure, rather than in multiple possibilities and softening perceptions.
Nonetheless, the differences and distinctions in terms of resources, supports and 'respectable routes' are consequential, serving to redraw the
boundaries of sameness/difference across class lines.

Respectable routes? Parental pathways and positionings

Interviewees discussed their varied pathways to parenting viewed as sus-
picious from varying perspectives including from within the lesbian
and gay 'community', where it was not easy to affirm the validity or
'respectability' of their choices. Nonetheless, many interviewees spoke
of being active choosers in planning parenting, foregrounding their

own sense of responsibility, as against that which 'just happened' all too easily. It makes sense for some interviewees to frame choices as good, solid sensible ones – this story was enacted, resourced *and* compelled, where the privilege of middle-class parents should be set against the context of institutional and societal prejudice; such 'performance' may be seen to constitute a disempowerment for middle-class interviewees. Yet in equating gay parents with thoughtful planning, a contrast exits between those who told of their transitions into parenting in quite different, classed, ways, where things 'just sort of happened' also intersecting with 'coming out' transitions and tales. The common ground of shared sexuality does not preclude a refusal to understand the choices of others. Importantly, these are not just stories which can be claimed in their circulation, rather they demonstrate the perpetuation of (un)entitled parenting performances and possibilities as well as the material inequality underlying them.

Where things did 'just happen', respondents spoke of going down the 'wrong route', explaining that this wrong turn had made them more resilient and resourceful. Jody narrates a sense of things 'just happening', similar to Kate's inevitable suppositions: 'I suppose I assumed I would get married and have kids and you know live a happy-ever-after-life I suppose'. This is not to negate or deny agency, choice and contentment within this, where Jody had 17 'quite good' years with her ex-husband:

> But it's not like, I wouldn't say I loved him, if you know what I mean I would just say 'like'. I thought, maybe thought I did 'cause I didn't know what actually love was 'cause he was my first you know. And then I had two kids off him which are now seventeen, eighteen year old but in that seventeen year I realised I was gay, you know. (Jody)

While Karen factually situates her ex-heterosexual relationship before 'coming out', for many others the weight of such a transition was emphasised in the discovery of who they 'really were'. This tale of self-discovery existed in middle-class accounts, where a certain knowing, reflexive subject position could be claimed (Gillies, 2006). It was not the case, within this sample, that only working-class interviewees had engaged in and/or had their children in previous heterosexual relations. But the ways these tales were related – or 'redeemed' – were interestingly 'classed' in the narration of things 'just happening' as against a sense of autonomy and agency, effecting a disruption with the 'past'.

Rather differently 'staying together' in the heterosexual family unit (Martin) was explained via the 'sake of the children', viewed to be in their 'best interests'. 'Coming out' and facing tremendous loss can be daunting even devastating, regardless of the kinds of cushions and privileges one has and such 'strategies' and slippages may tell of the desire to 'put a floor' on circumstances, to stop things getting worse and to secure the advantages one has (Skeggs, 1997). Yet often things play out differently, with a loss of status (or fear of) for some and a reinscription of the absence of status for others.

For example, the sense of things 'just happening' was also common to Martin's experience of being 'landed with' a typical 'old fashioned', 'catholic scenario' even in a middle-class context. In contrast to Martin's ongoing positioning through this, as he remains in a heterosexual family unit, Jenny dates this inevitable experience in the past: 'I had Monica when I was married, back a hundred thousand years ago!' While things were also rather regimented for Harriet, she is eager to retrieve her story of parenthood, emphasising that her child was not a mistake:

> I was married 'til I got myself divorced, you know, quite happily and it was, and then it just all sort of went downhill, he was in the army, I was in the army and I got out of the army to actually have children... I just sort of met women and you know... So that's sort of my sort of story into parenthood, you know, she was planned, it wasn't you know, just a mistake so to speak. (Harriet)

This would seem in many ways to be the ultimate in 'it just happened' narratives, a cascade of unplanned and unscheduled events which collided together to create the here and now. Carrie had her two sons in an ex-heterosexual relationship and told of being 'stuck' in poor employment, fearing being 'stuck' with the children, a fear which eventually inspired a life change, with the return to education and a 'coming out', rewriting sexual and classed paths. Nina also highlights material and emotional ties and constraints, accordingly postponing her own hopes and desires, not knowing what was worse – being heterosexual and unhappy, or gay and happy:

> I've always known I was gay but I suppose I tried to conform to the stereotypical 'normality', so I was in a long term relationship which resulted in both the boys and um I, he, my ex-partner was an alcoholic, and I stayed with him because I didn't know whether that was better than being in a gay relationship... It did because I just was so

unhappy when I was younger I think, that I didn't care very much and I fell pregnant when I was quite young blah blah, and it just wrecked everything and then when I fell pregnant it was a case of I wanted to go on and I wanted a career but then it was a case of I'll have a career when my kids grow up. (Nina)

Nina's repeated 'blah, blah' seems to convey the automatic, where the blanks fill in the known; the repeated experience of 'falling' pregnant discords with other interviewees' careful and 'creative' planning, often celebrated as a sign of innovative, if still difficult, differences. For Maureen, the sense of things 'just happening' then also became caught up with an anxiety that these happenings were, nonetheless, in the best interests of her children and, specifically, in relation to their 'need for a father'. James, Steve and David also spoke of the societal and familial boundaries of acceptance, and the ongoing pressure to conceive children in heterosexual relationships, articulating a sense that things might change for the next generation of gay fathers, who may not have to struggle with the same notions of acceptability. In doing so, they place their own movements alongside future imaginings situating themselves as individuals, even warriors, within a collective struggle, where the sense of being 'forced' into a straight relationship again discords with more 'dismissive' accounts of circumstances lived in and through:

> *Steve*: I think the next generation of gay fathers, it will be interesting to see how they…
> *David*: But I remember our friend Hugh who thought that we were kinda kamikaze, that we would eventually die out and I don't know whether he is right or wrong but I would have thought that the pressures that forced us into, eh, a straight relationship probably aren't there, in terms of society, as they were. But just because society finds it more acceptable doesn't mean it's acceptable to your family, you know, in a way I think there probably always will be gay fathers who achieve their parenthood in the route that we did, where we all had natural children conceived with female partners.

Steve and David also pointed to the material and spatial constraints against achieving a 'self-actualised gay identity' alongside parental possibilities, where you 'can't afford housing' (James) or 'the bus fare to Glasgow' (David):

Maybe your educational qualifications aren't very good and your mobility is therefore restricted, then your ability to develop as a gay person, with your self-actualised gay identity is going to be harder to achieve, if you can't afford or, you know, if you are not mobile it is going to be harder to establish that identity. Unless you make gay more acceptable all over. I think that's true, I just wonder how many people will be forced down the route we were forced down. (David)

Rather than things seamlessly improving, marking a moving, more accepting presence, interviewees struggled with the presumed (in)compatibilities between sexual and parental status, retelling the 'past' in relation to 'present' desires and smoothing out 'contradictions':

Everybody who knows that I'm gay if they'd just met me it's 'how did you get a baby if you are gay?' they don't understand that you can have been with a man or whatever, they want to know who my partner was, if we're still together and that's quite hard at times 'cause people don't really understand it...even though when I conceived Erin I didn't, I wasn't living a gay lifestyle, I was very much living a heterosexual married lifestyle. (Karen)

The fact that things can and do change appears to be a problematic one, with respondents reporting feeling tied to decisions, or non-decisions, made many years ago and which still impinge on their current identity and family situation. For all its self-proclaimed fluidity, people seem unwilling to allow sexuality to change much, especially when it is anchored in the concrete creation of a child. In managing the 'unexpected', other interviewees spoke of the importance of 'active planning', to reinforce the fact that parental decisions had not been taken lightly, and that their sexuality actually compelled, rather than negated, the following of proper, well thought through routes (Dalton and Bielby, 2000; Wilson, 2007). This parallels earlier comments regarding the relationship between the 'social' and the 'biological' in terms of how family is made and who counts as a parent – at once gays and lesbians are seen as too sexual (embodying the 'wrong kind' of sexuality), or too restricted by the biological to 'do parenting'. This leaves many contradictions, where parenting may be perceived as an entirely social, asexual project, which interviewees themselves negotiate, resist and repeat. Many interviewees spoke of being active choosers in planning their routes to parenthood, foregrounding their own sense of responsibility, as against that which 'just happened' all too easily.

Gemma claims an 'active choice' where family doesn't easily 'just come packaged', positioning herself against that which 'just happens' to 'het people':

> You make an active choice... and the vast majority of het people, it just sort of happens to them. You know, very rarely do they actively make the choice. It's interesting talking to women who go for fertility treatment because they are having to make the active choice. (Gemma)

Jacqui also foregrounds her own responsibility, contrasted with drunkenness and a profound lack of planning, recognisable in more conservative discourses. In both Jacqui's and Gemma's accounts it is difficult to reconcile notions of 'good planning' alongside other interviewees' experiences, where they would not be recognised via this 'redemption':

> I think that if you're going to that much trouble to have a child, it must be really wanted. I think that if it's a question of you going down the pub, you're getting pissed and you get laid and you come home pregnant, that child hasn't really been thought about or chosen, or decided on, or anything. I think that when gay people decide they want to have children they put a lot of thought and a lot of effort into it, so it's not just happening to them, they are making choices and I think that's a good thing. (Jacqui)

Immediate, even excessive, gratification is set alongside long-term planning and efforts. It is this reification of the children of choice as opposed to the children of folly which sits so uncomfortably alongside the acknowledgement of change and transition. How then to reconcile the child born within a heterosexual 'just happened' context with other precision babies?

The stories that interviewees tell of their own journeys (and those of others) do not exist in a void, untainted by societal expectations and pressures. Indeed, many interviewees spoke of 'community' responses towards them, as reinforcing – rather than dispelling – the presumed discontinuities between gay sexuality and parenthood. In some cases the 'authenticity' of sexuality, given heterosexual pasts and experiences were questioned, eliding the complexities of interviewees' biographies and identities. Such dis-identifications created boundaries as well as connections, and Elizabeth expresses this in terms of lesbian mothers having a bit more sense of the 'complexity of things':

You tend to click with people ... I think actually, probably it's the parents more who understand that side and understand the 'done the het bit, done the having children bit, done the splitting up bit', know what you're going through. (Elizabeth)

Jody speaks of the benefit of experiencing 'both sides' of life, preferring the gay 'dark side'. While all interviewees articulated their 'preferences', these were often dismissed, where their histories were somehow suspect and unattractive, as Steph describes in being 'some 40 year old heterosexual bag...', contrasting her own route to parenting with a more community-affirmed route, combining material, spatial and subjective (im)possibilities. Steph speaks of others who have 'always had that kind of world', living in close proximity and connecting in shared supports, donors and parental pathways, embodying a 'different model of being a lesbian parent'. The sense of being a 'bit on the margins' is echoed by Jess, who ironically declares that she is not 'a proper lesbian', having had a very different and not necessarily affirmed route into parenting:

But what I haven't done is therefore kind of gone and sought out lesbian support, lesbian mothers' support, because I think I would feel as though I was a bit on the margins of that. I had a very different experience. And politically, I kind of would agree with the lesbian mothers who'd gone the sort of, you know, donor route that somebody like me isn't quite what they had in mind when they had the group up. I don't have a problem with understanding that but the problems, as you have just heard, that come with changing your sexuality and having kids involved, are pretty hard as well. (Jess)

The specificities of pathways to parenting seem to open – or close – doors to community networks, knowledges and involvements, all the time negotiated with and against careful plans and inevitable happenings. Just as best interests, possibilities and perceptions, are variously classed, so too it seems are the construction of more or less respectable routes. And to complicate matters further, these sit alongside institutional de-legitimations, where class and sexual status is regulated, performed and dismissed.

Fit for purpose

In highlighting stories of choice and opportunity, research often points towards reflexive confidence and familial reclamations, foregrounding the experiences of those who openly choose to conceive as gay (Lewin, 1993; Benkov, 1994; Nardi, 1999), somewhat effacing distinctions and constraints. The 'opening up' of the possibilities for parenting is related in Weeks et al.'s (2001) research to access to community structures and knowledges, where such optimism challenges inevitable rejection of and exclusion from familial territory. Nonetheless, not all options are accessible or particularly favourable and in 'opting into' parenting many interviewees then found themselves engaged with various agencies who could deem them 'fit for purpose'.

It was mostly middle-class interviewees who found themselves in such positions, as working-class interviewees tended to have children in heterosexual ex-relationships. The evaluation nonetheless highlights the classing of prospective parents into 'functioning respectability', constructed via class, gender and sexuality, where the option may be to present and perform as such or risk rejection. Both subjective and material resources could be mobilised to effect this 'option', mediated by more or less sympathetic audiences and constrained by hostilities and institutional ignorance. Moving from adoption to experiences with clinics, in the purist of assisted insemination, the material and subjective costs of routes into parenting are again highlighted.

Of those interviewees who had adopted – or attempted to – many spoke of the tough process, including preparation classes, where their parenting abilities were, often not so subtly, assessed. Mel expressed various confidences in adoption agencies, negotiating seeming incompetence, in refusals to return phone calls ('I mean there wasn't even an answer machine, it just rang, a phone in an empty room I think'), to downright rejection, given Mel's lesbian status ('I was a wee bit taken aback, um, one agency wouldn't, didn't take on same-sex couples at all, they were very nice about it but that was out of the question'). Mel, although wanting to move areas, was staying put for the time being, unwilling to start this process all over again in a new locale. She was 'desperate' for a child and happy to 'consider almost any sorts of children' making the eventual match 'much easier'. Just to get an appointment involved much time and energy, consuming many financial and emotional resources, carried over in eventually finding a suitable agency, where intensive preparation classes were the next hurdle to overcome ('there were evening classes I think around two and a half to three hours, they were quite intensive...'). Despite such struggles and invested resources, Mel firmly believes that adoption is morally the right way, repeated in Sharon and Shirley's tale of choosing to parent where they were 'most needed'. It is hard to imagine that the 'moral' imperative can be invoked in working-class parents tales, even as it is (un)easily invoked in middle-class gay parenting experiences.

A couple of interviewees talked about being the first gay couple to pass through particular adoption agencies, being faced with a certain curiosity, both welcoming and unwelcoming. Dana and her partner were the first lesbian couple to go through the adoption process with one agency; while the agency itself was welcoming, if somewhat naïve in managing negative responses, the media hostility generated meant that they eventually had to walk away from adopting the child which had been placed with them. The process was a long, laborious and emotional one, with many 'losers'. It really is hard to underestimate the difficulties faced by prospective parents in this scenario, and that narratives presented are a far cry from a system of equality. Faced with court room and media interrogation, and with a bag placed over her head for attempted anonymity, Dana is still at least able to think of the positives, in paving a path for others to succeed, even as she went 'through hell in the process'. For Vicky and Wendy the process to be approved as foster carers took over a year, where 'all sorts of in-depth stuff' including sexuality was asked about. Vicky and Wendy's 'stable relationship' was ground for assessment, where social workers also interrogated on the grounds of 'health and safety', making sure children would have a united parental front, rather than a volatile mix. Dana also experienced this intensive gaze, choosing to get professional photographs taken, as part of a kind of parental CV, seeking to 'dot all the I's and cross all the t's'. Although similarly compliant, Mel is critical of such intensive and invasive evaluations, given the shortage of placements, where children are 'crying out to be adopted' in whatever circumstances, straight, gay or otherwise. While many could rationalise the explicit checks made and were willing, if not always happy, to go along with these, such checks and cautions could become more obviously homophobic in nature. It would seem that the best way to negotiate the system, to have even a chance of getting through it, is to acquiesce to all the demands placed upon you, however much they may rankle. This is an odd situation to be placed in and raises interesting questions about which type of people the system will reward. In being deemed 'fit for purpose', potential parents had to prove that they'd considered all eventualities and 'hazards', revealing the institutionalised structuring of proper planning, this time in relation to the consideration of gender-balanced 'role models':

I was kind of going, 'Pardon me?!' Loads and loads of, such emphasis on their role model. I know it's important but like that was the only thing that mattered and, you know, 'How are you going to deal with the fact that this child was going to be bullied because of his or her parentage?' And it's like, 'Well, how do we deal with any bullying?' You know, people deal with racist bullying. We thought, 'Okay, fair enough'. We got as far as getting to the panel and they said, 'Oh sorry, two of our panel members won't approve lesbians because of religious regions'. That's it. We then, of course, kicked up a huge big stink. (Angie)

Angie has to kick up a 'big stink' in order just to be heard – this is not an account of an entitled parent pushing her weight around but rather of someone fighting against huge odds. While Angie and her partner felt able to negotiate the system, drawing upon their shared knowledge of social work practices, they were nonetheless surprised and put off by complicated processes – not to mention the question of suitable clothing:

> ... We knew we were going to be their first gay couple, the first lesbian couple and I don't think they'd even considered gay men, but we thought, fine, okay, somebody has got to be first. The social workers were like, 'Yeah, yeah, we've done the training', so we started with our social workers and we came across some really, really bizarre attitudes.
> *Yvette*: Really?
> *A*: 'Why don't you wear skirts?' And I have to say, she was the most dikey looking social worker you have ever seen. (Angie)

The feeling of intensive evaluation was a common and mediated one, where Sharon and Shirley approached with caution, having done the reading. They did not feel threatened or challenged by the social work preparation course and in fact were able to 'challenge social workers' having an all-in-all positive experience. Few did report that things had happened 'fairly' quickly, 'without a hitch', often spoken with and against named difficulties, resolved in the final stages when things 'came together'. Nonetheless, the complexities of the adoption process were, for Sharon and Shirley, offset by the greater difficulties in having birth children and explaining the 'quite complicated' absence of a father. Interviewees, in engaging with various institutional structures, negotiated, resisted and re-produced normativity, where what was allowable and easier was constructed between institutional (im)possibilities and personal preferences – mirrored too in experiences of insemination.

From initial contacts, to follow-ups, engaging with clinics and agencies was often a fraught process, both financially and emotionally, beyond the costs of seeking sperm, where interviewees again reported various monitorings. In dealing with clinics, interviewees were also aware of the 'risks' and limitations, all of which made for costly circumstances. Michelle spent much money on tests and on repeated attempts, noting the limitations of frozen sperm, and the stressful 12 months of to-ing and fro-ing between cities to access the clinic. Lisa and her partner, Clare, had chosen a known donor and were trying to proceed via a clinic, as a less risky strategy. Yet its policy of freezing sperm to minimise risk actually increased their frustrations and minimised their own decision-making capacities, highlighting the distinctions between 'natural' risk and this 'mediated' risk and the varying viabilities between them:

> *Clare*: They are really, really clear about the fact that one man coming to donate to one family means the same amount of resource, creates a child for one family, and if that person turned up as an anonymous donor that could be used for up to ten families with the same resource of collection and testing so it's not something they financially want to put money in.
>
> *Lisa*: At the same time they have to test heterosexuals the same way and they do that for one family...The only thing they don't do is freeze it for 6 months, which you should be able to as a lesbian person who has a known donor say 'We don't care if it's not frozen, I'm taking this risk' the same way as the heterosexual woman is taking a risk with her partner...I mean they do inseminations, they do artificial inseminations on heterosexuals all the time, with the man's sperm, and that's exactly the same. It should be when a lesbian couple or person presents with a donor...But I think you should be able to say if you want to 'No, I don't care. I am willing to take the risk, I am willing to risk that' because that's what heterosexual women are doing essentially.

Women themselves were screened and monitored in engaging with clinics, jumping through various institutional red tape and being vetted with blood tests. The setting that Michelle describes is hardly a relaxed one, being told to 'get on the bed, open your legs', while, before getting to this somewhat uncomfortable stage, Sarah and Abi had to 'jump through all these hoops'. Such processes were emotionally draining, often resulting in tensions within relationships, where one partner felt the burden, bureaucratic and physical, more than the other ('I'd go up on the train to London on my own and have the scans and everything so she was very, she was not really involved at all and then she wasn't involved in the pregnancy particularly', Tracy).

Many humorously retold their negative experiences with clinics, where the outcome lessened the struggle. Others reported a more positive experience from the outset, which, however, seemed to rely upon a 'fantastic nurse' and the 'good few' experts, who were in the know. Contacts were also passed on through community contacts reliant of course in being part of such networks (Weeks et al., 2001). Stacy accessed the same clinic that she believes produces most of the lesbian parented children in the North East. The very professional touch perhaps reduces the negativity behind yet another form of screening, where those who 'don't want their sperm to go to gay couples' are removed from the available list.

Negotiations with health professionals and social workers could often be difficult and stressful, even if this computerised monitoring mediates the social hostility. It must be a little easier to read rejection than to have it said to your face, but nevertheless rejection it is. Getting the 'wrong', unknowing or awkward health visitor can be an uncomfortable experience and Kathy recalled being told that her partner's dates were wrong, an impossibility given that her partner conceived through assisted insemination. Often such scenarios were best dealt with through humour, which Kathy demonstrates, even as she outlines real anger and fear in being (un)able to perform a 'middle-class' status. Parental 'performances' are mediated, even rehearsed, in being able to tap into professional networks, even as Kathy is quick to emphasise that this would be her only chance – she could not afford other repeated journeys:

And when we went to the clinic, had to do that whole psychological talk to the psychologist malarkey...So we tapped into our social work friend she was like part of the Child Protection Team, she was like, 'Well, what we'll do, we'll do like a bit of an interview, like we do for people who want to do adoptions.'... I was like, 'All right, that's it, I'm not doing it, can't be doing role play, I'm not getting into this, bloody middle-class, bloody, bloody...' I was just all for moaning and Jill just said, 'You're right, just calm down'. 'Well, look at it, they bloody don't ask people this before they pop off to a night club.' So I was doing my [roar] Jill was doing the 'Well, we'll just go through some of them, we'll have a look.' But I was really thinking, 'Bloody hell'. Because I was thinking, '... we're never going to be allowed to do it and we've only got another option in Manchester and travelling up and down to Manchester isn't really an option, to do the insemination.' ... The clinic thing was quite bizarre. Because he did this whole thing, 'Unless my psychologist said that it's OK, we won't able to proceed with the procedure'. And the psychologist was such a stereotype of this really laid back hippy. She was just like, 'No, he has to say that. No, no, as long as you can answer these questions, no, it's nothing like the adoption procedure, it's what you're going to tell a rampaging teenager why there's no daddy.' And I thought, 'Well, I could go and ask at least ten of my straight friends whose husbands are no longer around or who never met their daddy.' And she was like ... 'Oh, you've obviously put some ...' You know, when we explained the support systems we put in place, she didn't have a problem at all. (Kathy)

There are various resources and constraints at play here where knowing how to perform, and being compelled to perform, sit alongside both the resourcing of this as well as its potential misreading and failure. Kathy, perhaps more uncomfortably than others, nonetheless succeeds in telling the story and again links – and possible distinctions – are invoked in telling sameness/difference between lesbians and single-mothers.

In managing such negotiations, Kathy, like others, gained the support and advice of many friends, also going to see a lesbian solicitor firm, buffering against such hostility. Similarly, many interviews made use of their own friendship networks, even getting involved in established networks, such as Pink Parents, while others spoke of more informal knowledges, passing on contacts and getting in touch via friends and being 'in the know'. Dana spoke of getting 'loads of lesbians' ringing up for advice over the years, absorbing collective information, strategies and recommendations. Protective networks of friends, created in the absence of and alongside supportive families, facilitated the exchange of information, from accessing and using clinics, right the way through to childcare responsibilities. A little bit of knowledge can be a very useful thing, especially in the face of seemingly systematic hurdles. Kathy had mobilised her friends to secure a certainty around childcare, with people she shared similar values with, seeking to avoid a traditional 'next of kin' model. This, however, had to be operationalised in legal consultations, where possibilities beyond initial parenting pathways were enabled through social and economic resources, as Kathy demonstrates:

> So before we took the steps around insemination, we had to know if anything happened to either of us, there would be adults who we wanted their values to be shared with the kids... Well, I didn't want to go into insemination thinking either of our parents would have control of our kids or siblings have control of our kids... and when we were talking about going through the insemination, we obviously talked to different people in our lives and get their ideas and opinions, just for how to go about it and the different... because it wasn't just plain sailing, a case of, 'Oh yes, we'll just go there'. First of all we had to find a blinking clinic that would do it, there was only two... then there was the financial implications, because I was on benefits, and there was lots of costs, if it had have gone on for quite a while. (Kathy)

Kathy's statement draws out the shared issues of problems and practicalities, even as these were variously negotiated and resourced, whether that be financially or socially, in isolation or in connection with community contacts and knowledges. At many points, interviewees' pathways to parenting, whether through adoption or through assisted insemination, could be disrupted, threatened by institutional de-legitimation, just as a professional performance could buffer as well as disappoint. The narratives of adoptions are at times harrowing and appeal to a very human desire to 'do the right thing' or to access that which does not seem that much to ask. And the repeated running into barriers, questions, accusations or ignorance is bruising, no matter how many friends and networks stand as buffers. Parental 'choices' were ever-framed through such constraints, present too in the selection of donors, and the negotiation of biological and social roles and (im)possibilities.

Like the letters on countdown? 'Picking' children

A major difficulty in 'picking children' was the financial cost in getting sperm, and in negotiating degrees of contact and 'risk', where lesbians of the 'liquid classes' were more successful in this (Agigian, 2004). Several interviewees had resorted to instrumental heterosex to avoid such costs or had at least considered this less costly option; Karen also envisages this as the most plausible route for her in the future, rather than using clinics or adoption services. This potentially fractures the story of things 'just happening', where the ease – rather than 'mistake' – of that route is recognised as enabling, rather than simply wrong. Karen has pondered upon other options, recognising that there are a variety of ways that lesbians can have children; having heterosex is, for Karen, simply more affordable.

The huge costs of accessing sperm via clinics were repeatedly highlighted. Faced with 'something like £600 a cycle', for insemination in a UK clinic, Lisa and Clare thought they'd upgrade and go somewhere else, although their ironic tone is hard to miss, 'So we thought maybe for a grand a cycle we'd go somewhere more interesting like Belgium' (Clare). Lisa and Clare note the ease in getting sperm *if* you have the resources (including time, knowledge and money), spending much time too on internet forums '...it's the easier way still to get sperm, even though legislation has changed here, if you have the money'. Sandra also found the whole process 'extremely expensive', working out at about £12,000, while Stacy detailed all the costs, including petrol, initial consultation fees, trans-vaginal scans and psychological testing. In her case this was just possible, given that she became pregnant first time.

Even when adopting a more 'DIY' (do-it-yourself) approach, via a known donor, Lisa and Clare still incurred huge costs in meeting accommodation and petrol costs of the known donor; the costs and travels had Lisa and Clare comparing themselves to a 'travelling circus'. Some women self-inseminated, using friends, engaging in a similar process of trial and error. Yet the informal nature of such engagements did not always result in a relaxed atmosphere, sometimes aggravating domestic situations, where Kathy comically describes 'some horrible sitcom' sitting in fluffy slippers and a night gown in her bedroom, awaiting sperm-on-wheels, while an argument about this brewed in the other room. It is similar to flat pack furniture; it is appealing because it is cheap and it all seems simple enough, but the reality can be a maelstrom of frustration, resentment and arguments over an Allen key.

Whether through a clinic or through informal arrangements, decisions about who should be the donor (whether that selection was based on limited biological information or on known 'qualities') were ever present, with interviewees deliberating on what made a father, whether they were necessary and what the problems and limitations of such 'necessity' may be (biological, financial, emotional) (Parks, 1998; Agigian, 2004; Clarke and Kitzinger, 2005). Some interviewees reported 'relatively easy' access to and agreement between themselves and sperm donors, often through helpful, facilitative friends and networks and Carol describes being 'incredibly lucky' in this respect. Clare and Lisa tell of simply being in the 'right place at the right time', where things happened 'accidentally' ('We're the first accidental lesbian parents!', Lisa), even as their plans had involved cross-continental travels. Lisa's self-appointment as the 'donor hooker' suggests a bit more effort in this 'huge process' than accident and luck alone.

As well as agreeing upon and finding a willing donor, other considerations also brought a series of barriers and tensions, especially the issue of negotiating the right amount of contact (Lewin, 1993; Stacey, 1996), whether that was no contact or potential contact in, for example, any child reaching a certain age and wanting to 'know a bit more'. For Cathrine, there was a certain confidence in feeling that there would be no 'third person' in her family, speaking of 'eliminating' involvement: 'In fact I'd probably want him off the birth certificate and we would do the supporting of the child.' It was hard to access to the right kind of donor and construction of this varied, where an ability to 'go it alone' also revealed the supports and resources to be mobilised in constructing an independent, rather than deficient, account (see Bock, 2000).

Lorna could not believe the monetary value and expectations surrounding sperm donation also feeling that she faced a hostile 'misogynistic' response. She had many resources to draw upon in creating her family, the sense of which continued to be positively affirmed. However, the cushioning perhaps provided by material, social and emotional supports was not enough to guarantee 'entitlement' to parental rights, as Lorna's experiences with searching for a sperm donor suggest, where she sensed that 'lesbians, couldn't and shouldn't bring up a child'. Having a circle of friends who had themselves been adopted, Lorna believed it important that her daughter can establish contact with her sperm donor at some future point, should she wish to do so. This possibility is separate from and not reliant upon financial obligations, where she has deliberately separated out the distinction between 'father' and 'donor' in this particular respect, while at once disputing and highlighting the importance of having a father:

> Me and my ex-partner decided to have a child ten years ago and we advertised within the gay community for a donor but found that full of prejudice, misogynist prejudice ... I found it quite misogynist and then also, selling sperm and one guy rang me up and said 'Well you wouldn't want think twice about spending a thousand pounds on a car, so why not my sperm' ... So it was through a friend of a friend and ... we made up our own contract and em, that gives our daughter the right when she is 16 to, you know, seek him out. He signed the

contract knowing that. Because I've got quite a few friends that have been adopted, one of the biggest things is the mythology of who their parents are and because of that and because of hearing their experiences we wanted to give our daughter the right ... Because he was heterosexual and we did think about if he couldn't have kids with his partner he might then have a need or a desire to look for his biological child. So that's why we put that in the agreement, and that was mainly it, about the right of the child ... I point out to our daughter he chose to be a donor, not a daddy. And again, that's another thing about my blood thing, again, everyone can be a donor not everyone can be a father and just because you happen to have a child doesn't make you a father. So just cause you distribute blood, it means nothing. Not nothing but it doesn't mean that you are a father. (Lorna)

Lorna insists on the disjuncture of the social and the biological, while this persists in 'mythologies' and in the potential laying and rupturing of claims. Lisa and Clare also described struggling with securing the 'right amount' of contact, imagining and balancing future desires, with possible threats to present family arrangements. The importance of space and place is evident where the emphasis is placed on keeping apart rather than keeping connected; a degree of security was felt in knowing that the donor was far enough away, literally on the other side of the world, meaning there would be no financial contributions or sudden physical appearances.

Sally felt that the lack of financial contributions suited her own – and the donor's – best interests, confirming her status as ready and independent, where a range of educational and employment-related 'readiness' featured, still affirming the donor as a 'bachelor around town':

I also wanted my own biological child for no other reason than wondering what he or she would look like ... Because I'm the biological mother there were no complexities at all, I was with my long term partner, Eleanor, we'd been together 6 years at that point, we both had very good jobs, she was a surgeon, I was in education management and materially we were quite sound, emotionally we were quite sound. So we decided to look for a donor ... we knew what we didn't want which was we didn't want anyone to have a financial commitment to the child because again we were both aware that that can create complications, rather than gain anything. So we chose Paul, through a gay dad's association, to be a donor. He didn't want to be a dad, he was still gay guy, gay bachelor around town, so he didn't want that to be interrupted. (Sally)

Sally's account, although initially appearing a self-confident assertion of the right thing to do and the right time to do it, is perhaps complicated by the negotiation of risk within this, the relative 'gains' and 'losses' where things could have gone profoundly wrong. Similarly, Sarah believed that herself, her partner and their donor had worked out a very 'clear and objective' arrangement before the birth of their child, which immediately became complicated and disputed as soon as Emma was born, with the donor taking them to court. Although things were 'eventually sorted', Sarah told of the uncertainty in operating 'without a framework'. Given her courtroom experiences, Sarah then chose to use an unknown donor for her second child, seeking to protect against such 'danger'. It is a relationship that is at once profoundly uneasy and yet profoundly necessary; this way of 'doing' family, of 'doing' conception must be negotiated at every turn.

Again, Kathy experienced an uneasy shift in what had been thought of as an objective 'sperm on wheels' arrangement, fractured by her early miscarriage and the emotional tensions which that brought, where claims were made on her 'child'. As a result, Kathy reframed her choices to prevent against a similar incident, 'definitely wanting it to be anonymous'. Now her children have a donor code rather than a social father:

> ...you get a little code, and you get colour coded sperm straw, and that's your colour and that's your code. So the kids know...If somebody says, 'Oh, your daddy', they go, 'Oh no, we've got DT01, that's our donor code.' So they just...from very early days, we made the decision that the kids wouldn't be under any false hope that their was going to be a daddy on a white horse coming over the hill to rescue them from tidying their bedroom tasks. (Kathy)

In contrast, other interviewees wanted contact with known donors, who could then provide a 'little bit of history', if children 'asked questions' at some point. The desire to 'know things' about donors, including physical attributes and personality types, also featured in accounts, acting to create family 'resemblances' (Jones, 2005). The issue of cost, investment and availabilities, raises questions about the scope and extent of family 'choices' and here it is interesting to note the ways that Sally explains her choices in terms of creating a good match, searching for a donor with relevant credentials, seeking to extend her family in the right direction:

> ... he was politically sound, he was intelligent and, eh, he's Asian and my partner at the time was, eh, very mixed race, all sorts of races from Scottish, Indian, Chinese, African. We wanted a sense of, we didn't choose the child because of the race, I mean we didn't choose the donor because of the race, we chose them for personality ... (Sally)

Such selections again highlight the relation of the social and the biological, this time in terms of which donors are chosen at once reversing and reinforcing the same distinctions that they, as lesbian and gay parents, are frequently positioned through.

Sally spoke of searching for and choosing the right donor, the right match, perhaps fixing things in a more conventional way than first seems. Here, having the money seems to free up possibilities rather than create confusing complications and Sally refused financial contribution from the donor believing that this would 'dirty things'. The disjuncture between the social and the biological is brought into sharp relief in Sandra's search, which paralleled 'normal' dating '... as if we were doing it in the normal biological way like a dating agency...' Many felt that shared 'political values' were important in the choice of donor, creating a commonality of 'liberal' morals, moving from physicality and personality to politics, where Sarah spoke of the importance of 'fairness and justice values':

> ... more left-wing politics, with a small 'p', and having a value around family life, which, again, didn't necessarily have to be based in biology, but a mix of people that can honour and love and commit to you, so his sense of kind of community and the value in that. (Sarah)

Interestingly, these seem to be very high standards to live up to and one must wonder if you would set out to look for a 'usual' sexual partner with such a precise and moral-based shopping list. And if you did, what you would end up with? While Angie's advertisement and search had not 'paid off' she was nonetheless warmed by the positive attitudes displayed by one potential gay father:

> ... 'White lesbian couple seeks donor' and then we interviewed a bunch of guys and came up with a very nice young man, actually. He was a lot younger than us and when we had this interviewed and

we sort of said, "Well what are your attitudes about child rearing?" and he just stood there and said, 'Well I'd hate a child of mine to grow up racist' and I thought, 'You're the one!'...but he wanted to have a presence in the child's life. I mean, I hope he's gone on to be a father somewhere else, but it didn't happen for us. (Angie)

In contrast, Joc took a long time to read donor profiles, feeling rather ambivalent about this 'odd process', echoed by Kathy in describing the selection processes as somewhat 'bizarre', opting for the middle ground of 'medium, medium, medium', where just knowing that the sperm had been 'cleaned and tested' was enough:

> It was just like...a very bizarre thing of ordering your sperm. Because we'd had talks about what, you know, it's not like America where you choose a pianist or an artist, or a poet; you literally get build, eye colouring, hair colouring, skin colouring, so we went for medium, medium, medium, blue, which seemed to be the only consistencies that were...in our family all of them are blue eyed, all of them are quite medium build, medium height, medium skin colouring, so at least the kids blend in, in some form, with everybody else... (Kathy)

Many were aware of the pressure upon donors and variously rationalised why some men chose to donate, from 'the kindness of his heart' to calculated biological/financial returns. Kathy notes the changing strategies, from going through 'tried and tested' routes to 'copping off' with someone: creative/inevitable pathways and possibilities again reappear (although rather differently) where the issues of finances, risks, possibilities, perceptions and best interests are all negotiated in (un)respectable routes into parenting:

> people started going a bit bizarre and doing inseminations in car parks in Glasgow where you would have people willing to donate but then you didn't know if people had gone through...you know, and you're asking a lot of the donor, like no sex, no drugs, do you know what I mean, before...So we were putting a lot of pressure on someone who had absolutely no part of it. So from both sides you could see the point of view but, no, most of the people now, that I know, have been using clinics or they've gone the other route and gone out and got very drunk and copped off with someone and gotten pregnant 'the natural way', as my mother calls it. (Kathy)

Kathy's account tells of multiple complexities, risks and strategies in negotiating pathways to parenthood, where varied commitments, investments and responsibilities are (in)validated by the construction of 'natural' routes. Once again we see the infuriatingly complicated 'nature' of things when placed in the context of gay parenting. There is no getting away from the fact that being in a same-sex couple can make things difficult in the mechanics of conceiving a child. The frustration of being unable to achieve that which comes 'effortlessly' to straight couplings is clear in these narratives and one cannot help but feel for those trapped in a moral, practical and bureaucratic maze for which there are few maps and fewer helping hands. The social and biological are both refused and reiterated in naming and doing family where it is difficult to navigate a proper, respectable pathway to parenting, complicated by the intersections of class and sexuality. Chapter 4 relates the intersection of class and sexuality in resourcing choice and equality in caring practices mediated too by institutional claims, entitlements and denials.

4
Family Fortunes

Disrupting the main attention spent on gender inequalities in heterosexual households, Dunne (1997) claims that there is an inter-relationship between lesbianism and financial independence. Being a lesbian becomes an 'economic achievement', also initiating and compelling more equalised caring practices, where a lesbian's partner may be her best friend, co-worker, co-carer and all round equality-enthusiast. Rather differently, Weeks et al. (2001) note the ways that their respondents, lesbians and gay men, strove to achieve more equalised relationships, even if desires were sometimes negated by actual practices (see also Jamieson, 1998). This implicitly suggests the complications arising from unequal material resources and a *difference* as opposed to seamless 'sameness' in varying family mis-fortunes (Carrington, 1999; Agigian, 2004). Rather than portraying lesbians and gay men as always, uniquely 'doing things differently' (Dunne, 1997; Dunne, 2000; Stacey, 2006), I instead probe at the complexity of childcare and financial arrangements and practices, which often involved complicated negotiations with ex-partners as well as with current partners, friends and family. The complexity of family practices queries Giddens' 'pure relationship' constructed in terms of adult relationships and only applicable to certain elements of family life (Jamieson, 1998; Gabb, 2004).

Many respondents spoke of the constant 'buzz' of children, as a background stress – and joy – of everyday parenting experiences. The practical costs of parenting were often too much to bear and many described feeling 'knackered all of the time', of going through 'a fucking nightmare', juggling work, unemployment and parenting. Emotional and financial costs were endlessly repeated as 'huge', 'enormous', 'gargantuan'. Many spoke of working less to care more, negotiating this throughout the life course and continuing to juggle respective priorities and financial (im)possibilities. The financial costs of parenting are, of course, significant. Yet this significance has arguably been sidelined, even as Lewin (1993) notes the struggle, across the class spectrum, to make ends meet; here individual struggles are set alongside mediating and constraining institutional frameworks which are often incapable of recognising, let alone facilitating, different family formations and practices.

This chapter explores the resources and capitals necessary in 'doing things differently', asking how desires and possibilities are constrained and enabled by material circumstances, social supports and institutional regulations. While the literature on lesbian and gay parents often centres creativity (Weston, 1991; Weeks et al., 2001), facilitating a more equalised division of labour, here both working-class and middle-class interviewees experienced a myriad of limiting – and facilitating – factors in allowing and disallowing such practices. The financial and emotional aspects of parenting are investigated, including attention to when things 'go wrong' as well as when things 'go right', exploring the ways that respondents 'do' family in terms of financing parenting, coping with and sharing caring.

The first section 'All lesbians are equal but some are more equal than others…' discusses desires to do things 'differently' alongside attention to the material reserves needed to resource equality. It emphasises that the practice of equality is not based solely on individual reason, merit or reflexivity (of which middle-class subjects are more easily recognised and positioned through). Rather, it is enabled and constrained by the structuring of expectations, resources, choices and finances. The section 'Try explaining this to the benefits office' elaborates on institutional (dis)engagements in claiming benefits, on 'living on nothing' and 'making ends meet' between one minimal claim and another. While many respondents had claimed benefits, some experienced this as only a temporary phase (or in the case of Child Support and Tax Credits as an *entitlement*) while others were financially dependent on benefits, and socially judged in their 'dependence' (Lawler, 2000; Reese, 2005; Gillies, 2006). The final section 'On the edge of family or streets ahead?' aims to explore the complexity of social networks, formations and geographical distance, looking at the significance of friends and family in compounding social capitals and connectedness, as against a sense of isolation, which ultimately makes it harder to do – and be recognised as (successfully) doing – family.

All lesbians are equal but some are more equal than others . . .

The notion of lesbian and gay families doing things 'differently', more 'equally' has widespread salience and some reported their intention to practice a more equalised division of labour with current and ex-partners. This sounds very nice in theory, but how practical is this within an unequal world? While Jacqui reflects on having equal responsibilities, she nonetheless states that she is the main carer, given her partner's long-term illness. Angie also tells of 'pretty amicable' conversations, where things work out on the basis of different skills and are subject to re-negotiation:

> There's some chores that one of us hates and some chores the other hates, like, she does nearly all the washing up, which I just skive out of. She has a tendency to asthma, so I tend to do the hovering and dusting type of things and I like shopping, you know, that kind of thing. So, it kind of works out and every so often one or other says, 'Well I think I've being doing too much', and there's a discussion. (Angie)

Sarah also speaks of a happy equilibrium, as '. . . 4 little cogs and we're all just working, sometimes together, sometimes independently', while Kevin circumstances were a bit more complicated, although the cogs-in-tandem model was attempted. Kevin spoke of thinking through the practicalities of care in the short and longer term, struggling to do things differently in the 'child rearing project' he'd entered into. Kevin initially moved in beside Sue, with whom he had a child with, so that they could operate a 50:50 model. Yet Kevin also felt it was important to move out after a 6-month period, returning to a relationship with his male partner. The 50:50 model is questioned and constrained by the fixity of the 6-month period that Kevin was willing to practice equality. While Kevin speaks of deliberate planning, others told of things evolving naturally, depending on different skills, adding up to an equalised division where partners 'played to our strengths' (Jess). At times, shared failure was teased and mocked where partners may not be the 'best cook in the world' or the 'best cleaner' but where contributions were appreciated nonetheless.

Notably, Rachel speaks of having experienced the 'female wife role', still having a pull in her current relationship, even as this is re-negotiated and 'balanced out'. Here it is seen that interviewees do not operate outwith or beyond gendered expectations and inequalities, but instead act according to these even within same-sex relationships, where some take on a more 'masculine role' (Gemma):

> It's like a second job, so then, after I've finished work here, then I'll go home and...well we have our routines...and I naturally found that I went into female wife role, whereas my partner didn't, but then again, she's never been married, so she's never done that heterosexual thing, but it pulls back and it does balance out somewhat. (Rachel)

The world is an unequal one, especially in terms of such roles and so it would seem to be a very big task to completely get round them. Some spoke of reversing usual gendered tasks (Dunne, 1999, 2000; Stacey, 2006), taking on 'male' and 'female' roles simultaneously, even as these proved problematic, both personally and in terms of broader social reception, where Kevin reported battling against 'stereotypes' as a gay man changing nappies in public places. David also spoke of being 'landed with' both male and female roles and getting on with it, where 'as a gay man one sort of has to do it better than others'. Some spoke of doing things equally with both heterosexual and gay ex-partners, while 'the only version of equal terms' which worked for Steph was a compelled one, where she insisted that her ex-husband financially provide and contribute. In 'doing things differently' Peter spoke of care and friendship provided by a male ex-partner who took care of Peter's child, opting into the fun tasks while not being needed in other roles, such as discipline:

> Even once we'd split up, he was still around and he was still, to all intents and purposes, he was still her childminder, so he would still pick her up from school on Tuesdays and Wednesdays when I was at work. And it was just never an issue. So he had good relationship with Cassie and I just let that play out and they continue to have that. And he never had to be the parent but he was still a significant older figure. He never had to discipline her. (Peter)

Here minimal involvements from 'cool' carers are likely to be acknowledged and praised as opposed to the automatic expectation that parents, particularly mothers, can and should care. That said, Kevin is the biological father of Jo but also views her brother as his son, acting as a 'pseudo-father' and 'picking up' responsibility for both. He notes the added benefits of including different adults in Jo's life, while the central decisions are still negotiated between him and Sue.

In speaking of attempts and practices of equality some interviewees still deployed the language of 'roles' and both consolidated as well as challenged normative gendered expectations (Jamieson, 1998). Martin explains that he undertakes these roles, seemingly challenging and re-inscribing normative notions, and continuing to live in a heterosexual relationship:

> I had no problems with being a housewife, except I hate cleaning. We negotiated that I would do everything indoor except some of the cleaning, and everything outdoors, and my wife would do the rest of the cleaning and be employed. She found it difficult, giving up 'her' domain ... Very few women were able to be friendly with me beyond pleasantries at the school gate. Both of us come from families where the women have been full time wives and mothers, and we feel deeply that the economic life of the country should be arranged so that one parent, doesn't matter which, can stay at home with children. We see raising the next generation as the most important of all jobs in society and think it should be treated as such. (Martin)

As Martin suggests in the school gate responses to his equal involvement, such practices are made (im)possible via the structuring of expectations, also demonstrated in relation to various institutional responses to lesbian and gay parents, in their attempts to 'do things differently'.

'Doing things differently' sometimes rests upon the same, continuing issues of finance and what is in the household 'pot'; 'We both roughly earn the same amount of money and it all goes into one pot, we share the finances, bills and leisure activities' (Jess). In some cases even splits were well resourced, also reliant open flexible working practices as well as an emotional commitment. The importance of financial circumstance and security in practicing an equal division of labour was often stressed, in accomplishing a good standard of living and being economically and emotionally autonomous. The financial aspect would seem to be the foundations of stability, a facilitative power which allows other aspects to go on smoothly. Mel expressed this as being 'financially Ok ... so that's relatively sorted'. Paula describes the ways that being 'independent' is framed through and contested by a series of gendered expectations and possibilities, where her mother suggested she might '... marry a rich farmer I think or something (laughs) which wasn't ever gonna happen'. Steph emphasises her separateness and independence, which facilitates a less complicated relationship, aiming to 'do things differently' and, like Paula, step outside of a 'straight model' with her current female partner:

> We are really very separate and independent with anything to do with money. We've done the right thing in not living together and trying to overdo inter-dependence really. Because we both came out of straight relationships where we had both felt frustrated by not having more say ourselves, so the last thing you're going to do is hand it over to someone else. (Steph)

In terms of roles and responsibilities, many spoke of difficulty of doing family, either as a self-contained unit, or as expanded across households and ex/partners. For Elizabeth, her partner's disengagement from her children meant a fracturing of family to the point where it was impossible to go on: Elizabeth's partner seemed to be waiting for a time when it would just be herself and Elizabeth, without the inconvenience of the children – a moment which, for Elizabeth, would never happen. Elizabeth explains this as 'a kind of division that ran all through the relationship' where things were not on an even keel with her paying two-thirds of the mortgage and most of the food and bills, and her ex-partner paying only for herself:

> ...in some ways that wasn't such a good thing 'cause it kind of reinforced the idea of her being like, we were a unit and she was on her own in a way I suppose. So she did only pay for herself and maybe the whole thing was kind of not as integrated as it could've been in that way. (Elizabeth)

Elizabeth connects non-contributions and the fracturing or consolidation of family to routes into parenting, noting that her children were always seen as primarily, if not solely, *hers*. She compares this with friends who had chosen to have children together as a lesbian couple, where things 'worked much better'. This situation whilst very difficult may not be that uncommon as partners, both gay and straight, have to struggle with relationships that come with children attached. It is a story which appears in so many varied contexts and which has a powerful pull on the imagination.

In new relationships some spoke of learning together, working things out in new arrangements. While Harriet speaks of working together, feeling relief in not being a single-parent, others spoke of their own and their partners' quite different ideas and desires in entering into – or exiting – family life. Janice's slightly older partner apparently desired the 'full Monty', children, partner and the rest, while Janice, having just stepped out of a marriage, is decidedly more cautious. Negotiations such as these brought into sharp relief family boundaries, often constructed through longevity, where commitments could be demonstrated, sometimes without the sense of what the 'roles' were. Sophie highlights the uncertainty felt in trying to create new 'roles', while fearing that her own, as mother, may be under threat (Lewin, 1993; Gabb, 2005):

> I think from her perspective it's probably quite hard because you haven't got a distinct role and you've gotta create that role haven't you really?... nothing is more fearful than the thought of losing my children, you know. And I would absolutely fight anybody to keep my children, I'm sure I don't need to explain that but, you know, it's a very sort of primitive instinct really and I felt that very, very strongly having been through that... I think I've perhaps relaxed or allowed myself to have some expectation that 'No they're not your children but you've chosen to be part of our family who were here before you, you know, it's a privilege and I'm prepared to let you share it'. (Sophie)

Others experienced non-involvement from new partners, where this was desired ('No, they were mine... they're mine and that's it really', Nina) *and* unwanted, involving emotional and material claims and negations:

> Unfortunately, the person who has not shown any support of all and who is a gay parent, is my partner. And that sounds odd to say that but I would never ask Gilbert to pick up Alistair from school or to come to Sports Day and I probably wouldn't ask him to me to lend £10,000! I actually realise that Gilbert doesn't want to be part of the family unit and that's my choice, that's what I've chosen to do. (Nigel)

As well as 'breaking down', things had to be 'worked up' and Susan spoke of the gradual changes in consolidating a sense of family, where her partner was thought to be struggling with new demands but was nonetheless 'sticking with it absolutely 100%'. In breaking up with partners, living arrangements and financial contributions had to be re-negotiated, ranging from amicable settlements, to continued conflicts, where things were a 'bit haphazard' (Gemma), resting upon unequal efforts. While Michelle's ex-partner had previously contributed equally, their break up had resulted in a termination of the 50/50 practice, to occasional weekend access. Stacy had also recently split with her partner but they both had joint residency orders. For Stacy, the emotional benefits of continuing a friendly relationship with her ex-partner are worth the economic costs of a less than equal division of care and expenses; she has some material signifiers of being 'well-off', such as her large house, but nonetheless has to shop in 'clearance stores and Netto and stuff...'. Classed (dis)comforts become strained, negated and reproduced in such moments, where claims and capitals are contested, stretched to their limits and accumulated.

Such issues were also reflected in respondents' break ups and ongoing relationships with heterosexual ex-partners, echoing profound similarities rather than gay differences; a break up may be a break up in any context, although it would of course be naive to idealise this similarity too far. Several reported good, amicable and supportive relationships, where support from ex-partner's families was also offered. Karen spoke of developing an 'ok friendship' out of previous tension, where Erin's father now comes around throughout the week and is still 'very much involved'. This is also echoed in Sophie's expectations that her children 'maintain a very positive relationship' with their father, meaning that she wasn't going to 'prevent their dad from being a dad'. For both Karen and Sophie, however, primary responsibility rested with themselves. In attempting to take on a more active fathering presence ('I didn't want to be a weekend father or pick him up from school and take him back'), Nigel notes that he may be viewed as not a typical father, producing a certain 'over-protective' fear. Kevin tells of his ongoing commitments, noting the ways that he has been positioned as the 'father figure' disciplinarian, perhaps as a result of his physical absence in the household. He is invoked in and disappeared from specific roles most recently in a smoking episode in which his presence/absence was alluded to in the threat of 'what would your father say?' Peter's own fathering changed from somewhat distant financial provider to the main carer as Cassie chose to move into her dad's house, rather than move abroad with her mother, stepfather and stepsiblings.

Several spoke of the difficulties in practicing equality across households, when everyday realities posed a series of complications, from technical hitches to physical impossibilities. These were negotiated across time and in relation to particular needs (such as the 'best interests

of the child') and circumstances. For example, Nigel's own fears about
and desires to be a 'proper father' were complicated by an incident
with the police and social work department, called upon by his ex-wife
who feared that her child was 'at risk'. This temporarily halted shared
childcare arrangements, which were only just returning to normal. This
example demonstrates the range of experiences and possibilities, the
potential for changes and fractures which may over time effect any
family, but which gay parented families, with their careful negotiations
and balances, may be more effected by.

Like Steph, others had thought through and even drawn up quite formal arrangements in sharing finances and caring, such as in shared
bank accounts and in wills. Yet this seemed to be more relevant to
this with more (resources/finance), who had more to lose in the lack of
such provisioning, marking a consequential difference between coping
and consolidating. Many spoke of the creation of sole and joint bank
accounts, where equality could be practiced and financed, with payments 'for the bills, the mortgage and that kind of thing' being deducted
from there. Although Sarah is more than willing to take her financial
share in contributing to child costs post break-up, she and her partner
both seem ambivalent about how exactly this is practically achievable,
whether joint or separate bank accounts are established:

> We have talked, but we haven't talked very positively about financing
> and I mean I want to continue to take and I will take my full share
> of the responsibilities, which will include finances. I think Bev does,
> but I think she's just worried about how we're going to do it and I
> think that some of that is needing to separate and that means, for
> her, emotionally and mentally having to close off a lot of things.
> And that, at the moment, includes our bank account, although that
> to me, that feels like a bit of an impracticality, but yeah, I mean,
> I'm still going to, yeah, hopefully take my... will take my financial
> share. (Sarah)

Such practicalities had to be worked out and re-negotiated over time
and across households, where the 'buzz' of everyday tasks could make
life do-able and manageable or complicated and complex. For example,
Kevin had been paying child-maintenance into a high interest account
for some time and had then moved to direct payment to Sue, when this
suited her, linking incremental increases to inflation.

In doing things differently, however, the resources facilitating such
'equality' were often downplayed, even as these seemed apparent,

where non-materialist sentiments emphasised another way of doing difference:

> Actually, I don't think it's important to have any resources, but it might make it better if you did. I mean, I know you can live on nothing and I have lived on nothing, and I'm, you know, my parents had minimal resources and I don't have much now, but actually it doesn't half make it easier when you do. I do find it easy to live on very little. (Gemma)

The 'nothing' that Gemma speaks of living on would, however, constitute a very big 'something' for others, revealing the respective relativities in considerations of 'minimal resources'. What one person may consider as frugal and minimal, others may see as being comfortable and ample. As a local government manager Gemma is on a good income and has capital in the form of her house in an exclusive high-income area. While Gemma speaks of her ability to live on virtually nothing, others spoke of 'downgrading' and not giving in to material desires, particularly those of children. Nigel has rethought what constitutes the 'good life', trading in his Lexus for a Ford Fiesta, Waitrose for Tescos, realising instead that the 'good life' involves caring for those he loves, including his partner and his son. While Nigel centres his own 'less pretentious' non-materialism, others spoke of this in refusing their children's 'needs' for the latest toy or designer clothing, thriftily shopping in charity shops and recycling across and within households. Karen emphasises the fact that she wouldn't let her child go without, at once responding to and deflecting the difference that her sexuality makes in this. Her tale of 'not going without' is very different from a self-congratulatory narrative of shopping 'thriftily' and changing consumption patterns:

> Children are very demanding. Em, now that she can pull things out and say 'I want this', it's a lot harder. But I do not think it makes a difference if you're gay or straight as to how much money you give your child. I wouldn't give her more just because I'm a lesbian parent, I would give her what I see as not spoiling her but not letting her go without. So she's got a nice comfortable life, she's fed, she's changed, she's healthy, she's clean, she's happy, you know, I don't ask for anything else for my child. (Karen)

Michelle notes the balance within a 'pretty average lifestyle' and, like Karen, notes the material impossibilities and unwillingness in 'spoiling' her child, where her child will learn life lessons in realising he has to pay his way:

> You pay for everything you can get, you know, you pay your way and if you haven't got it you save up and you do without. That's what I say to Jake if I can't afford it you can't get it and he understands that. (Michelle)

There are, it seems, different ways to 'do things differently', though not all of them may be recognised as a positive difference, and may well be conceptualised as a deficit. Differences – or 'deficits' – arise in the refusal (or consolidation) of normative gendered roles and the (in)ability to enact equalised divisions of labour. These can change with household formations and partnerships, financial facilities, as well as subjective desires, such as living a 'pretty average lifestyle', which may still be variously conceived. Such points of difference contend wholesale notions of intimate transformations (Giddens, 1992), and the significance of lesbian and gay 'sameness' within this (Dunne, 1997, 2000).

Try explaining this to the benefits office

In ex-relationships, both gay and straight, respondents experienced (non)contributions and 'point black' refusals. Gemma explained this in terms of her partner 'wanting to have a different life', and wanting to resource that through her *own* money, independent of any 'past' obligations. In highlighting the significance of the 'past', Elizabeth spoke of the financial ties to her now deceased husband, where his pension supplemented their children's education, a source of tension and pragmatic necessity throughout her relationship with her now ex(female)-partner. Some interviewees strove to achieve an equal distribution of resources and responsibilities post-divorce, which Edward celebrated in a matter-of-fact way, as a result of 'good planning' and 'reasonable' behaviour. Maureen praises her ex-partner's 'good behaviour' and lack of 'quibbling', almost expecting this as the standard response and feeling surprised in its absence. In contrast, the lack of such reasoned behaviour proved very difficult for Jenny, where the Child Support Agency (CSA) had stepped in to redistribute payments, amounting to little more than £40 per month. Vicky spoke of her own struggles in engaging with the CSA, initially as claimant and then as the pursued, with her own changing employment situation. Unwilling to pay, Vicky left the United Kingdom, and expressed her frustration at a punitive system, having sympathy for much publicised 'Father's For Justice' campaigners. While this at first represents a turn around from the 'typical tale' of loss, refusal and compulsion, Vicky is eager to demonstrate her continued financial and emotional loss.

Others spoke of not receiving – or wanting – any financial contribution from ex-partners and/or donors as this would uneasily increase claims on ownership, 'interfere' and 'dirty' things, as experienced by Sally. She notes that money 'dirtied' relations, fostering competitive investments in her now adult children's attentions, a position which she seeks to avoid in relation to John-Paul's donor, even as her financial situation weakens:

> ... with Patrick, John-Paul's dad, if he wants to give John-Paul clothes he gives it out of choice not from me going 'Oh, you haven't paid your tenner this week'. But at the moment, you know, since my partner died and that was five years ago now, nearly em, now and then I think 'Oh, I wish I had'. I wish he would buy a few more things but I'm not going to go there, if he can't do it out of the love of his heart. (Sally)

Sally then goes on to contrast the potentially 'luxurious' position of being able to 'choose' as a gay parent, with a sense of preparing for the financial worse and ensuring an independence as a potential single-parent:

> ... I suppose if gay people were in that luxurious position of choosing the arrangements we're going to have and, you know, at the end of the day we're making our own decisions and our own rights as parents and we don't have to be reliant on others. But I think anybody having a child then thinking one day they could potentially be a single parent therefore they need to know they can do it on their own, you know, financially. (Sally)

Sally foregrounds her own independence and responsibility (see Dunne, 1997), echoed in Chapter 3; in 'making plans' a very specific, well-thought-out, well-thought-through sense of parenting and self-hood is centred, potentially sidelining other interviewees' parenting as seemingly careless.

Financial vulnerabilities were experienced through various institutional structures, such as the benefits system, where child tax credits and unemployment benefits were claimed against an often unwelcoming, discriminatory system, which was unable to appreciate and respond to the complexities and needs of interviewees' family circumstances. Harriet complained of the complex system of benefits and tax credits, amplified when her partner became ill, even as it provided a 'little bit of extra money', while Janice spoke of living 'between benefits', feeling 'fortunate' that her ex-partner contributes, although things were 'very much in flux'. Such a sense of instability permeated financial claims, whether that be formally or informally and many spoke of fighting with the benefits agency and the CSA, where the (non)existence of fathers was variously disputed and entitlements fractured through notions of what families *should* be like. The benefits system is not renowned for its subtlety and appreciation of difference; the sexualisation of such questioning and judgement was specifically gendered where mothers were particularly interrogated about absent fathers.

While Carol felt confident enough to declare, when pressed, that the father was simply unknown and therefore could not be pursued for fiscal purposes, others were much more fearful of such a potential 'outing'. Whereas some were able to 'subvert' an intrusive system by claiming a lack of knowledge of the father, Michelle's experience highlights who is included into – or excluded from – official versions of *the* family. While Michelle wants her female ex-partner to contribute, the courts would prefer to search instead for biological connections, compelling a connection which does not exist, to the detriment of the social connection which may well do:

> On other hand, which really got my back up, is my ex-partner could take me to court and not have adopted him but I can't claim CSA, you know … It wakes you up thinking that it's a bit of an unfair system, that law will back her up to take me to court, cost me nearly £8,000 to fight the case, I didn't get legal aid. And yet all I was saying basically is 'Well okay, fair enough but has she, can she help fund Joseph. We both brought him into this world'. And it were like 'No she can't' and I thought 'Well, great' … all they said to me is 'Oh well, we'll trace his biological dad and he'll have to pay' and I went 'There's no chance', you know so I didn't even involve him at all. (Michelle)

Despite all the attempts from the CSA to ensure fathers pay out, many told of their 'pretty crap' procedures, ranging from intrusion to ignorance to incompetence. Rachel cannot afford not to 'stand up' to her male ex-partner, while her initial condoning sentiment perhaps arises from the real sense that men often do not have to try very hard, while Rachel pays 'the price for being gay':

> Yes he is, well he tries, bless him. The CSA are pretty crap and we've tried for many years to do things financially on our own agreement and he's not stepped up to the plate with that at all. He's completely taken the piss out of me and my partner and now we have a CSA case going through, for him to actually start to financially support the kids, because he doesn't. He sees them perhaps once a month. There's kind of like an expectation that I'll meet him half-way on everything, but as many a friend has said to me, I'm actually paying the price for being gay, which will put me into the position of a victim. And, yeah, I do agree with them. For quite a while I haven't stood up to him on lots of issues, but I can't do that anymore, because I can't afford not to. (Rachel)

Lisa and Clare also spoke of the complexities in negotiating a system, which was hostile to them on various levels, including confusion over their citizenship status; they state that they are 'fine' and managing, while making relevant points regarding the financial costs of being gay and 'foreign', excluded as they are from claiming Working Family Tax Credits. Choices and affordability seem shifting, where Rachel has moved from relative accommodation to necessary action and where Clare and Lisa are able to be geographically and economically mobile but are nonetheless 'fixed' in place. Just as there is no sufficient category to explain their citizenship and financial entitlements, Kevin also expresses his frustration at the benefits system where there was no category to explain and entitle his family:

> I'm not either of these things and they said 'Why not?' and I said, 'Well we both agreed that we would bring up this child living our independent lives so she's co-parented'. 'Oh, we've got no category for that'. So even in those Governmental terms, it's often very difficult to be acknowledged as a co-parent. And there was, and because you kind of, when we reached the stage where I moved out and Jo kind of had a co-existence, you had to do everything. (Kevin)

Resonating with Kevin's story, Steve and James detail the emotional and material costs in negotiating the CSA post break-up, seeking to

financially and physically provide for their children and achieve a 'level
of acceptance', which literally comes at a high cost:

> *James*: Sort of access issues mainly, yes, CSA...em, well from a per-
> sonal viewpoint you don't actually appreciate how much it costs.
> So you have to leave, 'cause that's just what you have to do. And
> then all of a sudden you've got to build up another home. Then
> you've got to find accommodation for the children.
> *Steve*: Yes, em, acceptable accommodation. You can't, it's not a case
> of if you want to access them, an amount of access to the children,
> then you have to have bedrooms available for the children, not
> just room for yourself where the children can come. It's getting
> that level of acceptance, you know. Which all comes at a price.
> *James*: And plus you've got to go through a divorce, a separa-
> tion, so that's costly as well as contributing to the children, the
> maintenance, it all adds up.
> *Steve*: I hadn't really considered the cost until it was highlighted that
> 'you'll have to consider x and y and z'. Because you are in the mid-
> dle of it, you can only see one thing at a time behind it comes
> something else. To sort things out, you can't afford to do it on a
> stacking system, it has to be a broad front 'cause it's all inter-related,
> you know. You've got to realise the full cost of it.

The complexities of such negotiations were difficult enough, increased
by the often explicit judgements faced in claiming benefits at all –
the idea that this was the wrong thing to do and that they had failed
as parents and people. The perception of benefit claiming and more
specifically benefit claimants is often very ingrained and all kinds of
perceptions and feelings come into play, which may make a potentially
difficult process even harder; 'when you're feeding four or five children,
um, and you've got your gas and electricity and all your other bills on
top it doesn't go very far' (Maureen).

Nina and Karen also detailed small cash sums which were to last the
week, feed themselves and their children, and pay bills. Karen despairs
at the endless negotiation, making clear that this is not a temporary
'aberration', an interruption to an otherwise 'gay lifestyle'; instead it is
her way of life, while Nina recollects and determines that she could not
return to such 'bleak' times:

> I had two children and I was on the dole I was despairing because
> how the hell can someone live off £70 a week? I just really do not

know, because I could never do that now. I don't know, it was so bleak and sad, I think, I don't know I've sort of blocked that time out because it was an awful time and I find a lot of my life has been blocked out because it was bleak, so I don't really think about it. (Nina)

Paula describes her one experience of living on benefits as 'horrible', which went beyond the money and included social estimation, while understanding and coping with this as a short-term issue, as a benefits claimant, rather than someone who was living on benefits:

> Well, at that point being asked, you know, so like how often I'd had sex to get pregnant. Or having somebody from social security landing at where you're staying at some sort of funny time of the day, I suppose to check up that you're living by yourself. But then the general kind of tone of any interviews that you have is you know, 'You're a piece of shit basically the lowest of the low'. So, you know, not having much money I mean it was a bit taxing you could either afford to go out and have a couple of pints of beer or you'd have a really good meal. Well you know but if you, but if that's short term and if you think that's short term and this is the middle-class bit for me I knew it was gonna be short term. Regardless I was gonna get some kind of work, that's the difference between being able to survive and it, you know, just being horrendous. (Paula)

Paula's experience, while horrific indeed, is somewhat removed from the ongoing, everyday experiences of those faced with similar judgements. For Jenny, her current unemployment means that things are often 'simply out of reach', although she is happy and 'pretty content' to live within her means. Maureen details the 'awful', 'stringent' budget on which she is expected to live, noting that this leaves no room for any extras or luxury purchases, there seems no choice for either a few beers or a good meal:

> The finances, it's awful, I mean financially we're sort of, we're coping, because we're literally got such a stringent budget. But it does mean that we are currently on half-term and we can't afford to take the kids anywhere. We've been ok with basics, but we've got no money left for extras, we haven't got any extras. We can't because obviously being on income support, we get sort of rent and that paid

but it means that everything else has had to take a backward step, we can't afford to do anything... Because of the maintenance support we get for the children we're entitled to £5 a week in income support, because what they expect you to be able to live on is £90. (Maureen)

Kate notes the cyclical pressures, such as Christmas time and the annual car test, compounded by everyday requirements, pressures and breakdowns, where everyday life is 'very much a struggle'. Many working-class respondents spoke of struggling and 'getting by', just managing 'at the moment' (Beth). Contrasting with the permanence of such daily managements, others situated their experiences as temporary, which for James is narrated through indirect experience in witnessing poverty and pressure in the gay dad's group that he is part of. There he is able to offer comfort '... letting them know that it's a temporary phase, you know, there is life afterwards'.

Again, Sally spoke of beneficial supplements provided through Child Tax Credits; perhaps the difference is that she was not completely reliant upon these, having a pot of savings and 'coping' rather than 'struggling', benefiting from family tax credits as an 'additional' resource, which could be saved. This is a difference not only in economics but in self-perception; she claims benefits as opposed to them claiming her as their own. While there was a struggle across the class-spectrum to make ends meet (Lewin, 1993), there were significant differences in the lasting effects and permanence of this, as against temporary – but still significant – episodes of hardship.

Interviewees discussed parental and sexual status in relation to reaching a 'pink plateau' (Gemma) further emphasising financial inequality, where Clare flatly stated that 'gay families have less money'. Just as finances were seen to be affected by sexuality, the gendered differentials in incomes were also discussed; lesbians in particular were felt to experience a 'double-glazed' ceiling income, where homophobia in the workplace was also a very real barrier in breaking through the 'pink plateau' (Taylor, 2007). Harriet narrates her own sense of financial loss, connected to wider societal inequalities where 'you always sort of find anyway that women earn less than men don't they?' Rachel also differently compares, measuring herself against a 'versed' and expected (middle-classed) notion of lesbians as independent and high-achieving, feeling herself to be falling rather short of this (Dunne, 1997). Echoing an expectation around gay independence, Nigel spoke of the disjuncture between the (male) 'gay lifestyle' anticipated and desired by his partner, who had 'done' his parenting, as against his own current parental 'lifestyle':

> I think the other thing about being gay and a parent, is the lifestyle. I don't mean sexual, it's just the perception that a lot of gay guys have got money and the 'pink pound' and amongst our friends, some have got a good income but that's not to say every gay couple has... I again have got a balance in that I've got, every second week my son's at his Mum's from Thursday evening through until next Tuesday so I've got that sort of breathing space as well, to do that. I can't have a gay lifestyle and support my son. I did have a very good job until the end of last year where I could actually have both my son and my partner, I could have the weekends away, the nice car, the nights out with gay friends, and still have that kind of process to support my son... We haven't got pink yachts but, it's just that gay guys do like smart clothes and they like going out to lunch at Harvey Nicks, but that's, I think that's a strain. That is probably a big bone of contention... And it comes down to two things. Time and money. Time that I could split between my son and him in respect of lifestyle and holidays. I used to have eight and a half weeks holiday a year and two bank holidays and it was great, and I also had a £60,000 salary to support that. And I managed it okay. Now, I go back to four weeks a year and half the salary. (Nigel)

Just as Nigel narrates a tale of varying priorities, a juggling act, with disappointments and failures, many spoke of struggling, coping and 'getting by', as opposed to those who 'always managed'. Beth speaks of being 'on the cusp' of (not) coping, where life is something to 'get through' rather than enjoy. The holiday scenarios that she imagines are rather distant from the gay spending invoked by Nigel, remaining out of reach for different reasons:

> ... I'm struggling, building my own career, keeping up with the washing and all that, the holidays, financially and every other way, or emotionally... I'll have to deal with it and I want to give them quality of life and some enjoyment, I want to give... You know, some things that you look back on and think 'Oh yes, that's when we went to so and so and we took photos' you know. 'That's us doing it' rather than just getting through the holidays. (Beth)

Everyday life could be facilitated by the smooth running of well worked out arrangements, and buffered by more or less confident negotiations with benefits system; more likely, however, were rather laboured involvements, tensions and disappointments. 'Lifestyles', either gay or parental, were frequently positioned at a distance, where the struggle to 'fit' in one category was thrown into question in occupying the other, whether that was in claiming benefits and/or residency, building careers (against a 'pink plateau'), or spending pink pounds perhaps in Harvey Nicks (or not). The difference between getting by and not, between having a lifestyle and just having a life is a profound one and one which must be constantly negotiated. Family relations materialised in such everyday spaces, encompassing (un)employment, consumption, leisure and care; the importance of navigating space can be seen in geographical (dis)engagements and (im)mobilities, where networks could be mobilised as facilitative in getting ahead or as preventative in stopping further falls off the edge.

On the edge of family or streets ahead?

Lesbian and gay families have been depicted as carving out new spaces and communities, building and advancing social capitals with creative, even revolutionary, glee. While such portrayals are indeed joyful they contrast somewhat with tales of communal decline, a depiction which variously combines classed and sexual 'failure' in the lack of social capital (Weeks et al., 2001; Gillies, 2006). When much can be read from locale, a focus on the intersections in constituting communities, neighbours and networks points to the varied abilities to inhabit, navigate and capitalise upon such space. Stephen tells of the possibilities in proximity, revealing a familiarly gendered negotiation of household terrain. His involvement was previously embedded in shared household activities negated by his departure and 'isolation'; but this now offers up possibilities for new ways of relating and 'having fun' (without the housework):

> My wife can phone me and say 'I'm bringing them round to you', they can come and sit with me for a short while or they can stay the night if it's needed. Em, I should be there for them to talk to, to listen to them, have fun with them, I don't think we had much fun when I was living at home, we seem to live quite separate lives Kelly-Ann would be on the television, Daniel would be upstairs on his play station or the computer and I would be getting on with life, and doing the washing and drying the ironing and the cooking and

cleaning. But now I'm here I've only got myself to wash, dry and iron for unless when they stay they need their clothes here so I've got a supply of clothes for them I've got a lot more spare time on my hands... (Stephen)

Although a struggle, Stephen was eventually able to resource such practical arrangements, now enjoying quality time with his children, facilitated by the separation. In other cases the lack of proximity resulted in difficult or impossible 'caring' and had to be terminated, as did desires for more involvement, leading Nina to declare it as 'just a battle' which she had 'given up really'. Movements *towards* and movements *away* from family were consequential in the search for a space, where Karen also spoke of the problems faced when attempting to get back on her feet post break-up. She is isolated from her family in staying beside her ex-partner, a proximity which gives him access even as involvements are somewhat minimal:

He said that he was going to be but only in the last two or three months and then only it's been like, getting Erin nappies and stuff and that's about it... me and Erin had to get somewhere else to live, we had to find somewhere new and find a bond and things like that to kinda get back on my feet. The thing is we've been in Cotton, he told me when we split up he didn't want me to move back to New Town because he'd never get to see her so I kinda so I stayed on with no real back up family support or anything like that, so he could see her. (Karen)

While some spoke of really being on their own, others listed the material and financial supports received from wider family and friends. Karen speaks of being socially, economically and geographically isolated, where her family is removed and she has to 'start again' in new places, dealing with circumstances she did not quite anticipate. Harriet also details the 'really hard' nature of parenting, complicated by the fact that her own family is about '50 miles away', while Kevin notes the importance of geographical and emotional proximity, where continued familial support after coming out represents the 'biggest vote of confidence': 'I would probably pay tribute to my family as being the biggest support network'. Many discussed the importance of support systems, effectively capitalising on, in some cases, multiple sets of grandparents; geographical distances were mediated by emotional commitments and a sense of the journey being 'worth it'. Material factors were also important, such as having the car or being able to afford the train fare, literally enabling physical movements and emotional supports35: it's very difficult to make the trek, to make it work if you can't even afford the bus fare and this must impact significantly on the sense of self and the sense of commitment to 'the right thing to do'. For Sandra, a two-hour journey is no problem at all, while impacting on the daily 'ins and outs' the effect is one where she feels 'surrounded by supports':

> ...Joc's parents are an hour away and my parents are 2 hours away, so they have both come up here at times of great need and also just visiting, but I suppose they're not there for the kind of daily ins and outs. Other friends, yes, I mean mainly kind of emotional support, rather than practical, but yes, definitely. (Sandra)

Gemma speaks of social networks and 'strong alliances' being more important than material resources, reiterating her earlier point regarding complete (financial) autonomy. However, the 'options available' that Gemma outlines simultaneously point to potential loss and gain, where 'choices' are made in the context of family negations. Gemma's network facilitates everyday parenting, occurring in a space which she specifically sought out and relocated to; perhaps it is not that 'the world is a much better place' in its entirety, but rather that the opportunities and alliances available in *this* neighbourhood network highlight specific relevancies of local space and place:

> ... it wasn't about the money so much, it was about having a network, and I think that network, you know, I had fairly good friendships with other kids' parents that are fairly robust, and they will pick them up from various things and you know, it's not about the money so much to be honest, it's about that network. And the world is a much better place. There are options available for people... That would be, for me, the most critical issue now, not the money, not the legislation, not the social acceptance *per se*, it's the actual network and whether that's available to people and what that does to family and you know, it's arguable that we would have lost the biological family anyway when I separated from my partner but, the fact that they were homophobic to begin with, you know, they didn't fight to stay in contact with the kids. (Gemma)

For Susan, an emphasis on locality is also important to the sense of support, where the lacking 'it' (lesbian and gay parents) is replaceable by supportive networks of heterosexual couples:

> Given the place where I live, it's not particularly prevalent in this area really but I have an enormous amount of very good friends who have all been absolutely amazing. I have a really, really good support network and none of which are gay, all are heterosexual couples and they're all fantastic and taken myself and my partner as a couple and have been brilliant about it. (Susan)

Paula's 'good social life' was facilitated by the childcare provided by a network of friends, relied upon as occasional 'baby-sitters'. While benefiting from similar arrangements, Cathrine hints at the slightly voyeuristic nature of support where co-workers and colleagues are 'fascinated' by her 'alternative' family. The idea that the babysitter, however valued, is metaphorically poking through your underwear draw must be an unsettling one. Where things depart from the norm, it seems that networks can be disrupted, rather than interestingly enhanced and many interviewees spoke of not quite fitting into everyday networks and activities and, as such, missing out on the material, social and emotional supports offered therein. Heteronormative by name, nature and numbers:

> Well, when you are a family, as in two parents, man and wife and children, you know that you fit into the sort of social norms of school activities, holidays...you might have routines where someone will drop in for coffee or you'll do something particular at the weekend, you'll be invited out for lunch, people invite you over to their house in the Dales, you'll do this and that. And you know, a lot of your friendships, if you were a friend with one or other of the couple, then they are based, they have the bedrock of the family, the whole family... Families are not going to invite me because I'm a single and I'm also gay. Who am I going to buddy up with? (Janice)

Janice's exclusion is also about being outside the model of sociable coupledom (invoked in Susan's account) – being gay *and* being single. For others too, being single was the consequential point of difference, serving to separate them from typical family activities, in some cases breaking with the past and all the supports situated there. Janice deploys a spatialised metaphor of being 'out there', conjuring up her expulsion from networks, demarcating physical and emotional distance:

> Now, when you split up, I suppose if we take sexuality out of the issue, when you split up, then a lot of that goes anyway. But if there are sexuality issues as well, you know, a lot of my friends that I'm friendly with, my straight friends, who I'm very close to, I continue to see them but not necessarily as part of the family group...I am no longer, we are no longer two parents and also, they are a bit less comfortable with me because they are, because I'm not who they thought I was and I'm a bit 'out there' you know? (Janice)

Janice speaks of her sexuality representing another 'issue', while others constructed their support systems, friendships and networks with other single-mothers, rather than lesbian or gay friends, where 'It's almost like two different versions of parenting and I'd be much more likely to get support from other single parents of whatever kind' (Steph).

Single-parents reported financial and caring struggles, noting constraints on their income and everyday impossibilities where care could not be shared or divided. Indeed, like Lewin's (1993) interviewees, many single-parents emphasised their single status as the most salient feature of parenting, 'regardless of what your preferences are' (Dana); 'That's the reality of being a single parent I suppose, for any single parent it's a sort of draining, the responsibility of it' (Michelle). Stacy relates a shift in feeling more commonalities with other single-parents, given that she is spending more time in childcare settings and having to mutually rely on other parents when, for example, children are ill. Such narratives of gratitude and 'luck' seem to have in them a degree of bitterness towards the lack of support from other gay parents and a surprise at the support of the straight community around them. They show that support networks can be varied and unexpected and that sometimes that which is on your doorstep can be just what is required. In emphasising her spatially situated 'luck', Gemma states that '... maybe I would find them anywhere actually, but maybe I wouldn't...' Clearly, geographical distances and proximities are relevant in the mapping out of families, friends and networks, where supports can be sought in new places and hardships and failures left in no-go zones. Yet such a depiction of (im)mobilities simplifies the complexity of interviewees' inclusions into and exclusions from family terrain, where being in the 'right' place is both a struggle and a privilege, involving the mobilisation of classed capitals and resources. The story of community-building, in centring a seemingly free-floating 'creativity' and a practice of 'difference', arguably sidelines such (dis)advantages, continued boundaries and demarcations. These are witnessed in interviewees' varied 'family fortunes' played out, on and against intuitional domains and domestic terrains. Chapter 5 explores the relevance of class and sexuality in parental choices and interventions in schooling.

5
Mixed Signals at the School Crossing

All interviewees had to negotiate the (in)visibility of heterosexuality as a structuring presence in schooling experiences, as well as the formal silencing of lesbian and gay sexuality (Epstein, 1994; Renold, 2000); yet strategies, resources and opportunities to *negotiate* this do contrast between those in different class circumstances. Sexuality is not the only ground for educational dis-affection, instead class may also solidify or smooth over differences in educational expectations, experiences and knowledges. Yet research highlighting the significance of class in schools (Hanafin and Lynch, 2002; Bettie, 2003; Reay, 2004) often seems separate from research demonstrating inequalities of gender and sexuality (Nayak and Kehily, 1996; Chambers et al., 2004); rare is the attention to intersections between class and sexuality, in the negotiation of identities and experiences within the school setting (Taylor, 2007).

In Devine's (2004) and Ball's (2003) research middle-class parents made strategic schooling choices, determined by evaluations of the costs and benefits of different courses of action, yet the opportunities and constraints within this enactment perhaps tell a more complex story about the intersection of class and sexuality. Here, lesbian and gay parents seek to 'resource' their children in similar and different ways to heterosexual parents but such strategies tell a complex tale in that these are not always successful, variously compromising efforts to protect and replicate class privilege and/or to simply 'make up' for a loss of educational and societal affirmation (Lindsay et al., 2006). Middle-class lesbian and gay parents face a more complicated journey in securing educational advantage in a context where their sexualities and family formations are institutionally marginalised (Wallis and VanEvery, 2000), while working-class parents may well share more similarities with their heterosexual counterparts, choosing to dis-engage with schools given that these are often felt as spaces of tension, disappointment and failure (Evans, 2006; Gillies, 2006).

This chapter explores the relevance of class and sexuality in parental choices and interventions in children's education. From accessing the 'right' school, to having no choice but the 'wrong' school, from the fostering and creation of suitable networks and knowledges (Byrne, 2006) to the limitation, exclusion and drawing back from such practices, both class and sexuality are relevant in the confidences, resources and entitlements, enacted educationally. Class and sexuality are intertwined in the construction of positive 'difference' and 'added value', where, for middle-class parents, difference is claimed and put to use, educationally and socially. Working-class parents are often acutely aware of their 'difference' as a division; while some are able to humorously undermine and challenge this association, others work hard to maintain the private/public boundaries between home and school, preferring an opting out, rather than classed – and sexualised – conciliations and arbitrations.

Access to social and economic capital, including knowledge mobilised and the manoeuvring of finances, affected school choices and experiences. Many spoke of their own uneasy transitions through school and again, the intersection of class and sexuality seemed to be a double burden for working-class respondents. This serves to situate current (dis)engagements across time in relation to class and sexual selves, as opposed to just emerging from nowhere, presenting at the school gates solely as lesbian and gay parents, without the ongoing weight of the 'past'. This placement may be read as both as an 'objective' situation, where schooling experiences determine employment opportunities, re-cycling classed destinations; it may also be seen as a structuring feeling, where working-class subjectivities are produced through exclusion from such space, in contrast to a middle-class entitlement to access and benefit from such a comfortable, known terrain (Bourdieu, 1984; Reay, 2004).

This chapter aims to unearth the significance of both class and sexuality in interactions with and experiences of the schooling system. The first section 'Low profile at the school gates' expands upon sexuality as the basis of educational inclusions and exclusions, noting the structuring of this beyond individual 'choices'; while heteronormativity is the dominant school profile, some are able to circumvent and challenge its governance, while others choose to keep their own low profile. The second section 'The ordnance survey of educational advantages' investigates the utilisation of classed knowledges in choosing a 'good school' and the positioning of children as in particular need of such 'good schools', given their family circumstances: this is, I argue, ultimately a middle-class privilege, even as it sits alongside a real, understandable parental 'need'. The third section 'Capitals, connections and critical masses' explores the consolidation of knowledges in networks of friends and family, where operating at and in certain 'professional levels' facilitates negotiation of the schooling system, from the recognition of a good school, through to the ability to challenge bad policies, especially in relation to sexuality. In relocating, mobilising classed and sexual knowledges and resources, middle-class interviewees often sought to secure their children's educational success – working-class interviewees typically spoke of 'local' schools, being 'good enough', where children would (have to) 'get by' (rather than excel).

The 'mix' which various parents seen as (un)acceptable is revealed in the section 'Pink schools or sink schools', echoing Byrne's (2006) research on the essentially middle-class balancing act of managing a 'good' versus an 'excessive' mix. It is complicated by the inclusion of sexuality as part of a desired diversity and schoolyard 'mix', for some, as against the distinction between public (school) and private (home) space, more common in working-class lesbian and gay parents' accounts (echoing, for example, Evans, 2006; Gillies, 2006). The last section 'Practically perfect?' explores a theme emerging throughout whereby children were variously placed as 'at risk' and in need of protection, as a result of anticipated homophobia, or relatedly, as able to reflexively manage this pressure and achieve because of or despite it. This middle-class placement contrasted with an expectation of 'toughening up', where children were not centred as reflexive subjects, confidently able to learn from and indeed embody difference as 'diversity', but rather as always dealing with difference as *inequality*. Such variations challenge the sexualised sameness/difference binary permeating discussions of lesbian and gay parenting (Clarke, 2001; Hicks, 2005) highlighting the significance of class in such constructions.

Low profile at the school gates

Against a depiction of middle classes selfishly and homogeneously replicating their own classed privileges in educational practices, such processes have to be situated in the context of anticipated and actual homophobia. There are many inflections of homophobia, ranging from everyday looks, stares and refusals to communicate, to more violent and explicit threats, all demanding a 'low profile' at the school gates. Many middle-class interviewees spoke of 'coming out' at the right time, mapped against important educational markers (e.g. after GCSEs, Highers/A levels, university), as 'overprotecting', 'overcompen-sating' with material/emotional support due to the added 'complication' of their sexuality and the pressure this was seen to put on children. 'Coming out' to teachers and indeed other parents was often undertaken as a 'just in case' cautionary process, where adults could be made aware and be on side in case of bullying, deflecting negative educational and social impacts. Within this context this specific instance of 'coming out' is for the good of the children, a valuable buffer against the potential disruptions caused by coming out in general.

In contrast to an emphasis on risks and threatened successes, other parents reported that their children were doing 'good enough', where they'd be capable of 'putting right' any bullies; rather than having an 'enlightened' educational experience – and an added, 'different' value – these children were 'coping' and 'getting by', learning also from parental mistakes. Carrie laughingly described her own negative experiences of education, saying that she was an 'odd looking kid with NHS specs and dirty elbows' now becoming the 'lesbian in the playground'. The feeling of not quite fitting in sometimes produced a sense of failed hopes to be put right by their own children's achievements, learning by their mistakes, as Karen and Jody relate:

> I do want her to finish her education, I do want her to get a steady career and if she wants to have a family, have a family, if not then have a nice, stable life for herself, you know? I don't want her to mess around with her life, I don't want her to sort of get into trouble 'cause that's kinda what I did when I was younger. I mean I didn't stay in high school, I left high school really early on, I moved out of my mam's home when I was 16 and I got my own place and I kinda struggled to get by. I don't want her to do that. I hope that she learns from my mistakes not to kinda dwindle her life away and just try to do the best for herself, whatever that may be. I mean if your best is working in MacDonald's and you know, then that's fine by me so long as she does to her full potential that's all I really care about. (Karen)

> I knew fine well she would have a struggle of getting somewhere in life or getting what it is that she wanted in life and she's even said herself when she left school, 'I wish to god I was back at school again, you know I'd done better at school'. Well I had always said the same when they were kids, you know 'I wish I had stayed on at school and done better'. (Jody)

Karen and Jody both spoke of their children learning from their 'failures' and expressed a sense of 'doing your best', even when this isn't necessarily esteemed, also echoed in other accounts of other working-class respondents. The desire to disassociate happiness or achievement from academic or economic success is notable, the assertion that the two do not have to go together, but with the subtext that if they did that would also be fine.

Maureen's response is more muted framed through the absence of hassle, 'I thought I would have a lot more trouble than I did', rather than the presence of welcoming arms. Kathy's experiences varied, from 'absolutely fine' to an altogether more negative response, where familial relations were negated. The sarcastic, humorous tone of Kathy's account suggests this is, however, something which she has had to get used to and manage, as have her children, again enforcing everyday 'outings':

> So school was absolutely fine: nursery school they loved, were really, really happy there. Moved to Primary School, fine apart from one teacher who did the, 'No, everybody has a daddy' conversation. They had a conversation about mammals, and humans being mammals, have daddies, and Celia put her hand up and said, 'I don't. I have a donor. It's not a daddy, it's a donor.' The teacher said, 'No, you have a daddy, you just don't know who.' And Celia was really annoyed and I went into the school, and complained to the headmistress. I said, 'I'm not even speaking to the teacher because she knows, we have been in and we have talked to all the teachers before the kids started this school'. (Kathy)

Other issues and identifiers also become relevant in navigating schools, teachers and playgrounds and Jenny reported that her single-parent status was often more salient in such encounters (Lewin, 1993), where teachers had been very supportive. Sally felt that being a single-parent meant that her sexuality was less of an 'issue' currently, not requiring a 'coming out'. Others reported that sexuality just hadn't 'come up', whether that was because of their own single status, their desires not to be overly 'political' and/or their unwillingness to make a 'big deal' out of 'nothing' (Michelle).

While Jenny's sexuality is somewhat irrelevant or 'disguised' when presenting as a single-parent, other interviewees had been 'outed', often post-separation, where ex-partners feared the implications – and potential failures – for their children's education. Nigel, in particular, had an especially difficult experience where his ex-wife reported his 'difficult' relationships, of which being gay was the latest and final manifesta-tion. Nigel approached the school head teacher, who reportedly handled the situation well, although Nigel's son, Alistair, was thereafter treated as special and 'in need', which Nigel then had to dispute. Nigel was able to continue longstanding good relationships with teachers and to re-negotiate these in the context of separation and living as a gay man, insisting that he still received school information.

Yet even with this ability to intervene, parents typically feared the 'fall outs' from 'coming out' to teachers, both educationally and more personally, anticipating educational and social 'baggage' and possible 'failure'; it was middle-class parents who vented such anxiety about their child at (educational) 'risk'. In contrast, working-class parents in fac-ing such 'risk' were less anxious, and more 'matter-of-fact'. It could be argued that working-class parents, who may have had a more ambiva-lent relationship with education, who may have had more experience of failure have a more realistic view of such things and therefore have less to fear.

Where children are thought of as targets there can be (classed) efforts in finding things out for the 'best interests of the kids'. Stephen contin-ues to receive reassurances, having good relationships with staff, but still worries nonetheless and aims to keep a 'protective eye' on the situation. While working-class parents did, of course, fear educational 'failure', they were often more realistic about its possible effects and consequences, limiting these in calls for 'toughening up' with realis-tic approaches and sentiments, rather than attempting to stave off and resolve 'risk' and 'failure'. Rather than projecting into the future and fearing when sexuality would become relevant, or 'an issue', Jenny spoke of managing the 'day to day', just 'getting along' as things happened.

For Diane, the size of the school provides anonymity, where there is no need to declare her individual circumstances. However, anonymity and neutrality are potentially ruptured in schooling activities, in, for example, making Father's Day cards, or when discussing family occa-sions, holidays and members (Gabb, 2005). Stacy struggles with making a 'big deal' out of the classroom slip up that wrote in a non-existent father. The teacher is aghast at her own mistake, while Stacy's response varies, naming *and* minimising such everyday encounters:

> I said, 'Look, I'm not bothered. It's just that I don't want him seeing all the other kids with this, I like my dad, and then he's got it and, therefore, he feels like something's been taken away from it. I don't want him ever believing that his family set-up is abnormal'. And she

said, 'Oh no, because we do families and we talk about, you know, I've got 2 mummies and blah, blah, blah'. And I said, 'Look it's absolutely fine'... they were saying, you know, 'What did you do at the weekend?' And he'd said, 'Oh I went to [city] with my mum'. And one of the other children had said, 'Didn't you go with your daddy?' And he'd said, 'No, I don't have a dad. I've got a donor'. At which point, they were all a bit like '...Oh, right'. (Stacy)

The gap between Connor's own understandings and certainties, amidst the 'confusion' of teachers and children, is, in this case, humorously demonstrated. Other parents spoke of the damage done to children in lying about their parental status, in simply keeping their 'mouths shut', while the word 'gay' echoed insultingly around the classroom. 'Lies' extended to maintain boundaries between home and school where friends were not invited home, given the possible breach to cover-ups and avoidances. These choices are weighty ones; the decisions made may have an enormous impact on the way lives are lived and the ways interactions are negotiated. Children are not the most discrete of people and the potential for slippage is huge.

The spatialised and temporal partitioning of home against school served to allay fears about possible bullying, though it was recognised that this boundary could easily be breached, with mum potentially becoming a 'monster': 'within the home we're fine, outside of the home, my orientation becomes a monster to them, which is really awful, because I'm their mum' (Rachel). Some children had been and were vocal in 'outing' parents (Gabb, 2005), and Carrie humorously de-centres the typical tale of hardship and struggle, telling her sons to 'get a life' and get on with it, now that all is known there is no going back. Her response is very different from frantic despair, intervention and mediating strategies enacted by some middle-class parents in seeking to secure against 'disadvantages', where her own direct and loud 'outness' is mirrored by her son:

He actually told his friends as well which was really quite funny 'cause then I had the mothers coming up to us and saying 'Eeh, you know I don't know am I supposed to tell your son off you know 'cause he's coming in the house saying you're a lesbian' (laughs) and I'm going 'Yeah I am, it's alright'... They said 'I don't know whether I can tell him off' 'cause that's what they did and it was being used as a negative rather than they were just coming, like kids at that age do, just share facts don't they?... some of the kids around the doors started to pick up on it and would give the 'Your mum's a dyke' and you know this and that. And it was kind of like 'Well yeah, actually she is but she would prefer to be called a lesbian' (laughs). (Carrie)

Importantly, the decision to 'come out' or not does not exist in a purely personalised void but rather relates to anticipated responses and resources – or lack thereof – such as books and even explicit policies, which reference welcoming attitudes to lesbian and gay parents (Wallis and VanEvery, 2000). This points to the continued efforts still needed, as several emphasised, even in a post-Section 28/2a UK context. These negotiations may be understood in the context of managing 'mixed signals' from schools themselves that were seen as still floundering even with the repeal of Section 28, where 'things haven't really moved on' (Jess). Margaret also makes clear the difference between a passive inclusion based on the removal of discriminatory legislation and a more active inclusion, which requires 'more of an effort'. For Sally, the decision to 'come out' is situated in the ability to accommodate her family situation, via appropriate books, for example, and non-heterosexist sexual health education. Sally has a background in education and accordingly feels that she can mount the right 'non-aggressive' challenge.

Carrie reports an excitement amongst school staff aiming to cater for this new and novel scenario, ordering in new books and reporting their efforts with glee, swapping information and reading 'articles in the paper about lesbians'. While Carrie was touched though somewhat amused by such new purchases, others were more scathing of the 'contrived' nature of such inclusions, expressing doubts about particular books' scope and relevancies as well as expecting more embedded inclusion, rather than what was felt to be a rather tokenistic addition and *enclosure* of lesbian and gay parenting within the pages of specificity. Such books, named as 'expensive' and 'too American' (Kathy), also seem contrived in the retelling of a very specific narrative of routes into parenthood (via 'daddy machines') and family composition, eliding the complexity and diversity of lesbian and gay parented families, where sexuality may also be 'incidental', only a small part of the story:

I think one of them is called ABC Family and it's like A is for something, but on each page there's a different family set up, doing the activity they're talking about and then there's the Daddy Machine,

which is about 2 children that have got lesbian mums, who decide
they want a daddy, so they make a daddy machine, but the daddy
machine goes a bit wild and churns out 50 daddies. And all the
things the daddy can do, they realise that mummies can do and so
they put all the daddies back into the daddy machine, apart from the
first daddy that came out, who strangely enough, goes and lives with
the man next door! But it's nice. And I've got them books for when
they're older. There's one called *The Duke Who Outlaws Jelly Beans*
and it's short stories, but again, it's not... *There's Heather Has Two
Mummies* and I don't want that, because it's really like they've written this book, basically, about lesbian parenting, whereas I'd much
prefer to have books that just happen to have a lesbian character in
there. (Stacy)

School resources and policies ranged from the glowingly 'perfect' to the
startlingly imperfect. Margaret and Rachel detail school bullying policies, believing they deal with the issues, without making 'a big deal'
out of it and here again the balancing act of making visible that which
can be stigmatising is revealed. However, Mandy went on to speak of
intervention by educational psychologists and behaviour mentors, suggesting that special attention is sometimes warranted in light of the
difficulties to be expected. The negotiations of identity and outness,
of disclosure and discretion, tolerated or begrudged, can be a tightrope
and the school yard a battle ground for the most 'normal' and 'mainstream' of children. Kathy relates internal school policies to external
provisioning noting that not many people have the 'know how' to
access such services, where the links between schools and services are
often unknown:

Again, it's about communication, there's no network that people
can tap into, like a website and find out what's happening... Not
everyone knows that Mesmac can go into schools and talk about
homophobic bullying... And I think it's easy if you're in the know
to be able to say, 'Oh, I could ask someone at Mesmac what to do'.
But if you don't know that or if you're by yourself, it can be quite
scary. (Kathy)

Kathy illustrates the importance of networks and knowledges in mount-
ing educational challenges or in simply surviving in 'scary' places, with
few support systems whether they are institutional or interpersonal.

The ordnance survey of educational advantages

Models of 'good' and 'bad' parenting are often mapped onto social class and sexuality, with educational responsibility, success and failure bound up in such constructions (Evans, 2006; Gillies, 2006). Many interviewees spoke of being and feeling 'just as good as' if not better than straight parents. In fact, telling the story of being a good parent in the context of legal and social discrimination becomes a necessity, often awkwardly experienced at the school gates (Hicks and McDermott, 1999; Stacey and Biblarz, 2001). For example, Ann spoke of feeling 'under the microscope', showing no chinks in her armour as she faced (and felt she met) the 'huge pressure to be this perfect parent'. Nonetheless, for middle-class parents this pressure mostly mobilised as a fear rather than an actual intrusion and they spoke more confidently of being able to make the right educational choices for their children (Ball, 2003; Devine, 2004). In the selection and monitoring of children's schooling, sexuality was not the only grounds for advantages and disadvantages: many middle-class interviewees spoke of consulting league tables and Ofsted reports as well as being concerned with anti-bullying policies.

For Angie, a good school is one that fosters individual abilities and personalities, matching her own 'liberal' education: '. . . where he's interested in lots of things and his personality can blossom, his interests can be fostered, his capabilities, whatever they might be'. Lisa also communicates her desires for a 'liberal' school which adopts a holistic approach to teaching, compounding academic achievements through a diversity of pupils, families and teaching agendas, where her child is still fostered as an *individual*, within diverse surroundings: 'I hope that it's, that she has good teachers, good classmates, and teachers in a real diverse setting where diversity is celebrated where her family is discussed as examples . . .'.

The importance of a good education was often emphasised by middle-class parents and anxieties over and victories in getting into the 'right' school were commonly aired. Sue celebrates her children's entrance to a 'very graded' 'top school', in the 'top 5%' in the UK'. Yet, awareness of different gradations of successful and failing schools, gauged through Ofsted reports and published league tables, often generated a fear around 'political' changes and disruption, leading 'good judgements' to be troubled. Joc reported being nervous of changes in schools' admissions policies, which would make her daughter's educational chance somewhat of a 'lottery'. Just as Joc has been able to 'select', albeit nervously, Jess also speaks of doing her homework and selecting a better school outside of her immediate catchment area, capitalising on family connections:

> It's really important that they get a good education and it has affected the choice of schools – they go to one just outside of the catchment area. We researched the local schools, their dad's a teacher and so we made him do his homework and read the Ofsted reports, which then enabled us to pick a school with good results and a nice feel. It's a state school but we've been selective. (Jess)

School visitations pre-entry were common amongst middle-class parents, where journeys were made with the knowledge that such schools were on the map of educational attainment. Angie explicitly, and somewhat embarrassedly, named such visitations, judgements and knowledges as a 'middle-class' practice; for Angie, however, such strategies become necessities as she hopes to guard against educational failure, anticipated as a potential fear of Thomas' possible learning difficulties as a potential 'inheritance' from his biological mother. Very specific language of educational 'success' and 'failure' is utilised and understood, where Angie is considering a specialist Steiner school. Angie's experience of educational managements points to the complex considerations and demonstrations of rightful educational places, which are able to accommodate difference: the anticipated problems emerge from Thomas' possible learning difficulty, carried over from his 'old' family, as well as difficulties associated with his new family situation. In negotiating similar dynamics, Clare admits that such selections are a bit 'ugly', available to her as a middle-class mother, feeling a bit 'classist' in negotiating such ugliness:

> I think you need to have kids to really see some of that, you know, when you're looking ... It does bring that, like they've got schools, you know, you'll send children to where you think they are going to fit in more so I do think that that comes out. But it's a bit ugly. And I think nobody wants to talk about it because it's just so 'ugly'! (Clare)

In contrast, other, predominantly working-class, respondents were more uncertain in exercising a selective discernment, speaking instead of their children's 'just being happy', where they could be provided for, socially as well as educationally. The value in proximity was gauged through access to friends, where their kids could enjoy the company of others living locally. Mostly, working-class parents spoke of local schools as the 'obvious' or only 'straightforward' choice: '...I didn't think about it really. I'm not sort of a great pick and chooser' (Katerina). Here, the local was 'good enough' for parents and children, while middle-class parents spoke of the local as sufficient when it was also a 'good school' – entry was not automatic but was instead sited as suitable only when it 'worked' educationally. Beth explains that although her children attend the local comprehensive it is, as a comprehensive, still acceptable and while 'disadvantaged' children attend, they are not in the majority and the convenience of the 'local' mediates the more off-putting aspects of 'disadvantage'.

Nonetheless, there were contradictions to be negotiated in accessing even a good school, where the school ethos did not quite match, support or endorse interviewees' family formations. Stacy wants to send Connor to a good school, but is cautious about the good Catholic school, hoping his friends will act as a buffer against any school bullying. Stacy positions lesbianism and Catholicism in opposition, but is hoping to work within this – rather than move away from it – aware that the local school is really the best. Yet many middle-class interviewees did speak of making deliberate movements and relocations to 'good areas' with corresponding 'good schools', which would be able to guarantee educational success, an extended acceptance to lesbian and gay parents and a response to homophobic bullying. Gemma recognised her current local area to be a 'lesbian' space and moved accordingly, repeated in Tracy's choice to relocate to a gay area, believing this would offer her child a comfort in not being the 'only one'. Kathy tells of more 'push' than 'pull' factors, seeking to avoid school bullies through a change of school, where 'bullies' are situated and removed in the departing working-class area.

Relocations require material resources and Sandra, while having sufficient resources to move at the right time, to the right place, is ever anxious about what could have gone wrong in being stuck in a 'dead-end' area, priced out with nowhere to go:

> In our area you had to be, at the moment, while catchment areas are still in operation, you had to be within 200 metres of the school and our previous house wasn't and we were in a bit of a dead-end area for schools, so it was very important. And we said, if we didn't move now, we wouldn't be able to afford it, we'd be priced out of the market. (Sandra)

Joc named such an ability to relocate and search for the right place and right school as a 'tough' middle-class choice and a 'harsh reality' at that. It was, however, a choice available to her and she was not '... going to compromise on her education for my principles...' Lisa and Clare are living with the consequences of being 'priced out', living in between a good and bad catchment area, wishing for entry to the right side of the road, being relegated instead to the wrong side of the street:

> *Lisa*: She starts nursery in August.
> *Yvette*: Oh wow!
> *Lisa*: Well, if she gets in. She's on a waiting list for both of the schools.
> *Clare*: ...I mean, we've got two schools by us, we are just out of catchment for the one where...
> *Lisa*: That we wanted to send her to...
> *Clare*: Yes. And the one which is in catchment seems a bit rougher. And you know, we've been to both of them and been to the one that we want and said 'Do you mind if we bought books in?' And the school that was less diverse and, I think probably, the schoolteacher said, 'Well it depends if it would be appropriate'
> *Lisa*: 'Well as long as they are age appropriate'.
> *Clare*: Maybe some of the political correctness I suppose. Still, a bit of class diversity makes us feel that there's a chance that she'll be... You know, other friends have been to the one we want...

Lisa and Clare want to avoid the 'rougher' school in their immediate catchment area, but do not necessarily have the resources to move, to actualise such avoidances. Lisa explicitly names this as an issue for gay families, who may well be more financially vulnerable, yet other classifications in her account also appear, as intangibles where the look, feel and even light all convey gloomy prospects:

> Gay families have less money and so you end up when you are looking at the class thing, where you end up living, sometimes is not, like, we don't have the same options around schools because of your financial situation... And where we are, we are in a catchment, and we love the area we live in... we would pick to live here, we would just like to be on the other side of the street to get her into the other school catchment. But, for me, I am, I've have gotten quite panicked because I went into the school, I'd only been in two nurseries and I went into the school and I really just, my guts said 'Don't put your kid in this school', for whatever reason, you know, some of it felt a bit

rougher, it's a lot darker, there were kids sitting in the office... I really don't want her going to her school, and so financially, that puts us in... We can't really afford to move necessarily and when you cross the street, when you get in that catchment, houses go up by £50,000. And that's Eastside, it's just getting across the street costs that much more because it's called Park View instead of Edge Hill. (Lisa)

Others spoke of the luck of the draw, the doorstep challenge which only a few could successfully win – Peter, for example, was 'in luck', where good spots 'just happened'. The 'lucky' and 'mobile' spoke of the pleasure and good planning in being able to 'escape' state schools and choose private schools instead, when money had been carefully saved and 'ring-fenced' (Edward). Several interviewees also spoke of protecting children via private education, even when this was 'against their principles': their children's education was something they were unwilling to compromise or risk and often their sexuality was described as an added burden potentially impacting upon their children's success, which they therefore had to 'compensate' for.

Lorna, for example, speaks of giving her daughter 'confidence about her mums as a same-sex couple', protecting against the 'uneducated', in the wrong ('inner-city') space, which was seen to be failing Rose emotionally as well as educationally. Such 'failure', for Lorna, justified a moral compromise in sending Rose to a private school. Lorna is also able to pay the high fees for private educations, resentful still of the fact that as the non-biological mother, separated now from her child's biological mother, she doesn't get 'any credit' for this investment, even though '... the financial issue of private school is hell, actually but once you've made a commitment you've got to stick with it. It's like £9000 a year.' It may be difficult to conceptualise such debt as a wholesale privilege, complicated further by the particularities of family circumstances. Nonetheless, resources are mobilised and put to educational use, marking a significant advantage.

Even so, Gemma questions the degree of protection that a private education can offer – perhaps it is all smiles and little substance but, with the anticipated educational success, Gemma situated this as an acceptable form of homophobia. Being 'right on' in certain circles means silent smiles, no admissions and no engagements with *the* issue:

My other daughter goes to a school... which is a selective school and it's a girls' school and it's a much more suburban and traditional girls' school where the word 'lesbian' doesn't get mentioned. But bizarrely, they do have lesbian staff and they do, I mean, they do make an effort to come and talk to me and stuff so that's quite nice. (Gemma)

This is echoed in Lorna's account where 'Parents are too "right on" to be homophobic, even if they are (laughs)...I mean they're a little bit middle-class, rich, trendy and they wouldn't even dare admit they are homophobic (laughs). That's a generalisation on my part.' Perhaps a generalisation, but it would seem that, in some cases, money does buy educational success, if not love.

Capitals, connections and critical masses

Many middle-class interviewees were or had been active in schools, confident of support mechanisms and aware of others 'in the same boat'. Such parents could seemingly assemble parental networks, and mobilise social capital to achieve educational inclusion. Others, mostly from working-class background, preferred to engage only when necessary and maintain home/school boundaries. Yet the ability to engage in as against a desire to maintain boundaries shifted across time and several interviewees spoke of being excluded from school participation post-separation and in times of relational crises. Like many others, Jacqui and Lynn told of supporting the school, taking part in usual activities of parents' evenings. Carol and her partner's involvement preceded their daughter's entry to school and Carol spoke of interviewing teachers, making sure everything was in order for a successful school entrance and experience. The ability of the school to respond to and welcome Carol's lesbian parented family is a vital part of their inclusion:

> We went together and made sure that they understood who we were and wanted to gauge what their response to us would be as a family and what they would, how they would handle any issues that arose...she [Head teacher] also added that she positively welcomed the idea of us as a family in the school and would be happy to tackle any issues and raise, you know, the issues of lesbian parents with the kids as a part of their development which was great. (Carol)

For Carol, the relationship between school and home is a very important and highly constructed one, with expectations and demands placed on the system and the individuals within it. While there was a range of involvements and engagements, Kevin captures the sentiments aired by mostly middle-class interviewees of feeling an entitlement and ability to engage with and challenge the school, described as easy because of the certain 'professional level' that he is coming from, meaning that '... it's not difficult to have a conversation with the Head teacher, certainly not for me, and say, "This is what I think you're not doing right" ' (Kevin).

Many respondents spoke of intervening in and challenging schools policies, yet there was an articulated awareness about the differential abilities and effects of this, between those who (but for sexual status) spoke the 'same language' as schools and those who saw themselves in perpetual conflict with schools and who were unwilling and unable to negotiate effectively (Agigian, 2004). For example, Nina spoke of going to the school in a flare of anger – and of the subsequent view of her as 'troublemaker' to be dismissed – in contrast to Nigel who, like Kevin, spoke of himself and his ex-partner's 'professional' approaches, where it would '... not be difficult to have a professional conversation with the Head teacher'. Speaking the right language, behaving in the proper manner and fitting your face in can be invaluable resources but ones which may be impossible to learn. Diane speaks of her parental status being almost negated not only just through her sexuality, but also through a series of classed dispositions and performances:

I don't do school very well and my partner's quite, you know, quite good with school. So she tends to speak their speak if you like (laughs). So she speaks to them and they automatically assume that she's the mother. (Diane)

While Diane's approach is to disengage somewhat, humorously though knowingly surprised by her own erasure in not 'speaking the speak', Nina has adopted a more confrontational approach. Likely, this will not be seen as the correct 'speech' – or act – but Nina has had enough and is working hard to maintain the boundaries between school and home, seeking to retaining a public/private distinction (even as this is not achievable):

I went down guns a-blazing which I think took the teachers by shock I think because I don't think they were expecting it... I said 'Look, if you don't deal with it I will deal with it in the school playground, away from the children obviously, but I don't talk about who other parents sleep with and I'm not having them 8 years old telling my son who I sleep with in bed'. (Nina)

Rather than feeling a comfort in crossing public/private spaces, for Katerina the welcoming approach by a lesbian teacher is viewed as slightly suspicion, a case of sharing too much too soon, becoming a 'bit weird' and out of place. The issue of sexuality often forced 'interventions', where 'You have to really be an advocate for your child though, I think even more so when you're a gay parent' (Lynn). Nonetheless, there are varying classed (dis)comforts in effectively negotiating these, dependent upon having the 'correct', legitimate knowledge, confidence and resources. Others did not want to get into the 'ins' and 'outs' of the school system at all, preferring instead to maintain boundaries between familial and educational spaces. For middle-class interviewees caution and fear was often dissipated in effecting changes and challenges, as opposed to underscoring a continued sense of never quite being sure, or still feeling at loggerheads ('guns blazing'), prevalent in working-class parents' accounts. Being comfortable and confident in your own right to speak, your right to be heard and the 'rightness' of what you are saying, can facilitate change and therefore reinforces your sense of rightness. Turn that round and the opposite is true.

In expressing a confidence, Sarah speaks about finding out how schools would deal with homophobia, and support her as a lesbian parent. Similarly, issues of bullying, support and inclusion will be 'one of the first questions' that Tracy asks in visiting potential schools. Such concerns and anxieties were projected onto the future and were, in some cases, ever present from the first thought of having a child:

> ...I am fairly confident about negotiating it with the school itself and I think it would be naïve to be over-confident about how the wider community are going to react and, yeah, I have concerns about that. And I have concerns about how that will impact on Emma. I mean we thought about that a lot before we took the decision to have a baby. (Sandra)

It is clear that such knowledges do not emerge from nowhere, instead 'tactics' are generated via classed knowledges and resources (Ball, 2003; Devine, 2004; Byrne, 2006) and more middle-class parents spoke of being connected with lesbian and gay social networks, who were able to provide support and information. Through her own friendship networks, Gemma had received recommendations about a particular school with a 'number of lesbian teachers', while Margaret was reassured that many of her own friend's children attended the same school whose parents were 'professional lesbians so we are kind of in the same boat really, and they don't have any problems'. Gemma has relocated to an area where the local school has other lesbian parents and lesbian teachers and where recognition becomes a 'very positive' given. Support is described in familial terms; her daughter had both her 'school family' and her 'real family'. The capitals and connections with others served to embed herself and her daughter in the school and in the local community. Similarly, through the lesbian 'grapevine', Sarah became aware of a good, oversubscribed school where the new (lesbian) Head was spoken highly of, as 'fully supportive'.

Peter also spoke of the importance of affinity and not being alone, though his account also highlights the significance of gendered responsibilities and negotiations at the school gate, where he may well be alone numerically:

> I can't remember how it came out, but because either me or James was picking her up half the week, we kind of figured out that there was a small network of other gay parents. It was mainly lesbian Mums. But suddenly there was this feeling, 'Oh! We're not alone'. And nothing particularly close grew out of that, but you know, there was this kind of constant little drip of affinity and it just made us feel quite comfortable. And it was a nice school, very mixed primary school in a really sort of ethnically and class diverse area, so again, a nice sort of broad belt of kind of types and tolerance and so it was certainly not an issue there. (Peter)

There are indeed other salient points of sameness and difference in meeting with lesbian and gay parents. Explicit classed knowledges existed alongside sometimes implicit sexual knowledges, where glimpses and nods at the school gates signalled possible similarities. Rather than there being explicit and obvious connections, others spoke of more subtle and silent signifiers, suggestive of potential commonality, while still protective of privacy. For Peter, like others, the 'strength in numbers' was articulated alongside a general sense of diversity, a comfort gained from sexual, ethnic and class 'mix'. Again the idea of balance and mix comes through the right combination of sameness and difference so that there is diversity but not danger.

Pink schools or sink schools: Difference, distinction and deviance

Reflecting Byrne's (2006) research, many middle-class interviewees spoke of desiring and achieving a good educational 'mix' for their children: yet this mix was to be managed as a balancing act between addition and excess (Skeggs, 2004). Searching for the 'right' school implicates both class and sexuality often involving, for middle-class parents, relocations to be the 'right' catchment area, as previously witnessed. Sarah views her family as one of 'difference', conceptualised positively as an addition, which others may identify with and/or learn from. The resulting 'mix' has all round benefits:

> Because we see ourselves as a family of difference, because that brings barriers and challenges and trouble of its own. One is, hopefully, there maybe... the school will be looking at how to work positively with difference and to take up those challenges, and I think that has been borne out in reality. And, yeah, I guess because, we would like our children to be able to see that difference positively, not just the particular difference they might identify by themselves, but the difference that they, hopefully, may begin to identify, in other children and other children's families. (Sarah)

For Paul, one school represented a lack of 'mix' and, even though it was one of the 'best schools', it had been rejected, given its homogeneous Christian composition, where there were only four 'non-whites'. Against monolithic compositions, the existence of a 'broad spectrum' encompassing a class and racial mix was viewed as fostering and welcoming difference, of which many interviewees felt they added to. Paula described the 'lovely mix' within one school, although one may question the extent of this mix, based as it seems to be on quite specific university surroundings, where the children of lecturers mostly attend. Sarah describes and welcomes the 'richer mix' of children from all different racial and class backgrounds, where its oversubscription acts as testament to its success (Byrne, 2006; Gillies, 2006). This school operates at just the right scale. Sophie also speaks of her school as reflecting and including a rich mix, from the very wealthy to the real poor, bringing differing contrasts and an enabling 'range':

> ... you've got the range from those that come from you know very wealthy er well off families with mansions and then you've got er a couple of kids that live in caravans. So you've got the complete, a real contrast and everything else in between. I perhaps didn't appreciate that they would be exposed to, to such a mix of friends. (Sophie)

Lisa, however, articulates a more uncomfortable sense of gains and losses in such 'mixed' settings. A 'broad spectrum' of children from differing backgrounds and family settings is seen as beneficial, and an indicator of possible 'tolerance' and inclusivity, while such features are seen as compromised in an excessively 'working-class setting'. Lisa herself falters in what she suspects may be quite 'classist' sentiments, viewing neither a monolithic middle nor working-class setting as appropriate, and hesitating too over implied issues and resources in a more classed and ethnically diverse setting. Here minority ethnic and working-class children embody more 'need' and potentially distract from that of her own and her child's, while the right balance could work for rather than against educational success:

> ... It's interesting to have worked out the class stuff here and at times feeling classist, but... I don't want Alice on either end of those, I don't want Alice where all the middle class goes, I don't want Alice where there's only working-class kids. For me with her, what we've talked about is wanting her to be somewhere where there is a broad spectrum of children... I don't want to send her to a mono-cultural school on either end of the spectrum... Thinking about schools has been quite an eye-opener about looking at different things differently. I want her to be at a very diverse school but once you start getting more diverse you end up having different languages and once you have languages, some of the school resources then are finding translators... If they are not getting the resources for that, then there's always the money going into English as an additional language support. We have the benefit of a diverse classroom, but it isn't properly funded, what's happening then in terms of commitment to afford to get the books they want, do they have to make choices around that in order to have additional support? (Lisa)

Lisa and Clare claim that they are looking at things differently, through a new parental lens – while they welcome some 'mix' of difference, there is a cut-off point to this; where once the 'local' was described as (culturally) 'diverse' it was then rethought of as deficient, where the economic is foregrounded in the discussion of (lack of) material resources. The ethnic mix of the area itself is welcomed by Clare where there are 'families from all over the world' but she fears being 'stuck' in the attached school, unable to get out should such a mix stop being conducive. This is a complex negotiation, a fragile balancing act and the narrative reflects this tightrope: not apologising for the very precise demands but aware that the rejection of certain options has an implied judgement on those who constitute that group.

In common to Lisa and Clare's desire for something more than a 'mono-cultural' experience, Carol speaks as deliberately choosing a 'tough but good' school for her first daughter, believing that an inner city school – albeit one with adjoining tree-lined residences – adds that which predominantly white suburban schools cannot:

> It was a deliberate choice . . . we lived in a place . . . on the other side of the city which is considered much more, what's the word, 'desirable'. Predominantly white and we hated it, it was dull and boring. We'd always liked Hatton Vale you know, and gone across there for curries and stuff like that . . . we lived there a couple of years and then we decided to buy a house, tree lined right in the middle of town it was really, really good. So it was inner city schools that she went to, tough schools you know but good schools. (Carol)

For Sophie, the educational and spatial 'mix' works in that her child is still able to get on at his own (quicker) rate, and is not pulled down by the slower children; he can still shine and his specialness is measured from their 'otherness'. However, the boundary between acceptable and unacceptable 'mix' seems to be a difficult classed and racialised balancing act, where too many children embodying the 'wrong' kind of difference threaten to disrupt discipline and educational distinction. The 'naughty' boy had apparently been placed beside Jacqui's child 'because they wanted her good behaviour to rub off on the lad and I just felt that he was stopping her from getting on with her work'. Rather than encompassing a (good) 'ethnic mix', Lorna alluded to the mix within a comprehensive school becoming messy and unmanageable, diverting resources away from their rightful place (students that worked hard). To resolve this, Lorna sent her child to a private school.

However much of a 'mix' parents may welcome or seek to manage, these exist alongside institutional structuring and (mis)management, where there may be an enforcement of sameness against anticipated diversity, even with the 'mixed' composition of schools. Kathy had stated that her children did not have to engage in the apparently collective – and compelled – prayer, equating such procedures with a general lack of respect for difference, whether that be sexual or religious:

> You can't sit and tell a class of 60% Muslim children that they're actually Christians at heart. So it wasn't that she had a specific thing about lesbians and lesbian parents, she just had a thing that was she was a

Christian, therefore she had certain values and she wanted everybody else to reflect those, and unfortunately that's not real life. (Kathy)

Kathy also speaks of the 'West End drain', representing the flight away from poor or failing schools, where difference cannot be recuperated and put to educational use; instead its 'sinking' state represents unacceptable educational failure. While Kathy has endured this, given that her children were succeeding nonetheless, and given her own personal politics and commitments, it has now become too much and too threatening. Her children have had a diversity of experiences, which she wishes for others, just as she seeks to protect her own, who as the 'gifted and talented' were being 'used' to 'pull up' other children. Karen's comments reflect those of others who feel that their children are being 'put to work', strained educationally and suffering from classed (mis)placements, disruptions and failures; sexuality also impacted on perceptions of educational risks and anticipated 'failures'. Here we see once again issues such as entitlement, right, benefit and compromise coming together in a very practical context. School may not be the great leveller and not all differences can be covered up by a uniform.

Practically perfect?

Notwithstanding (in)adequate provisions, many middle-class parents centred their children's ability to make good choices about who, if and when to tell, to come out, even as 'failure' was both feared and managed; they were reflexive choosers who had been properly prepared, briefed with possible consequences. Others advised caution and carefulness about who to tell, where the fear of 'widows [being] put it' (Jody) was very real. For Jody, the awareness of physical threat co-exists with the emotional necessity of '100% trust', while for others, the emotional benefits and consequences were centred. Here children were invested with a capacity for 'learning from it' (rather than 'dealing with it'), spoken of as a safety in numbers where children could protect one another:

> ... Generally what happens is that they get shat upon by all the other kids, you know, if they say anything, then the other kids will round on them and say 'Shut up. Behave!' and that works really well ... (Gemma)

Such 'networks' were generated and sustained by children themselves, as protective 'little communities' (Sarah). Others spoke of their children as being properly prepared, acting as individuals able to tell or not, where decisions were then 'entirely up to them' (Lynn):

> But I think the important thing that I said to them was 'Not everybody sees it as okay. Some people struggle with it and you have to be prepared to deal with that and about differences, not everybody accepts differences and it's about how you have to sometimes expect that people may then share their views with you'. And I think it's important for me to do that, it's about preparing them really. But I certainly wouldn't want to put the responsibility on them or the pressure that they shouldn't talk about it, because it's nothing to be ashamed of. (Lynn)

Kathy spoke of the constant renegotiations and the reflexive practice required of her, even at six o'clock in the morning. Telling the family tale can happen in the strangest of times and places, instigated by apparently innocuous incidents, which nonetheless have the power to suddenly demand the uncomfortable truth or more uncomfortable lies:

> Celia quite clear, she's like, 'Well, if they don't like I've got two mummies, then I don't want to be their friend.' But Harry's much more, 'When I said I like pizza with no toppings, they said, that's really gay.' And I was like, 'Ah ha'. 'So as soon as they find out I've got gay mummies, then what are they going to think?' And I was like, 'OK, well this is at six o'clock in the morning, I need to think about this one' I said to him, 'Harry, you don't on your first three days [of school], have to tell everyone your life story, but don't lie. You don't have to tell them, but just don't lie. So if they ask about your family, you have to think about what you want to say. It's ok not to say I've got two lesbians who I live with, who are my mums, but what I don't want you to say is my dad doesn't live with me. Because you don't have a dad and that will be a lie and lies catch you out.' And I said, 'If anyone doesn't like it, and they give you hassle, we have to deal with it when it happens'. (Kathy)

Responding to such everyday incidents may well necessitate a reflexive practice; yet set against an emotional reflexivity, Carrie argues for another kind of reflection, which is ongoing and part of 'toughening up'. Her son 'got stick' at school and used to ask why she had to be a lesbian, failing to see that this comment was itself part of the problem:

I say to him 'Do you realise you know by acting like that or coming out with that you're actually, it makes me feel like you're being homophobic' and he gets really pissed off, 'Well I'm not, cannit be' and all that kind of thing. But I have to sit down and explain to him that he can't rest on his laurels... But he got stick at school and he got a lot of shit and he had to deal with it... I mean he'd come home sometimes and I remember once when he said he says 'Oh mam, why do you have to lesbian, why can't you just be like everybody else, you know, and I wouldn't get this crap' and I just looked and I says 'Well what a boring life that would be (laughs) just think of all the wonderful women that you've met' and he was like 'hmmmm'. I said 'You've had fun on the back me being a lesbian so don't complain about it!' (Carrie)

Sally also feels there is a worth in 'toughening up', forcefully 'coming out' into the face of adversity, even as she now operates a more cautious approach with her younger 'more feminine' son, who seemingly represents a more fragile pupil:

Em, I think one of the first things I said to them around when they were being picked on at school, originally they said 'Don't tell people you're gay' or whatever and I said 'Look, if I was black would you try and get me to turn white, or would you say to those racists get lost? Would you toughen up and fight the racist or would you try and put me in a little box?'... They said it helped them so much in handling bullies, just by being able to say to whoever, the bully, whether it's homophobia or racism, 'You've got a problem here, it's not mine'. (Sally)

Dealing with adversity was not always needed, especially when having a lesbian or gay parent had a cool cache, a currency of difference and value, in the movement from primary to secondary school. For Peter, things have seemingly moved beyond 'cool' towards a stance of indifference, where it is '... not an issue for them', the teenagers in Cassie's peer group. The 'enlightened' experience, for Lorna's daughter, is as a result of being bought up with 'no deception', where things can be openly declared:

Rose, as a child from a same-sex couple has no qualms, she educates people. She has no, I read one of her letters she is writing to a pen pal and the pen-pal, she always puts I've got two mums... matter of fact.

And one of the pen pals from Sweden or somewhere, don't know, said 'Why have you got two mums?' and I read the letter back going (laughs) 'Because they got married', we had a ceremony years ago before we had her and she just doesn't understand why people don't understand. Not in a naïve way just 'people always have kids when they get married'. She educates, because she's been bought up with no deception, no qualms on anything, if one was to hide it from her she would think there's something to hide, she doesn't (laughs). (Lorna)

Rose is seen to embody and *do* diversity, educating others by her very presence and refusal to hide. In the above accounts the idea of a good 'mix' again emerges – from the desire to be a bit different and not the same as everyone else, to the child as educated, embracing and indeed embodying 'difference'. Nonetheless, there are limitations to – and exclusions from – this certain kind of coolness, where the 'mix' appears only at a surface level, as witnessed in conversations about private schools as rather 'PC'. Here Tracy bluntly declared that '...you know, there's nothing cool about being gay it's just a fact', where sexuality was seen to stand for nothing other than itself, as against an embodiment of diversity, epitomised in children's educational potentials and experiences.

Clearly, lesbian and gay parents do not arrive at the school gate from 'nowhere' – instead, they embody and enact 'past' knowledges and entitlements, interfacing with financial capitals. There are 'mixed signals' in the reception of such 'entitlements' where parents are still often operating in the context of institutional hostility. Yet working-class parents are faced with a double burden of hostility, unable to relocate and spatialise their claims, or recuperate through notions of a 'good mix'. It is not that such parents are 'stuck' in place but rather they are unlikely to be recognised in discourses and research which foreground agentic capacities, movement and 'good parenting'. Chapter 6 continues this theme, exploring the desire for and construction of 'good' parental space.

6
Privileged Locations? Sexuality, Class and Geography

The negotiation of everyday space is often difficult for lesbian and gay parents across the class spectrum, also complicated by complex child-care arrangements and legalities, negotiated across household, regional and even international borders. The difficulties in being a parent are multiplied manifold by the addition of a sexual-spatial dimension. However, these difficulties are not always cross class constants with many middle-class interviewees frequently attributing homophobia to working-class others, apparently separating out such structuring features in individualising these to a certain sector of society (Moran, 2000; Taylor, 2004). A more complex tale depicted the variously classed forms of homophobia, from a subtle silence to a strident scream, complicated in the geographic structuring of inter and intra rural/urban divides, where more cosmopolitan places were thought of as 'streets ahead' in their diverse 'tolerance' – such places were both protective and privileged locales, structured through classed inclusions and exclusions. Sex and the city would seem to be more than just escapism, representing instead the belief in the importance of geography: it's not what you do, it's the place that you do it (and the group you belong to whilst doing it).

Many middle-class parents articulated a desire for a 'good mix' in their immediate localities and neighbourhoods, again expressing that diverse settings would sit alongside and enhance their own difference; clearly though, not all spaces or all inhabitants were equally desirable, different or diverse. A mix is good, but sometimes the mixture can be a little too rich, or too dry. The ability to occupy correctly 'mixed' space is a classed process, where a 'mixed' terrain, as opposed to a homogeneous middle-class setting, was considered beneficial, even necessary, in facilitating belonging. Perhaps unsurprisingly, working-class parents did not speak of accessing 'diverse' settings, but rather often spoke of being unable to attain safe spaces, with good facilities and amenities. And sometimes a safe walk home trumps a pond of ducks and a good deli.

Parenting priorities were significant in forming all interviewees' sense of space but where 'green spaces and parks' may feature on the everyday maps of some parents, for others there was void of such enhancements. This is not to say working-class parents exist in some no-go landscape, marked by exclusion and absence. This was not, primarily, how working-class lesbian and gay parents expressed and experienced their sense of place. Significantly, the sense of being unable to move and accordingly coping with such limitations contrasted with another sentiment, articulated by middle-class parents, that limitations could be challenged, movements could be made and, ultimately relocations could secure a safety, even as these remained costly.

Access to and experience of lesbian and gay networks, whether that be in commercialised scene space, or in parental community groups, was also affected by local provisioning and funding, a case of accessing what was on offer where, often situated in specific city space. Many articulated a sense of division within such places, where differences were particularly discussed in relation to class, affecting composition, activities and ultimately networks and supports. The illustrations offered of group dynamics clearly show the potential, stated or otherwise, for classed conflict within groups. Issues of location, access and differential availabilities themselves reveal inequalities in the creation and compounding of 'social capitals', in 'diverse', well-'mixed' settings. Further, the articulated purpose of such groups also classed accounts, in highlighting children's *needs* for such networks, where middle-class children were spoken of as embodying and requiring a special difference. It was middle-class parents who sought to ensure an (educational) exposure to a spatialised 'mix', which was simultaneously 'different' (from the heterosexual norm) and 'like us' (as essentially middle-class), in their attempt to buffer against anticipated homophobia: the same but different, educational but safe, enriching without endangering.

This chapter will first explore the desire for and construction of 'good' parental space, investigating notions of a constructive, enhancing, educational 'mix', following on from discussion in Chapter 5. The first section 'Location, location, location – geographies of choice (or not)' will also look at the relevance of local amenities and resources in space. While some could move away from 'lacking' spaces, others' strategies consisted of 'making do' and 'getting by', often negotiating difficult circumstances, such as the pursuit of 'decent' council housing. In the second section 'Happier in Hebden Bridge?' strategies of relocating, also complicated by divisions of labour and childcare responsibility across spaces, are considered. Some respondents spoke of being 'in-between' space, experiencing a conflict between private/public space and their parental/sexual selves, ever aware of monitoring and geographical segregations of acceptance. The third section 'A league of their own' discusses the perceived benefits of involvement in varied lesbian and gay parental networks and interviewees' observation of points of sameness and difference within such spaces. The last section 'Networks, knockbacks and nice times' explores the classing of lesbian and gay networks and, relatedly, the intersection of class and parenting in changing non/scene space, where such groups often remain voluntarily run and therefore rather vulnerable. In such circumstances, it is difficult to express a straightforward sense of privilege, access and capitalisation. This chapter, like respondents' own varied (and unequal) movements in space, takes a tentative step forward in charting complicated maps, intersecting class and sexuality.

Location, location, location – geographies of choice (or not)

Geographies of choice were mobilised in desiring a 'good mix', where middle-class parents articulated such 'mix' as a sometimes obvious marker of the degree of cosmopolitan 'tolerance' – as against a working-class 'backwardness'. Working-class parental experiences contrasted to the extent that 'mix' was described as an everyday reality, a 'mix and match' of circumstances, compelling an everyday 'getting on with it', rather than a measure of 'diversity' in and of itself. This is perhaps the difference between the jumble sale and the vintage shop, a similar set up but a different motivation for rummaging. Such classed experiences and articulations lead to a consideration of 'difference' as facilitative or impeditive – sexual difference was often invoked as requiring access to a *different* space, encompassing more than sexual difference. Sexuality was situated 'in-place' in such mixed territories, while working-classness was decidedly marked as 'out of place', as an excessive threat. Working-class parents often expressed a pragmatic desire to relocate to more well-resourced areas, for the sake of themselves and their children, yet did not inevitably seek to 'escape' existing spaces, finding value and a sense of belonging. It would seem that working-class experience in such situations is often one of recognising the best of both worlds as opposed to seeing only the greener grass on the other side, appreciating that while a relocation may offer tangible benefits, that which would be left behind also has a lot to offer.

Carol tells of her previous, and preferred, 'culturally diverse' area, where her child learned and indeed embodied a different value:

> Hatton Vale... is predominantly Black and Asian and it's a fantastic place to live. It's very culturally diverse and you can get all sorts of exotic foods from your corner shop... and people are pretty well accepting and tolerant of each other. Where we lived was a little tree lined street and was pedestrianised and it was lovely, it was a good place for kids to play. When Abby was out playing in the lane she would hear some homophobic abuse of one kind or another because gay was then, as it is now, used as a term of abuse... and Abby always tackled it she has a very strong sense of justice and always, always tackled it whether you know it when she was six it would be big hulking thirteen year old boys and she would take them to task. (Carol)

The mixture in Sarah's area moves from a sense that 'isn't totally in an area where just professionals live' to a numeration of ethnicity ('It's about 70% non-white, but very mixed. There's a lot of Caribbean people, lots of Latin American people and recently lots of Eastern European, quite a few Somali people'), sexuality ('it is a real mixed bag, and a fair few gays and lesbians as well on the estate') and poverty ('It's a very mixed area, inner-city, sort of lots of poverty'). A geographic and social merry-go-round to rival 'It's a Small World'. Both Gemma and Paula speak of their areas as 'very mixed', while going on to say that they are 'mostly white' and 'middle-class'; perhaps diversity is recognisable as positive with such a numerical safety-net that it is, after all, just the same.

Paula's strategies of assessment before 'coming out' are understandable, she does not want to risk telling the wrong people but what is interesting to note is the ways the 'right people' are easily aligned with profession status to be de-coded at the 'good' school gate:

> Sandbank was quite a kind of mixed area and you could choose whether you were gonna be friendly with people or not. But when you have a child you, you kind of you're gonna meet these parents regardless and em, sometimes it's sort of okay and sometimes you just decide not to say very much. I just try and figure out where their politics are at and how kind of em 'right on', for want of a better description, people are and it's very hard to say what the clues are... I mean, it is fair to say that people involved in social work you tend to

be a little bit more broad minded . . . so you kind of think, guardian reader type you know so you make, you make it based on those sorts of clues. (Paula)

Sarah again describes living in 'very middle-class area, it's full of social workers and teachers' yet doubts if acceptance exists on a wholesale basis. She is critical of middle-class 'tolerance' yet at least believes residents will be receiving if not absorbing equalities messages: 'they will be getting lots of messages from their employers about equalities'. It would seem that the *Guardian*-reading social worker will indeed inherit the earth, or at the very least a nice house in a decent area. At the same time as centring this place as very middle-class, sceptically aware of its limitations, Sarah still emphasises the good 'mix' of the area, with a range of prices available to a range of people, from public sector workers to those in need of council housing. Sarah's physical and subjective situation in space literally changes in relation to those around her, as she expresses being 'obviously' on the lower income bracket, while still seeking a garden, an acceptable level of diversity and a good school:

Because we wanted a bigger garden and we lived in a part of Birch Field, again, a very diverse area, but lots of cheaper housing, so it had a lot of lesbians living there, often because we are in a lower income bracket. Lots of large racial mix, sort of African, African Caribbean families there, so we were basically looking for a bigger garden and this is the next price range up and still in this side of the city and near a main road, so easy to get into town and what have you. We also had friends up here who knew the area. We knew that the schools were okay – that's about it really. (Sarah)

Interestingly, all lesbians are situated in the same financial boat, if not the very same place. Sarah is also aware that her previous area would be perceived as 'professional' and 'middle-class', although she experiences her own movement within and between that as quite 'confusing' and 'contradictory', preferring not to assign via class, still aware, however, of the better choices on offer:

I find it quite confusing or contradictory . . . you see, I live in an area now where I am surrounded by others who are professionals and would be seen as middle-class and previously we lived in an area where, again, it was big classes of working-class area and I'm now moving back into an area which is very much on the edge of there, of that community...However, I also very much recognise that living on a lower income and often, therefore, you are living in areas on the outskirts of cities and everything that comes with that, that exclusion from society. It will fundamentally affect your opportunities in life and your children's opportunities in life and, therefore, those factors you may start trying to attach those to a model around class, etc...which allows me greater opportunities and greater choices and allows me then to aspire to living in this area and to send my children to a school, which isn't totally in an area where just professionals live, this is very much a mixed area, but it gives us choices. (Sarah)

Sarah seemingly more readily identifies with locale than class position but her account then goes on to detail the intersections between class and parenting (im)possibilities, and the compulsion to 'mix' with others, noting varying geographies of choice within this.

Angie speaks of relative safety and danger, and the shifting notions of harm, retelling her own childhood spent commuting to school, in contrast to a frequent over-protection in contemporary times. The need for a certain freedom and 'exposure' is spatially situated in the good 'mixed' area, where she lives, contrasted with suburban isolation and homogeneity, even as she fears 'pretty rocky' times ahead, symbolised in teenage gangs. While the neighbourhood terrain can be rather 'rocky', Thomas' difference and the difference around him is almost spoken of as facilitative, enabling resilience and compounding emotional resources. The overall positivity of 'mix' is again expressed by Clare and Lisa, who speak of open responses from neighbours in such an 'in-between' space, which is contrasted with both homophobic housing estates and the unknown wealthy areas:

Clare: There is a sense of community around here. When we first moved in, the neighbour popped her head out of the window and said 'Oh, Alice's got two Mums has she?' and she was actually quite open and fine about it here. It's really nice. And you know, we bumped into the 7 year old next-door at the movies yesterday with Alice and she was with a whole bunch of friends and she said 'Alice's cool, she's got two Mums!' and announced that to them all! (laughter). It's quite a non-issue around here.

Lisa: But I think that goes back...I think this is an area that's very economically diverse, I think it is quite a mixed area and so I think that means more things go in general. And people are just a bit more comfortable about everything in an area that's more diverse.

Clare: Yes. When I think of the two sets of friends that we know who live on housing estates, it's less positive for them.

Lisa: And we don't know anyone who is living in really, really wealthy areas, do we? (laughter).

Once again, a mix is a good thing so long as it is the right mix. Not too rich, not too poor, just diverse enough. The difference articulated seems to be in a certain 'struggling' comfort as opposed to uncomfortable struggles, where too much poverty cannot be conceptualised as diversity. Susan also speaks of being 'in-between' the elite and the masses, though her own geographical reach seemingly extends across these two spaces, where she is in the 'midst of everything' from 'where the footballers live' to 'some of the most deprived areas in the country 5 miles away'. This sense of 'in-betweenness' is spoken of as a facilitative gauge, rather than as a fixed measure of placement, of being 'stuck' in space.

Extending notions of 'mix', both Gemma and Peter spoke of living in 'bohemian' areas, with the right politics, values and deviation of difference ('it was a cheap and kind of Bohemian place to live and you just network, the networks you're involved in feminist things', Gemma). For Peter, this 'bohemian' atmosphere mostly centred around London, and was lost in his relocation to Scotland where apparently 'there's a narrower band of standard deviation in Easter Hill and it's much more white, it's much more, the area we're in, middle-class and just a little more conservative'. It is interesting to consider how willing Peter is to situate himself on the margins, given that he is still seeking a ('like-minded', 'open-minded') 'sameness' and access to mainstreamed 'good' space with a 'good school'. His fatherhood compounds his networks, rather than negating these, while parental considerations (e.g. schooling) also make it harder to 'start again' in a new place:

Even before I became a parent, I was already building up a community of like-minded people. Again, not necessarily queer, but just alternative, open-minded, arty, interesting people. That was kind of my peer group. So Cassie was then born into that community so there was a ready-made family, as it were . . . And when I did start working, the people I met were nice but they were much straighter, they seemed to be, and again, I'm using that in a much wider sense, not just sexuality. Just the standard deviation of deviance in Easter Hill, it's, (laughter), it's much narrower . . . which is part of the reason why we're thinking of moving because Cassie's now finished school and I'm meeting people here that are much more my kind of person. And it just feels a much more conducive environment. I think that's one of the reasons, Easter Hill is quite a conservative city. I mean, I've met the Gay Fathers group, and you know, there's some nice guys there, but again, nothing has really taken off and maybe that's also to do with my engagement in Easter Hill and I'm a bit ambivalent about being here. (Peter)

Peter foregrounds Cassie's needs in his current location, while still being geographically mobile and able to access networks across spaces. Parental and children's needs were constructed from personal and parental roles and preferences, with many pointing to the relevance of resources and amenities in the creation of 'nice', 'safe', 'child-friendly' space (Devine, 2004), where children could go out to play and 'explore' in, for example, a 'nice little cul-de-sac' (Harriet). Both Janice and Jess are surrounded by nice green spaces, facilitating social and educational pursuits in terms of 'playing with other children'. In moving to a terraced house, Janice still feels that the children are 'missing the outside exploration space' even as they have a park nearby in a 'really pretty area', while Harriet speaks of a 'good area' as encompassing a good school, good transportation links and networks to other places. It may even have that duck pond. All such facilities and resources do, as Nigel claims, make parenting life much easier:

We've worked hard to get this house. Cotton Hill, this area, is a very good area. It makes it easier being a parent. There's not a drink or drugs problem, there's not teenage pregnancies, there's not hooligans etc. The area is quiet ... it has made being a parent easier than living somewhere like, say, Windy Rise or somewhere like that. I don't say that from any point of being elitist, but it has made it easier. There are good schools, there's good amenities, swimming pool, the shopping centres. It is actually quite a good place to bring a child up in. One down side is, lack of interaction. It's actually quite cold in that way ... We, I've been in the street for 15 years and I'd say that even now I'd be hard pushed to name you two of the houses that have got kids. It's very cold like that in respect that the people don't interact much. That's a little downside and I think it's probably just snobbery, I think it is. But yes, it makes it easier being a parent, living round here. (Nigel)

Nigel mobilises a classed comparison between the 'good' suburban area and the somewhat infamous council house estate (where 'teenage pregnancies' and 'drugs' are situated by comparison); the lack of human interactions is replaced by the material resources and amenities in the area, adding to a sense of safety and ease. Sometime the quiet life is the good life, especially if there is somewhere to take the dog for a walk. Yet the variety of middle-classness is hinted at here, where city cosmopolitanism may be seen to contrast with suburban frostiness and a lack of interaction.

In contrast, working-class parents spoke often of the 'buzz' of human interaction in noisier, differently 'mixed' areas where parental fears often involved negotiation of physical violence, poverty and exclusion. Nina's sense of safety in space arises more from her children 'opting out' of local 'gang' culture, although this remains a possibility and is mediated in sending them to local clubs, where they will also be away from her for some time. This is not intensive 24/7 parenting where activities are carefully selected and a future envisaged, rather this is about staying out of trouble in the here and now:

> I may be lucky because they don't generally go out and hang round in gangs and stuff like that, um, like a lot of children do. Sometimes they'll get on my nerves if they're round me 24/7 um, that's something I'd rather do, or that's why I send them to clubs or I give them money to go and do things, so as not to hang around the streets. (Nina)

Jenny's sense of place arises from a commonality, where there are many single-mothers on her estate; where some might see such council terrain as a deficit, devoid space, Jenny feels that its particular composition is a 'bonus' where two mothers can only be seen as a positive:

> ... we live on a council estate and really, all of the parents around us are single women bringing up children on their own, so two mothers, bonus. (Jenny)

Two for the price of one can never be a bad thing within this context. Like Jenny, Carrie speaks of the pleasure of sitting on her own and her neighbour's doorstep 'people watching', as the main summer activity. This sense of commonality is in marked difference to the safe anonymity described by Nigel. Kathy articulates a more complex geographical positioning, feeling that her specific street is more than acceptable, contrasting somewhat with the area as a whole. She speaks of the changing (dis)investments in space marked, for example, by educational expectations and resources, desires for more space ('bigger gardens'), local affiliations and allegiances – depending too on 'what you are used to'. Kathy describes her current situation as somewhat of a 'fantasy league' where lesbian households are in the majority on her particular street:

> And I'm quite comfortable in the West End. There's some parts I wouldn't feel comfortable in but I think there's some parts of every-where you don't feel comfortable in. We live in a closed off end of the street, so the kids are allowed out to play certain parts. Some-times you get people sitting on the top bench drinking, I don't think that may happen in Garden Row as much, but it happens where we are, you just have to deal with it. Yes, it has placed restrictions on them, yeah, we had a spate of, years and years ago, we went through lots of burglaries but we haven't, touch wood, had any issues around our sexuality. (Kathy)

Kathy then goes on to detail the commonalities of parental status in affecting a sense of being in place ('I'll just chip away by saying, "Hello" and make them acknowledge me. But that's not easy for everybody and it's not safe for everybody'), as she organises an oversubscribed art group, serving to build alliances and deflect attention from what she might do in bed. She has sought to make local connections based on childcare, seeking to invest in her space, while she also mobilises a classed com-parison in situating the West End against the middle-class suburb of Garden Row. Kathy has been able to create a protective zone within the West End, aware that her experience perhaps differs from those who have experienced homophobia, living just a few streets away. The estab-lishment of safe space is, as Kathy suggests, rather difficult when stuck in the 'middle of nowhere', in an area which is deemed too working-class and where she would be somewhat out of place:

> I'm quite happy staying here but I think it's because of where we are, I might have different opinions if I was stuck in the middle of Low Gate. So I think it very much... I mean, I wouldn't like to live on Grangefield, where I know there's at least four lesbians living, because I couldn't stand living beside the Anglo Asian club and the social club next door, because all of the people going in there, I would have real issues with their behaviour... So I couldn't live there and I don't

think that's safe for anybody who's walking backwards and forwards, who looks different, acts different. I think a lot of people get abused and I think the lesbians who live there are one of them. (Kathy)

In occupying variously classed space, interviewees discussed constitutions of good or bad 'mixes', often highlighting their own and children's 'needs' for a protective, protected 'safe space'; it was middle-class parents who were able to mobilise their geographies of choice and, if necessary, to relocate to more lesbian and gay friendly areas.

Happier in Hebden Bridge?

Relocations were made to areas with recognisable lesbian and gay spaces, where such movement not only required financial resources but also involved varied subjective tensions and (dis)comforts. Interviewees spoke of reconciling parental and sexual status across different borders and here the classed aspects of homophobia, as spatially specific, were highlighted. Relocations were negotiated in relation to childcare responsibilities, where some had moved to 'lesbian and gay' areas in order to be in similar, safe surroundings, seeking to provide a sense of security and protectiveness. For example, Ann spoke of the importance of being somewhere where there were other lesbians and where she could be 'part of that fabric, it's all much more common, there's that support network' (Weeks et al., 2001). Moreover, Rachel's sense of not being the 'only gay' is evident in her thoughts that a 'little village' of gay parents may well be forming in her territory. Gemma also spoke of relocating to a lesbian friendly space where 'there are certain areas and certain places that I wouldn't have entertained going. I thought of the issues with homophobia and things like that.' Such 'certain areas' are constructed as empty *and* excessive, devoid of the necessary supports and replete with menacing presences.

The sense of comfort gained from such relocations is mediated by financial resources, where money simply makes possible the movement in and out of space. Sandra's account foregrounds material possibilities, hinting also at the way class features in the construction of good, liberal people and places – differing from those who may shovel dog poo through letter-boxes:

My cousin is also a lesbian...when she first had her daughter, her and her partner had dog poo shovelled through the door and they had people slashing the tyres on their car, they were physically and verbally shouted at, all sorts of things – horrendous … I think in some ways it gets easier the more money you have as well. So they've managed to move into a different area over the years and where you have more space, less contacts with the neighbours and you're more likely to see people that you kind of speak to, that you're more likely to get on with, people are a bit more liberal. (Sandra)

Sandra tells of the ability to be selective in her neighbourly interactions, seeking out 'like-minded' 'liberals', where the sense of movement includes financial possibilities as well as moral, behavioural, 'liberal' compatibilities. Again, this is echoed in Paula's tale of safety, security and comfort in creating just a 'basic' standard, where 'a lot of money' is nonetheless needed:

… because you're talking about having safe, secure pleasant housing and well you know how much that will cost in presumably a nice pleasant, safe, secure community neighbourhood or whatever. I think that is incredibly difficult so it'll cost a lot of money I think to be able to provide those sorts of things, you know, it's not necessarily, it's not about lots of material things but just to provide the basics of what I've said you know to feel to feel comfortable and safe. (Paula)

Having lived in the West End for many years, and feeling committed to such a space, Kathy articulates an uneasiness around the implications of moving away, 'ranting' with 'posh rage' and telling of 'culture shock', alongside her desire for a south-facing garden:

And yes, it's going to be a cultural shock for us, moving … I do a bit of … I have 'posh rage' … I'll start that rant, so I know I'm going to go to Garden Row and I'm going to have to watch doing the, 'comparing to the West End.' 'There were neighbours in the West End, could go to the shops …' (Kathy)

While Kathy copes with her 'posh rage', classing the two areas and finding deficits in the middle-class suburb, Harriet speaks of making the right move, moving away from the 'rough area' to an 'absolutely lovely' one, with a good school. While this represented a reconciliation of the bad against the good, others expressed a tension in occupying space, navigating both parental and sexual identities and feeling caught awkwardly between, where the city is 'poor in terms of the lesbian community' but where the children are happy nonetheless. Here the narrative is one of splitting and compromise.

Parental identities and responsibilities were ever present in the navigation of everyday space with some more than others, able to establish and consolidate what they considered to be acceptable, child-friendly spaces. Edward, for example, spoke of establishing a 'Golden triangle' post-divorce, linking his son's school, paper round and homes, as he sought to prevent any unsettlement. Many experienced a 'downgrading' in space following the break-up with partners, where the division between households and the resultant fracturing of cohesive responsibilities in one place could produce a sense of displacement. Kevin resolved such tension in moving closer to his children, even as this was not his preferred location. More complexly, Clare and her partner, Lisa, were compelled to traverse not just regional borders, but international ones, caught between international legalities, residences and respective citizenship status. As Clare and Lisa suggest, the ability to live and be in place is constrained by everyday inclusions and exclusions from discriminatory legislation to hostile attitudes. The decision of where and how to live is seldom as easy as just making a choice and making it be so.

While some spoke of the worth in 'being open' and challenging negative attitudes, from throwaway comments to stares and violent incidents, others told of being 'closeted' 'for the sake of the children'. Michelle speaks of 'being open' and just 'getting on with it', where nobody then 'seems to matter at all'. In contrast, Sophie preferred to just not 'draw anyone's attention to it', letting neighbours 'draw their own conclusions'. In making decisions to 'come out' or not, respondents spoke of negotiating different forms of homophobia as informing their decisions. Jacqui, for example, felt compelled to 'come out' and report the homophobic abuse that her daughter encountered in a violent attack, while Diane somewhat minimised the general round of name calling coming from a somewhat expected source – teenage boys. Even in 'good' places, respondents spoke of the frequently more 'subtle' signs that they were not welcome at all times, in all places, with the desire for a 'good mix' being somewhat compromised. Sandra's account also illustrates the variety of middle-class positions and responses, from raised eyebrows to enthused inclusions:

> I don't think you're ever safe wherever you go... But I've never had anybody make direct comments to me about our situation, but I think we've had people not want to talk to us about things, we've

had people avoid us in our local area. But most people have been fantastic and actually enjoyed the novelty of it, as well as being able to kind of tick off on their box, 'oh good lesbian lovers, oh yes nice one, we know lesbian lovers'. But I think we've had a few people raising their eyebrows, yeah...Often those people are very conservative, but we do get people looking, you know, it's up to us, we don't know how to interpret those looks, but I would assume some of those aren't particularly friendly, either that or we're asked if we're sisters. (Sandra)

Ticking someone else's box can at times be rather tiresome, with the relegation to 'sisters' a distinct disappearance. Diane tells of moving from a council estate where she experienced homophobia, to a more 'family area' where she keeps herself to herself, not quite integrating into the 'very strong community' around her and feeling 'quite isolated'. This is a complex progression to chart, with mis-fitting movements marking dis-associations in both spaces. Out of the frying pan and into the void. Diane's spatialised tension points to different classed movements (made clear in her council house swap), intersecting with sexuality, as space is moved into or away from. Just as Sandra ascribes a certain subtle hostility to the conservative nature of the area, others detailed the classed specific forms of homophobia across different areas, where middle-class respondents frequently attributed more obvious homophobia and generally 'backward', 'traditional' values to working-class areas and inhabitants: 'I don't like reverting to stereotypes but maybe the South Yorkshire Neanderthal man still dominates the household, family life, you know, northern values and attitudes' (Jess). Mandy also describes the vocalisation of homophobia as a result of the spatialised absence of the good 'few and far between':

Because we are not particularly feminine looking, people do shout 'Fucking dyke!' or whatever as you're walking along the street. It quite often happens in town. If the children are with me then I just completely ignore it because I don't want to draw attention to myself and I don't want to put my children in a situation where there will be some kind of aggression that would then cause distress or upset. So I just kind of laugh it off. And if the children have heard it, if they mention it, I just say 'Well that person is not very well educated and they don't understand that everybody is different'...Again, mainly because it's mostly a lower-class and working-class background of people. The professional, educated are few and far between. (Mandy)

Where are all the social workers when you need them? Off reading *The Independent on Sunday* no doubt. Just as Mandy equates the lack of education with homophobic attitudes, more existent in 'lower class' individuals, others spoke of the varying classed forms of homophobia, aware of its existence among middle-class individuals. Nigel, for example, spoke of the suburban frostiness faced and '... the silence, that's it, lack of interaction', contrasting with the area as an ideal place for children. The classed comparison which Nigel invokes between suburbia and a block of flats in Park Row hints this time at what might be better in working-class areas:

> And next-door, they, Fred hasn't actually said so much, but Philippa his wife has sort of said he finds it difficult and we went to the supermarket and saw Fred and said 'Fred, this is Gilbert' and he walked away... But across the road they just openly ignore me completely, but to be honest, having said that on the door-step at the same time, I'll kiss Gilbert goodbye, on the door-step, and I don't see why I shouldn't do it. It's just the way I am and I don't have to hide... Gilbert says I should be a bit more subtle at times but it's my home... If we lived in a block of flats or somewhere like Park Row it might be a bit different, but because it's somewhere... As I say, it's a bit cold and people don't interact but it's really public and... I wouldn't say it was difficult but there's an element of freezing out a little bit. (Nigel)

Sarah also reported that her next door neighbour wasn't quite able to meet her eye, even as a polite 'good morning' was exchanged, while shared child activities offered connections with others in the neighbourhood, bringing connections and eventual ease. This sentiment is mirrored in Sandra's experience where 'fairly traditional country ladies' in her holiday home now 'adored' her little girl, and Sandra received their seal of approval as a 'good parent'. Kevin struggles to describe the particular form of homophobia, which has changed over the years, whereby his family, once a spectacle, is now welcomed and no-one needs to worry:

> In a very quiet way, they've acknowledged that this is a different type of family, because the school is around the village, and the village, you know, you can't hide these things in a village really. And I think people kind of looked upon the whole experience as a kind of spectacle in a strange kind of way... Fourteen years later, the children are

fine and everybody thinks now that there was nothing to worry about and that it's gone really well. But at that time, fourteen or fifteen years ago, especially in Wales, nobody else had done it in Wales, and it was a real sense of, 'Oh, you shouldn't be doing this' and there was, and it was very difficult to get that whole sense of support. (Kevin)

Silences were often equated with a 'small town mentality' existing in some rural areas, where '... everybody sort of knows everyone else's business' (Harriet) contrasted with (correctly) 'mixed' city spaces. Harriet lives in a rural community, and although generally happy with this, she notes the lack of information about any possible lesbian and gay parenting groups, reflected in Lynn's remarks that there was just nothing really to comment on – or find controversial about – a previous, rural location, similar to Elizabeth's sense of the 'respectable' 'retirement town' where she lives. Diane laughs that herself and her partner are most likely to be the only gays in the village. One would hope that they were not actually the only women in the village, as that would be a whole different chapter:

> *Diane*: We're obviously the only two erm you know the only two women (laughs).
> *Yvette*: In the village.
> *Diane*: Right. It is a bit like that.

Single-parent status was often discussed in relation to a negative 'difference' or deficit, something neighbours were curious about where this, rather than sexual status, became the most significant feature of being in or out of place. The story of the single-mother council-house-dweller is relocated in this rural context, but the curiosity and hostility seem no less real:

> ... it's mostly straight community that I'm aware of here that I mix with and obviously the parents as well and erm they usually have a problem with the whole single parenthood regardless of sort of sexuality which wouldn't come into it anyway. But they sort of say, 'Oh, did you know you were going to have a child?' And, you know, as if it's sort of like a choice you know, the choice to be a single parent sort of thing so ... and they ask really out rightly, 'oh will you have any more children then?' which it's such a very sensitive question when you don't know somebody. I'm always very sort of open I just say you know I'm not with, I'm not with Martha's father, at that first meeting

that's what I would say because I don't want any more questions of that nature and I think it's quite sort of over familiar really. (Jenny)

As the urban/rural was often invoked as a significant difference, variations between urban areas were also discussed, where different urban locales were placed as differently welcoming, cosmopolitan and accepting, discussed by Lisa and Clare in relation to Glasgow and Edinburgh. Glasgow in its entirety is depicted as more 'backward' than its capital counterpart, being 'quite far behind politically' in contrast to 'open-minded' Edinburgh (see Taylor, 2008). Poor Glasgow, always the bridesmaid, never the bride, not even at a civil partnership it would seem. Edward also spoke of the different climates and support groups in different cities, repeating Lisa's ideas that city space varies in terms of resources and choices, explained in part, for Edward by the reluctant 'nature of the Glaswegians'. James, Steve and David also talk about the differences between city spaces and the gay parental supports on offer, providing a slightly less individualistic analysis than Edward's ponderings, relating the significance of financial factors and access to social supports:

> *Steve*: ...I don't think many people realise 'cause if you are moving out of the family home you've got to set up another one. It's a struggle to bring kids up in general, without having to set up another home. There were a lot of financial issues there, it was another set back.
> *James*: And again it's always, it's always in the mother's favour. It's really biased with regards to the father, so again not only do you have limited access but...
> *Steve*: There were certainly more poverty issues in the Glasgow group...There were quite a lot, well the incidence of mental health was far greater in Glasgow than in Edinburgh. We used to get references from the Samaritans, which never happened in Edinburgh.

> ...

> *David*: But the minute you're outwith Edinburgh or Glasgow, we were trying to set something up in Dundee and 1 guy turned up. Well we all know there's more than one gay dad in Dundee! But trying to get people to come along to any support group like that was almost impossible. Also tried in Aberdeen, didn't get anywhere either. Very different. To an extent it seems to be that if you

haven't got a visible gay culture. Otherwise it's very difficult to get established.

While Steve, David and James detail the different receptions and support structures in different city spaces, Mel failed to access support in London. It would seem that geography by itself is not enough to facilitate easy access into these varied and various structures which are contained within it. Being in the right place at the right time may not be enough. She knows that lesbian parenting groups do indeed exist, yet feels unwilling to go to these, not having 'the nerve to turn up' even as she expects it would 'be nice to get that little bit more support from families who are in similar situations'. Mel's hesitancy reveals the emotional mediation of space, even when resources and supports exist; routes may be blocked into – and things may not always be happier in – Hebden Bridge.

A league of their own

Respondents spoke about the benefits accumulating to themselves and to their children in being involved in lesbian and gay networks; it was predominantly middle-class interviewees who detailed their beneficial involvement in networks, which were spatially situated, mediated by involvement too in online spaces and communities. Many such interviewees articulated this as an anticipated exposure to a 'good mix' of diverse people and practices, where non-scene space extended to encompass child activities and entertainments. As well as the benefits for children many spoke of self-benefits, again emphasising the practical and emotional supports to be gained in such involvements, such as access to good 'role models', a sense of affirmation and access to shared information for specific 'needs'.

Ann, for example, told of being part of a 'rainbow families' groups which could provide positive role models for her child, against the general negativity often experienced by and directed at lesbian and gay parents. The group then provided alternative and protective spaces and examples, where both Ann and her daughter could feel positively included, through a shared sense of 'sameness', as well as an added 'mix' gained in having a range of (straight and gay) friends:

... we're going there Sunday morning in Brighton so all sorts of things are kind of coming together and she spends time with my friends like, the lesbian friends, well friends in general find, you know...be they straight male friends that I've got, and also with lesbians so she's getting that whole mix. (Ann)

Ann also emphasises the importance of friends in preventing isolation, in just getting her out of the home. The 'normal' everyday activities were also seen as important, where lesbian and gay parental experiences could just be seen for what they 'normally' were, as opposed to being a radical difference (Clarke, 2001). Parental groups, in being very much about such routine, everyday aspects of parenting, were seen to 'very much normalise it' (Joc), 'because of the visibility, the openness' (Steve) again conveying this sense of 'normality' to children:

...being able to talk about experiences and you know what to do in different situations what do you do about the education systems, what do you do about the schools how do you approach it you know all that stuff. Again it's the balance between wanting your children to grow up knowing who they are and feeling good about themselves and their background and not making them a target for stuff that goes on in schools. (Carol)

Sarah also highlights the practical supports, where information is swapped: 'you just share a lot of things about what happens in school and what could happen in school and what have you'. Continuing to demonstrate the importance of practical and emotional supports, Sarah spoke of being part of a formal parenting network that pooled resources and even provided grants. She highlights group specificities and the particularities of needs and identities, framing this positively where there seemed to be lots on offer and something for everyone including '...a Bisexual Mums Group and a Mixed Heritage Families Group as well'.

Lisa and Clare speak of their disappointment that the lesbian and gay parenting group didn't work out, as it could have offered Alice much needed benefits, offering an exposure to diversity as well as a sense of similarity ('We felt it would be nice if Alice could see other families like this, and she still does, even though it's not through a formal setting', Lisa). Kathy also highlights the self-benefits, evident in parents' own experiences of 'coming out' into a broader community and finding dual affiliations in shared gay and parental status. Here, Kathy reveals the importance of accessing community knowledges and resources, such as the guide to good (gay) parenting, where parents may be struggling in a heteronormative context, illustrated by Kathy's questions:

> What is the difference between a residency order and parental rights? If you can't afford to go to a solicitor, you don't know or you don't want to go and look stupid. So if there was something, either a book-let, 'The Guide to Gay Parenting' or something that was easy to read and not the jargon reports that you get out and it's Appendix 7 ... But there needs to be something that the kids can tap into, as well. And the books, I haven't seen any of the books, 'My mother's a great big lesbian, she keeps having sex.' Just not out there. You just don't get them on Amazon, you certainly can't get them in Waterstones. But there's got to be something about having a central point, a central area, where people can get information, even the kids can access it without having to ask their parents. (Kathy)

Interviewees also spoke of the self-benefits, and the support offered by such groups in 'coming out' and negotiating parental and sexual sta-tus, featuring especially prominently in gay men's narratives, where, for example, Nigel spoke of his disappointment that his current part-ner, Gilbert, did not attend or support his own attendance at the gay dad's network. Steve, David and James highlight the many issues faced in dealing with parental responsibilities in a gay male context, speak-ing of the similarities across spaces, set against limited resources and lack of networks (see Stacey, 2006). Interestingly, David also disputes the sexualisation of gay male space, challenging a common association, potentially negating the parental focus of this group:

> *David*: It wasn't somewhere to meet someone for casual sex. It was putting a space out there for people to actually make friendships.
> *Steve*: Uh-huh. And share problems and hopefully find solutions, which we've all been through various permutations.

While 'various permutations' are highlighted in the above account, interviewees also discussed the varied and fracturing points of difference; it was not all seamless 'sameness' and smiles, where social connections or capitals could be easily accessed and opera-tionalised; there were limitations to 'doing things differently' in accu-mulating friendship networks and community knowledges (Weeks et al., 2001). The divisions and distinctions within lesbian and gay community spaces led Carol to wonder about 'how many ways can we divide ourselves', drawing upon a specific politicised feminist discourse of changing the world – if only commonalities could be embraced.

A significant division within lesbian and gay community space was the dis-associations between those who have children and those who do not, with parents often feeling resentful about their exclusion from traditional 'scene' space. Elizabeth speaks of 'veering towards' other parents who she had more in common with as a significant point of sameness/difference in accessing social support networks:

> I wasn't really aware of many other people at that time, we became more involved with other lesbians with children since we've split up I think. The group of friends that we had I suppose, I then kind of veered more towards the one's that had children so she stayed maybe more with the one's that didn't. I think in a way there's a kind of I think in the lesbian community there is a bit of a division kind of over lesbians that have got children and lesbians who've never been in a straight relationship or haven't got any children anyway. Or even with those lesbians, who've had children with their lesbian partners there's more of a sort of, there's something in common with people that have got children. (Elizabeth)

Elizabeth's account suggests that lesbian parents may well be in a league of their own, where potential points of sameness/difference are complicated by sexual and parental status. The politics of identity are profoundly complicated by the marker of children, which even when situated outwith a heteronormative context still serves to create strange bedfellows. Again, Steph speaks of being 'on the margins' of support networks, given that 'kids are involved'; she highlights her own route to parenting as somehow not corresponding with the politically preferred (donor)route. While Steph highlights the felt significance of specific pathways to parenting, Ruth outlines a more wholesale division in different 'scene' spaces between those who have children and those who do not. To reproduce or not to reproduce would seem to be both significant and a signifier of identity and allegiances, creating commonalities and camps which may run across the fault lines of sexuality. Carrie's version of the extremities of differences (paraphrasing the response from both sides of the parenting fence that 'I don't want anything to do with *them*') is reflected in Peter sense of division once held by himself and now held in tension, of the 'non-breeders' and 'breeders', separating lesbian and gay spaces. Peter is currently having another go at gay dad's networks, feeling a certain 'tribal' pull towards it, despite his frequent lack of commonality with members, and a sense that he is just like straight dads:

> And we talked about that thing of finding your tribe, because, as a gay father, in Easter Hill anyway, there's more in London culture, but in Easter Hill there was the sense that you belonged to the 'other' tribe, you were neither one of the 'breeders' or one of the gay community, there was a sense of, you know, finding it quite difficult to find that affiliation. And so we had that in common, the fact that we felt kind of slightly freakish to both communities... But part of me sometimes thinks it would be as meaningful to talk to a straight guy just about being a dad, because most of the issues I have with Cassie, not that there are many difficult issues, but they're about being a father and being a good father... The idea of being a gay dad, I don't quite know what that would mean. I know what being a dad means and I know what being gay means, but what does being a gay dad mean, other than as a kind of demographic stamp? But in a way, being gay other than, I don't know, something like the matter of choosing Cassie's dress colour, I don't know... (laughter). You know, some of those clichés probably do hold true. (Peter)

Kevin speaks of breaching – and reconciling – the boundaries of acceptability between gay and straight communities, where although gay men 'love children', having children constitutes stepping across community lines:

> I think there was a sense of, from gay men, there was a sense of anger, thinking, 'You've done this and we would have wanted to have done this but we've just not been brave enough to make these kind of things happen'. So at one level there was that, and then there was just the whole 'You must not do this... you've crossed the line'. (Kevin)

The (in)compatibilities between gay male culture and parental status are also expounded by Steve and James where it is often seen to be 'odd in gay man's culture to have kids' (Steve):

James: And you do feel very much like an island, you're not fully accepted into gay culture because you've got these responsibilities of children and gay culture is obviously a sexual culture, than straight culture, so you feel very alone.

Steve: You get bounced between one and the other, gay then straight...The gay friend of mine they're not really interested in the family life.

Steve and David spoke of the difficulties in establishing a parenting group without examples, where they often were left in a league of their own:

David: There was nothing for gay men, absolutely nothing. For lesbian mothers...

Steve: Yes, there's a model there.

If there is one thing that some lesbians do well, it is to set up mothering groups. The differences in terms of gender are, it seems, still prevalent, even as these are humorously outlined. While Carol pondered over 'how many ways' different divisions could fracture communities, David plays with points of 'sameness':

Steve: Even in our community there's prejudices, which I found really odd, there's a hostility.

James: I think it's just the same as any other community, gay men don't like lesbians, lesbians don't like gay men and they all hate trans people.

David: I've got a lot of lovely lesbian clients, I like lesbians. Basically I'm a frustrated lesbian (laughs).

The above accounts tell of the points of sameness and difference which are relevant in accessing lesbian and gay networks and in gaining a parental comfort – or otherwise – in these. Class was a significant barrier to entry, literally affecting the take up of social space and the relative (dis)comforts produced therein. Such groups were classed beyond membership, composition and location alone, affecting what was done and who was welcomed, suggestive of a more complicated amassing of 'networks'. Lesbian and gay parents often articulated being in a 'league of their own', fractured by internal and external differences and distinctions.

Networks, knockbacks and nice times

Class was often considered a significant barrier to accessing groups, shaping their membership, location and activities. Interestingly, Ann spoke of the lesbian and gay parenting group as just like the (straight) mother and toddler group, similarly shaped by gendered composition. Yet in consolidating points of sameness, points of difference also feature more subtly, echoed in Lisa's account of 'Stockbridge ladies', in gay parenting networks, who were spatially located and placed as a certain class of women. Clare and Lisa's account demonstrates the intersection of class and parenting, encompassing values, lifestyles and preferences, creating a classed 'culture clash'. The exclusion which they detail functions covertly, constructed through seemingly individual preferences, while serving to consolidate 'proper' (middle-class) parenting practices. It is the gay parenting group which 'brings out differences':

> *Clare*: You know, like when you've just come out, it's really cool that you are part of this cross-sectional grouping, you know, you're meeting people from all sorts of cultures and classes and the thing you have in common is quite central to what you are going through... you also have just joined another community, come out into the parenting community, a bit like owning a dog (laughter)...
>
> *Lisa*: But also you have this community that ends up being things you don't want to expose your children to, like, you wouldn't have your children exposed to comes up, those where you're thrown into group, like an LGBT group... And I think that really hit our group at one meeting where there was just this clash really of the group.
>
> *Clare*: Yes, it was just clashing values. All of a sudden there was this whole group of people and some of them felt that it was really okay to, you know, we're having a picnic in a park, to also be smoking in front of the children or leaving the children to it and beat each other up or whatever, and we're talking about... 'Oh it was so fun getting so drunk last night, snogging on the dance-floor, blah, blah, blah' (laughter). It's like 'Hey! Oh my God! Well maybe this isn't the best kind of chat for these kids to be around'. And then you had people on the other hand who were really trying to initiate games for the kids, just a different sort of environment and you could see that it was just a sort of...
>
> *Lisa*: Culture clash.
>
> *Clare*: A clash really...

Lisa: It was at some points good. In general I think it is very good and...I think it's best for children to have a really wide variety of people. So yeah, I mean it's really hard...And I do think some of the class stuff has come out and we were less aware of that as a concept until you see it. The picnic, the picnic was quite an eye-opener, you know?

Class was seen as relevant to group activities and the behaviours deemed (un)acceptable; rather than creating a 'mixed' space differences of class seemed to cement division and 'knockbacks' rather than smoothing over variations, where one group would leave when outnumbered by the other:

Lisa: If there are more middle class parents there and so the more working class families, they don't come back...

Clare: Yes. All parenting groups are like that, it's not just LGBT ones, so you'll get people saying about finding a group that matches, you know, not being the 'Stockbridge Ladies' or, you know...Most parenting groups parent, you know, here, what I've heard, are very middle-class.

The reality of parenting groups being 'very middle-class' may itself be evidenced by the non-involvement of most working-class parents, where groups may be composed of more 'academic' 'middle-class' sorts (Beth). Both Carol and Nigel express a sense that groups are 'middle-class' somehow operating beyond numerical composition, to include values, politics and activities, where class is the one gap that cannot be bridged or blended in. Carol suggests that this has been ever-present and ongoing, where the 'awkwardness' of class extends beyond finances alone, given that generally 'middle-class people feel in a position of privilege'. The moral weight and variety of class is illustrated in Nigel's detailing of the look and feel of class 'levels', as well as his own hesitancy. The flattening down or heightening of class is contradictorily related in Nigel's account as he attempts to uncover the particular significance in relation to lesbian and gay community formation:

Interestingly, the diversity stops at the class barrier. It's definitely middle class and up, and what I mean by that is someone who might be a white-collar worker. I've never seen what I would term a working-class guy there. Again, just to clarify that without being...possibly a builder or someone who has got a certain income level. I think another thing that interests me is with the gay community is, I wouldn't say it's classless but there's a definite dearth of levels, a definite... It's almost that you are driven more by looks and by age and money as in by what car you're driving, but I think in the gay community almost like flattens down to right down to probably one or two classes, whereas how many classes have you got, you know? You've got loads of different names. But I think in the gay community, it's actually going to be more so because it is quite a cynical world. If you're not good-looking and got a good dress sense, well, that's all that matters. (Nigel)

At once Nigel foregrounds and undermines the relevance of class in gay community formation, suggesting the lack of layers, while emphasising the superficial layer of outward appearance as paramount. It is this inability to get to grips with class, to fit it first within a gay and lesbian context and then within a group context which is characteristic of these narratives. Class is at once there and at the same time not; it is both salient and silent. The effect of it may be clear but the pronunciation of it is often less so. Paula and Angie continue to note the lack of diversity in networks, composed mostly of 'social worker types', leading Paula to wonder where working-class lesbian mothers go and the lack of 'ease' in being unable to access supports, where '... class might affect those sorts of choices'.

In contrast to a professed desire for a 'good mix', a lack of diversity was often experienced in accessing groups which, according to Rachel's experience, are rather homogeneous: 'it's not completely all white, but it does seem to be, on the whole, I think, middle-class. You go round the table and everybody's a social worker or a volunteer or something like that...' David replaced the word 'class' with 'culture' in detailing points of difference within the gay dad's group, yet his account is remarkably similar to that of Lisa and Clare, who explained class division as a 'cultural clash'. Nonetheless, Steve, James and David are quick to defend the common parental 'playing field' they have helped to establish, where points of sameness are viewed as more relevant than possible differences, including classed ones:

Steve: It's really diverse. There's no boundaries. We have common problems, you know. All having difficulties with these common problems, irrespective of salary or income. It's not an up, down thing.

David: Even that guy who came out of prison who came along. I don't think anybody in the group encountered any prejudice because of who they are. They were coming into this as another gay parent. People were meeting on quite a level playing field irrespective of background.

James: It was more of a question of 'look we're all in this boat together'.

David: The biggest benefit of the group was a collective sigh of relief that there was somebody that spoke the same language as you.

James: Yes, and I had experienced what you are currently going through and came out the other end.

Steve: Yes but you are also trying to rebuild your life, aren't you? You are trying to find another relationship. The gay culture, well at that time, was very bar orientated. You can't really take your kids to go out and find true love.

. . .

David: And it's not classed based. All come along, all sorts of occupations, livings.

James: But all enduring the same sorts of problems.

David: What certainly started to strike me was that the majority of the time you could have removed the word 'gay' entirely and it was really just about how the parents tried to deal with their kids.

James: Hmmm, yes.

David: I mean the gay issue, in many respects, never really arose.

Steve: Well, apart from 'coming out'.

Within the tone of this conversation awkwardness is clearly to be heard. The very fact that class is the unspoken elephant in the corner, something that doesn't need to be mentioned, reinforces the importance of its presence. Running alongside the salience of class, spoken or unspoken, with the formation and function of gay and lesbian groups are the issues of space, economics and the interface of the two. Groups that operate within the context of actuality, for example non-virtual groups, must have a concrete space in which to operate. Given that the majority of available space has either an economic or cultural price or expectation attached to it, the implications for group formation can be significant. Not everybody will fit in everywhere, for a variety of reasons.

Divisions occurred between people and places, expressed also as a divide in time between 'now' and 'then' as a contrast between more or less politically aware and active times, constituting a lack of space and a movement from 'networks' and 'nice times' to personal and political 'knockbacks' where 'there isn't the networks that there once was' (Kathy). Peter and David also comment on the exclusivity – and inclusivity – of commercialised scene space, where finding affinity through parental and gay status is somewhat of a 'lottery win', a chance finding with huge stakes. While David notes that gay male culture is 'very bar orientated' where 'you can't really take your kids to go out' he, together with James, disputes the relevance of finances in going out for a drink, even without children ('we just drank coke all night or we took a bottle of water'). Nonetheless, finances were clearly important in creating lesbian and gay spaces of both a non/commercial nature, where parenting groups in particular tended to be run on a voluntary basis and were therefore particularly vulnerable to under-funding and unstable numbers. Dana had watched the large women's group, which she helped establish and run, slowly diminish over the years, leading her to ponder about the lack of involvement from younger women, whereas others lamented the lack of time in being unable to participate and commit. Other groups had folded and then been re-launched under another name, only to face the same fate. Such stories suggest that networking relies upon the creative but often unstable efforts, which often exist without formal structures or funding, meaning that they can come and go with attendees. Again, this complicated the accumulation of capitals even for middle-class lesbian and gay parents, suggesting an intersection of sexuality and class in varying (dis)advantages.

Nevertheless, classed distance – and proximity – was negotiated in ways that ultimately served to distinguish and resource middle-class subjects. Again, the classed boundaries of (un)acceptability are expanded and contracted by a focus on the relevance of sexuality in the constructions of (un)desirable 'difference'. Diversity is frequently coded as a liberal middle-class knowingness, spatialised in the specific 'cosmopolitan' terrain of the inner city. Bodies and values coalesce in the construction of boundaries of (un)acceptability, where lesbian and gay parents' concerns for an 'accommodating' location may be seen as a manifestation of classed – and sexual – desires and constraints. Chapter 7 explores the complex negotiation of civil partnerships and the classed claiming of legal territory which materialises and legitimises certain families.

7

Just Cause or Impediment? Costs of Civic Acceptance

Much has been written about the 'costs' of same-sex marriages and civil partnerships, focusing on both material and symbolic gains – and losses. The practical gains in accessing rights may be positioned against an erasure of different ways of living and loving (Hull, 2006; Naples, 2007; Shipman and Smart, 2007). Family units are brought into being and indeed negated in interaction with institutional frameworks and through legal and material (im)possibilities. Here it is possible to view The UK Civil Partnership Act, and other similar legislation which formally recognises lesbian and gay partnering and parenting rights, as actually *materialising* family, making that which was sidelined and under-valued included and recognised.

The ability to consolidate partnerships in terms of legal, material and emotional 'unity' is significant to the naming and doing of family and specifically in doing parenting. 'Stable relationships' may be formally recognised, even welcomed in, for example, adoption or in the everyday spaces of parenting, where the 'other mother' at the school gates suddenly becomes official and validated. The 'stability' apparently welcomed by official sponsors and individual parents also hints at something less welcoming, where stable becomes standardised, reproducing new partnership and parenting hierarchies (Richardson, 2004; Cahill, 2005).

Legislative changes enforce a reconsideration of family, especially for lesbian and gay families who are faced again with naming, creating and challenging, with the weight of success (anticipated from their supporters) and the burden of failure (endlessly declared by the less enthused). Such negotiations are indeed complex, as lesbian and gay families seek to survive and thrive, to 'put a floor' on their social circumstances (Skeggs, 1997) and indeed capitalise on such legislative changes. Herein lies a consequential classed difference between those who can afford to conceptualise such changes as beneficial, particularly in relation to finances, but also in relation to social status, respectability and esteem: to have a new currency is a mobilisation and mainstreaming of class privilege, as it is of sexual status.

This chapter explores such a mobilisation, aiming to keep in mind the complexity of middle-class and working-class respondents' tales. For example, legal incorporations often did not represent wholesale citizenship inclusions and were often used strategically in, for example, the avoidance of inheritance tax and the assurance of material benefits, as well as the emotional comfort to be gained in being officially deemed 'next of kin'. Nonetheless, such real and valid concerns sit uncomfortably alongside the fear expressed by others that, rather than accumulating through access to pensions and shared resources, they would be financially at a loss. In such circumstances, the costs of civic acceptance include more than the celebratory parties, involving the social costs of (still) not quite measuring up to friends and family.

The first section 'All legal and above board?' charts the varied familial (in)validations as expressed by interviewees, many of whom spoke of desiring 'normality' (Richardson, 2005). The ability to have a civil partnership then represented a legitimisation of their family structure and relational possibilities, encompassing both their partnership and parenting choices. This leads on to an empirically grounded revisitation of 'sameness'/'difference' debates, exploring interviewees' sense of whether or not civil partnerships are the same as heterosexual unions; whether they are better, different or still unequal. Physical and emotional opportunities and constraints become more pertinent in contending with the practicalities of everyday life, including childcare responsibilities and financial necessities, as explored in the section 'For richer, for poorer'.

While the legislation may be seen to positively materialise connections and creations for some, others experience this much more negatively, fearing a dissolution of their partnerships, as regulated and constrained by benefit and housing provisions. Gains and losses are again witnessed in the section 'No longer living in sin?', where anticipations and celebrations are framed through consideration of friends' and families' reactions: the trope of 'in the best interests of the kids' again reappears, where the foregrounding of parental roles and responsibilities sits alongside partnering (im)possibilities. Relational hopes, and failures, are discussed in relation to some interviewees' repetition of 'been there, done that' ('Once bitten, twice shy'), where respondents are situated in terms of their relational journeys (including heterosexual relationships), rather than emerging in this new legal context as lesbian and gay partners and parents.

All legal and above board?

The pull of being 'normal', of receiving state validation, was repeated in respondents' celebration of the UK Civil Partnership Act and all the good it was seen to bring in terms of social recognition and legitimisation (Clarke, 2001; Hull, 2006). Edward spoke of his friends as recently becoming civilly partnered, explaining that this makes good sense given that they were '... living together already and have bought a house together and they have two sets of kids coming to stay with them. I think that, you know, it's empowering to have the right'. The empowerment seemingly lay in 'having the right' like their heterosexual counterparts, serving to 'legitimise it a bit more' (Mel). Diane notes that it depends on where you are coming from ('suppose that would depend if you're heterosexual or not the way you view that'), feeling an unchanged security in where she is coming from ('I think that gay and lesbian people have a legitimate relationship anyway'). While not 'a great supporter of marriage as in institution, full stop' Joc still spoke of the appeal and joy in being '... now allowed to be on an almost equal footing as heterosexual partners'. Jody repeated a 'simple as that' view where lesbian and gay parented families should have the 'same rights as straight people'. The same, almost equal, legitimate, very similar to straight people.

The comfort in being 'normal' lay in suddenly having a language through which they – and their children – could be understandable. Prior to the legislative change language could be uneasy, highlighting the difference in the lack of accessible and understandable terminology to describe relationships. Nina, for example, stated that the legislation showed her children that 'everything's normal' and that 'we are almost equal', while Kevin details the significant emotional validation in now being able to 'make the feeling official'. Crying the day that civil partnerships became legal, Jenny detailed the 'deeper level of commitment' now enabled and demonstrated in legal undertakings, as well as heightened levels of confidence arising from legal affirmation:

> I suppose if you felt established and sort of had more recognition and more equal status in that situation then, then yeah I suppose you'd feel more confident in lots of ways. (Jenny)

The comparison with heterosexual 'normality' is invoked by Stephen in comparing the now equally 'firm and solid' commitments which lesbian and gay men can now demonstrate, as their heterosexual counterparts always could. Civil partnerships are welcomed if 'you're so much in love with each other and you know that your relationship is firm and solid as solid as a heterosexual marriage could be then I'm really, really happy with it'. While Jenny cries tears of joy, Peter rationalises this as simply a sign of 'civilised society', which endorses multiple versions of family and partnership. Yet, another take on this exposes the construction of validity (rather than simply arising from civil society) revealed in Kate's statement that 'I don't think they necessarily make them more valid because that's to say that they're not valid in the first place': Kate's critique arises from a contentment with what she already has and an ambivalence in potential gains and losses, of a material and emotional nature. Yet validity and legitimacy have significant material effects, ones that matter to Angie in the realms of parenting and adoption. Its 'real importance' is grounded in the mediation of parenting by social, medical and welfare services:

> I mean I can see, immediately, the difference in how seriously lesbian and gay couples are being taken as, potentially, adoptive parents, just because it has been legitimised, like the state is saying, 'These are okay'. So the questioning that used to go on, you know, the real bottom-line question about, 'Is this an okay thing to do?' It's like, well, 'It is, and it's legal'. So anything that questions it, immediately falls into ranks of discrimination. (Angie)

While Angie details the institutionalised benefits in being legitimised as 'ok', Mel details the personal benefits in not being the 'other', the last tick box in monitoring forms. When compelled to tell a 'good' coherent story, neatly connecting parenting and partnership, it *is* consequential that things are all 'legal and above board' where apparently 'deeper levels of commitment' are measured, even if problematically so:

> ...actually wearing a ring's quite nice really, it does sort of legitimise it a bit more. It's actually the nicest thing of all, is when you fill in those forms and you're asked whether you're married, single, divorced or separated and I always just used to write 'other' and circle that. It's quite nice now that you can either write, well most of them don't have civil partnership on it but when people say, you know,

are you married or single and you say 'Well, em, civil-partnershipped em, sort of married I suppose', so that does feel quite important actually. (Mel)

Mel's sense of being able to name and consolidate her family also featured in Maureen's account where her own and her partner's children were able to see themselves as family: 'They call each other brother and sister now, all five of them.' The sense of things coming together, facilitated by the legislation, accords with Nigel's sense that post-marriage, his sister's family now represents a tied and coherent unit, where 'there was a big knot being tied in the big family unit and it was all kind of nice and neat'.

While Nigel expresses a 'nice and neat' view, some respondents struggled with a sense of the sameness or difference to heterosexual marriages, as a radical alternative or as simply not good enough. Lynn views civil partnerships as a positive thing, although details the difference between them and conventional marriages conducted in church. Others also spoke of feeling let down that civil partnerships didn't go far enough and were still not equal to their straight counterparts, summarised by Martin in his contention that 'I don't see why gays and lesbians shouldn't marry on the same terms as straights'. Tracy was forthright in expressing her anger that it was definitely not the same, constituting nothing more than a legal loophole:

When I first read and heard that we were going to be allowed to have a civil partnership, I was really angry, I felt like it was suddenly we would be able to sit at the front of the bus. I felt that we were being offered a loop hole in marital law that you know doesn't apply to heterosexual couples and that I just felt so angry. I said to Kym that I never wanted to have a civil partnership because just out of principle that we, we weren't even being offered a marriage contract, it's not even called a marriage contract. (Tracy)

Judgements encompassed both practicalities and principles, where it was noted that it may not be everything but it was a start – one which was welcomed given the wait. In attending a talk on civil partnerships given by UK activist Peter Tatchell, Carol tells of the impossibility in filling all the principled arguments, against her desire to finally be legally included. Her voice seems to carry an emotional resonance apparently against academic abstraction, where rather than being 'legally incorporated', Carol's wish may be read as simply wanting to marry her partner:

> ... 'I've waited eighteen years to marry this woman and if I have to wait until every box is ticked on that sheet of paper of yours we'll be dead, so we are going to have our civil partnership in June and we are gonna do it'. And everybody applauded ... I know that there are a lot of misgivings and there are a lot of things that they need to put right but it's a step that we thought would never happen, I never believed that in my lifetime lesbian and gay relationships would be legalized in the same way ... (Carol)

Carol's equation of being 'exactly the same' is mostly a positive one, while Lisa and Clare are more sceptical of the reach, politically and practically. They note, for example, that provisions and recognitions stop at national borders. Others asserted a need for a different way of doing things, sceptical of the reach or desire of a mirrored model. Paul, for example, stated that marriage in general needed a 'makeover', citing high divorce rate and financial dependencies:

> We have such a high divorce rate, so that the whole marriage, relationship contractual system is really in some kind of disarray and I think needs some sort of makeover. But I don't have any solutions, I'm not quite sure whether, you know, we may need to make less of marriage as it were, so that marriage can maybe be a sort of civil partnership that then maybe can be ratified at some sort of point in terms of a longer term. (Paul)

Angie also spoke of doing something 'completely fresh', viewing the ability to do things differently as a strange reversal of usual discriminations, where it was heterosexual couples who could now not chose to do things differently through a civil partnership ('I do think it's a shame that it is only available to gay couples. I think it's a strange bit of homophobia in a funny sort of way'). The ability to and value in departing from the marriage model was repeated by Elizabeth and Diane, where an alternative way of life was in jeopardy, threatened by assimilation into a 'traditional' way:

> I think that part of what lesbian and gay couples have got is also a sort of alternative way from the heterosexual marriage and I don't think that we should just be sort of seduced down the line of you know 'oh

you can do the same and it's like a marriage' and you know and turn round and say, like an honorary heterosexual couple in that you're a married couple. I think that then we could lose, just some people will be losing what we have that's kind of alternative and different and showing a different way of having a kind of family unit...but in terms of I mean in terms of the legal side the financial things and everything I mean that's all a great step forward. (Elizabeth)

Elizabeth notes that it can 'depend' on circumstances, practicalities and, of course, the couple themselves. But her comments about the potential negation of a 'different way of life' point to the reduction of possibilities, increasing the dependence on a certain model, even as this can be seen as 'a great step forward'. Dana also struggles to reconcile similarities and differences, negotiating the 'traditional terms' as legally laid out:

I think it's good that the lesbian and gay community can have a way of committing to each other but then I think it's very, very different to marriage. I think marriage is a very traditional thing and that's all to do with ownership and there's no way that civil partnership can ever be the same as marriages in its traditional terms. (Dana)

Others were more forthright in their rejection of civil partnerships, fearing these to be 'just like bad marriages' producing a certain 'squeamishness' (Steph) in witnessing them. Paula spoke of the legislation critically as enabling only 'second rate marriages', which she would refuse in her unwillingness to model herself 'on straight society'. For Sarah, the trouble in re-creating marriage is the 'terrible misogynistic history' which marriage represented, which cannot be easily displaced in attempted 'makeovers', while for Steph the problem lies in the entrenchment of a 'two-tiered world' where some faced being placed firmly in the margins, as others are rescued and redeemed as now in the mainstream. Once again the good homosexual is placed in opposition to the bad one and sides must be chosen, or allocated. The option of civil partnership can be seen as making this differentiation more concrete, for now gays and lesbians can either commit and settle down or live in sin. And do gays and lesbians really need more sin?

I think the danger of it is that I think it's fantastic for people that want to do it, I've been to lots. But I think the danger of it is that it's creating a sort of two-tiered world where you are kind of jolly and out and no problems and equal to straight people and then the kind of slightly grotty ones who decide not to. You know, like an underclass, and I'm in that! (laughter). I'm in that underclass...again! Back in the margins. And I think, I mean, that's one way of looking at it and also, because I've done that, I've been married and I spent most of my adult life married...you're not really going to start wandering back into that world and, you know, I don't care about the legal and the financial links really. (Katerina)

Others also refuted the benefits of legal and financial links, claiming civil partnerships to be a 'meaningless formality', nothing more than 'a bit of paper that isn't going to make any difference' (Jenny). The ability to enact changes and choices is shaped by the weight of expectations, as outlined by Sophie, who is pleased that there is a choice, even as she is sick of people asking her 'if' and 'when', seemingly weighed down by the expectation that now she can, she actually should. In negotiating such expectations, Sophie tells of refusing 'someone else's dreams', refusing to tick the (wrong) box. Kathy also makes clear her 'adamant' resistance, rejecting the option even as it is legally available, apparently all 'above board' and desired by her children:

We did talk about it, because the kids would like us to do it. They think if we were married then it would be easier to talk to people. And I said, 'Why? Isn't it enough that you love someone?' And Harry said, 'Yes, but it's the law, if you're married, it's the law.' And I was going, 'Yes, but there's a phrase, "the law is an ass" ', he doesn't get it right all the time. He was like, 'I don't get that, what do you mean the law's not right?'... I was going, 'Well, it was law for years that gay people were wrong and they were locked up in hospital and really badly treated.' And he was like, 'No.' So then we have to you know, explain... (Kathy)

The tensions between possibilities and practicalities were ever present in interviewees' accounts, as desires were enabled – and constrained – by what was on offer, simultaneously viewed as a benefit and a limitation. Vicky and Beth's experience is one of being caught between varied religions, personal and legal camps, where having the 'bit of paper' is invested and fraught. Rachel and Kevin express a sense of things being 'double-edged', where heteronormativity constructs and constrains and where the appeal of being 'normal' as well as the ever-present threat of being out on a 'minority limb' is ever negotiated, as is the desirability of 'sameness' (Richardson, 2005):

> It's double-edged again, because it's not the same, you're still differ-ent. It could make it worse, to be honest. For my daughter to be able to say, 'Yeah my mum is civil partnered to a woman', it's just not going to happen. From a gay perspective, it's addressing a balance, but from a hetro-normative base, no, it's still very much out there on a minority limb and I think that's probably where we will remain, in my lifetime. (Rachel)

Rather than experiencing an easy assimilation, Rachel hints at the costs and consequences. The double-edgedness features again, where Kevin claims that the financial concerns, familial desires and a personal sense of 'difference' are probably 'a middle-class thing':

> A lot of my friends see it as a very middle-class thing, it's about prop-erty and all the usual middle-class notions. On the other hand, for me, it's about protection of some of the people I love. I think we're at the stage where it's starting to plan a Civil Partnership and it just seems to me a great opportunity to have a wild party and a really good time with the people who are important to you...The kids are really into it, they like the idea and think it'll be fantastic. So it feels a bit more like a celebration than a Civil Partnership. But I do have this very different sense of what it means and should we be doing it. (Kevin)

It would seem then that the reception of civil partnerships is most definitely varied. The various arguments about equality and same-ness are countered by more combative voices and their wholesale rejection of the 'marriage' aspect of partnerships. What is telling is the extent to which the economic aspect has come to influ-ence discussion and opinion, the practical benefits and disadvan-tages perhaps being more quantifiable are therefore more debatable than the abstract ideas of worth and citizenship. Of consequence were the financial and parental benefits to be gained by some in entering a civil partnership, where 'next of kin' could rightfully access resources and enact responsibilities with regard to partners and children.

For richer, for poorer

Interviewees spoke of the materialisation of family in securing financial provisioning, and thus their own and children's material well-being, contrasting with those in more financially adverse situations. The potential negative impacts on resources and entitlements were considered in relation to new legal responsibilities, applicable whether or not civil partnerships were undertaken. While the benefits could be perceived and realised as a 'great step forward' (Elizabeth), securing 'the practical things' (Carol), the complexities and tensions within this often lead to disadvantageous circumstances, experienced most by those who were the least well off.

Sandra told of the financial benefits as significant in her decision, whereas other interviewees spoke of a possible reduction in their benefits, fearing the occurrence of this even if they did not have a civil partnership. Against this, others spoke of the practicalities of everyday life simply becoming much easier. While Gemma is critical about the implied economic dependence 'being seen as one entity', she feels this is outweighed by economic benefits. Harriet's statement captures the sense of civil partnerships acting as a safety net should the worst thing happen, enabling her to make claims on shared resources, such as pensions. The ability to make legal claims on, for example, residences and pensions constitutes a very significant change where the claiming of such could be expressed as a political fulfilment as well as a protective buffer:

> I'm sure there are other good reasons but at the moment that's the only one I know about. But as for needing a piece of paper to say 'You're together' then no but for any legal reasons when it comes to your will or your death or hospital or anything like that then yeah, the recognition of it ... I don't know if my twin told you but her partner died and the legalities that she had to go through and if she'd had a civil partnership she wouldn't have had to do that. So, spiritually no, politically yes. (Lorna)

Lorna notes the material worth and legal responsibilities contained within a piece of paper; if she'd had a civil partnership, her ex-partner would have now been compelled to pay child support. Similarly, Mel discussed the importance of financial security as significant to her own personal sense of family, as well as figuring in adoption procedures, with the ability to jointly adopt being 'extremely important' in terms of becoming a 'real family'. '...and having rights over each others, you know, money and finance, and so on' (Mel). Others mentioned the avoidance of inheritance tax, where disadvantages could be reconciled through legislative benefits. The negotiation of legal loopholes was often a tricky business, protecting against relational breakdowns and disappointments, and safeguarding income. While Tracy is disappointed in the limitations of civil partnerships in not equating to full marriage, she has come to realise the financial benefits entailed:

> ...I realised that for financial reasons it's better to have a civil partnership than not because of inheritance tax, you actually get the tax benefits as a married couple and also parental responsibility of children. You don't automatically get parental responsibility you get something else that and then you apply for parental responsibility but anyway we never did it so consequently Kym hasn't actually got any parental responsibility over the children. So I can deny her if I want to, which would seem very cruel and heartless of me but you do cruel and heartless things sometimes when these things happen. (Tracy)

Protective necessities reappeared in Derek's account, where he sought to protect his current male partner against his ex-wife and any financial claims that she might make upon Derek. Reversing gendered disadvantages, David, Steve and James also spoke of the insecurities and vulnerabilities to be negotiated via children and ex-partners, something which David is adept at, given his employment as a solicitor. He relates the devastation felt when past relationships leave nothing and where the (financial) consolidation of years is wiped away in breaking up:

> *David*: I think that's the job, that's very much part of advising people what will happen. People that are doing civil partnerships, having to say to them 'Look somebody else is going to get this money'. The hardest part of my job is saying to someone that after 10 yrs you are homeless.
> *James*: I've made my will with my children, will inherit one third and my (ex) partner will inherit one third, but my partner doesn't like the thought of death and therefore hasn't made any will. So that then makes me very vulnerable.
> *Steve*: When you look at the tax consequences.
> *James*: Why would you volunteer to pay 40% of your wealth if you can avoid it by doing something else?

Lorna tells of the law getting in the way, complicating as well as easing matters, noting that solicitors may well be the main financial beneficiaries. Her scepticism suggests a 'knowingness' not unlike David's where financial and practical concerns are weighted and navigated:

> I'm not the marrying type. But I think the tax benefits, the inheritance benefits, great. But in relations to solicitors making a hell of a lot of money off us when we split up, it's all shit. But in relation to the law or the state recognising us, it is fantastic. But again in custodial battles, I don't know, the law can sometimes get in the way of what is naturally ok. Em, whereas, my sister they had a family before the marriage laws came out they all shared the same last name, they changed it by deed poll so they didn't need the law to do that. (Lorna)

Rather than foreseeing financial benefits, capitalising upon shared income and resources, others spoke of losing out and facing greater financial risk. Both Elizabeth and Vicky were reluctant to consider legally 'coming out' in enacting a civil partnership, given that they had financial ties to ex-partners and would lose out in terms of pensions if they effectively re-married. Edward summarised the obligations and benefits arising, concluding that he was 'not the marrying type', where civil partnerships entailed 'great responsibilities as well as rights'. Janice and Jacqui both spoke of being financially worse off and facing complicated renegotiations with benefits services. Here circumstances are related as particularly tricky, both materially and emotionally, where much appears to be at 'risk' and complicated rather than clarified in legislative change:

> ... I think it's just a particularly set of pieces that I have, components that I have and finding somebody who will understand everything who'll be enough for me to trust and engage with. But from a financial point of view, I don't know what the issues are. I know there are issues about you know, two women living together and the Children's Tax Credits and those sorts of things, because I have a friend who has just broken up and is having to change everything back, all these sorts of issues. (Janice)

For Jacqui, the oppositions to civil partnerships were not just theoretical or principled but rather thoroughly practical, where once 'dis-counted' partners are assessed for benefits purposes, even if there has been no civil partnership. Jacqui details the gendered dimensions of this and the risks around income and housing:

> ... because when we were together, because it was a long time ago, because the law didn't accept that lesbians could have relationships, if one of us was working and the other one was on benefit, neither of the two were connected, even though we wrote on all the forms. So, in terms of financial, lesbians are now worse off financially, because of the Civil Partnership. If you are two lesbians living together and one of you is working, they would be expected to support the other one. Unfortunately, women's wages aren't as good as the majority of men's so we're not in a position maybe to support our partner financially. I'm not saying all men are. There are men that, you know, will struggle with that as well, but it wasn't the same for women. So, in terms of financially, I think we're worse off. But in terms of more equality, and obviously you can make that commitment to your partner, there's all the issues about if one of you dies and, you know, you've got a joint tenancy or a joint mortgage or whatever, it clears up a lot of those kinds of issues ... like with most change, there's good and there's bad (laughter). (Jacqui)

For every downside there is a silver lining and as has been shown, economics can have an enormous bearing on a relationship. The change in benefit law, while on one hand signifying a recognition of gay and lesbian relationships, has perhaps been detrimental to the very people that can least afford to lose. Sometimes acknowledgement is not that welcome. Rachel also echoes the 'good' ('I wouldn't imagine they would be taken back to their father') and the 'bad', noting that while custody claims are more secure, finances may be less so in the closing of a legal loophole, which meant partners could claim benefits as single people. This is echoed by Beth, where the loss of benefits confuses the gains to be made: 'I'm a bit confused about this really but nowadays if you start, say if I started living with a woman, I would no longer be able to claim my benefit'. There were many dilemmas to be puzzled and maybe solved, some new, some ongoing. Some interviewees were able to capitalise on personal and professional networks for information and advice, operating against the sense of confusion expressed by Beth. An interesting feature of the legislation is detailed by Edward, who speaks of avoiding inheritance tax in entering into a partnership with his son, who he is not legally or biologically related to, potentially capitalising on a rather queer twist:

> There would be no direct benefit except that if I was on my deathbed, with a terminal illness, in the next year or so, I could in fact enter into a Civil Partnership with John, my son and hand him this house and avoid inheritance tax. There's a twist! (laughter). Imagine his Mum's reaction! John's first reaction was 'Bring it on!' (laughter). But that's just a little quirk of the legislation. You just have to not be related. (Edward)

While Edward speaks of capitalising on the legislation, others spoke of feeling 'no difference' that they were well resourced in any case and things had been planned and provided for. Sam owns her property jointly, can nominate any partner or person on her pension so it 'makes not the slightest bit of difference'. That said the feeling of difference could operate on both symbolic and substantive levels, where interviewees spoke of finally belonging, being and feeling included.

No longer living in sin?

Some interviewees expressed an altogether positive feeling that civil partnerships were long-awaited and revolutionary in their potential, given the social approval of 'no longer living in sin'. Yet even celebrations brought tensions – as well as reconciliations – as family and friends sought to get in the party spirit. The sense of family could be consolidated in such ceremonies and legal undertaking where, for example, children could be given roles in ceremonies to emphasise their importance in new family formations. Others spoke more lightly of ceremonies as simply a 'big party' and a chance to celebrate with meaningful others, while the costs of such celebration still had to be met. Here the practical constraints as well as enabling factors became obvious. Those more critical of civil partnerships were inclined to view these moments as a welcoming celebration and consolidation only for some, those who could and would 'buy into' such a model: gifts were offered, and cakes eaten. Yet this perhaps does not represent such a change, where interviewees spoke of always celebrating family occasions and a sense of togetherness; what is of significance is the supports, resources and affirmations – both financial and emotional – which respondents had different access to.

In celebrating the passing of the legislation and subsequent official partnerships, interviewees struggled and celebrated with family and friends, who often came together in such moments, even if such 'coming together' represented a moment of tension as well as festivity. Carol reports that although her friend was less enthusiastic about the concept, in practice she was more than keen to celebrate, raising a glass in a celebratory spirit, while having political reservations. While most of Carol's biological family were not aware of her partnership status, she had included those who she considered her immediate family in the ceremony, inspiring a rethinking of family and who she 'really cares about'. For Carol, the Civil Partnership Act represents a movement into the twenty-first century – while her partner's parents have been dragged into this century, others reported that guests were entirely supportive, where ex-partners were friendly and encouraging presences.

Mandy tells of the ceremony being the same as a heterosexual couple's wedding and her description certainly evokes traditional ideas, even as her and her partner's outfits would suggest otherwise. On the one hand, Mandy appears to be 'doing things differently' in the wearing of suits, but even such transgressive practices are situated within a fairly normative context of gift giving, cake-cutting and familial approval. It is a ceremony, a way of being which would probably be familiar and understandable to most people. Mandy also spoke of the joy of her children who could get similarly dressed up and included:

> They just thought it was fantastic. 'Mummy and Christina are getting married!' and it was 'Let's get the Next catalogue out and let's have a look at dresses!' and so they had bridesmaid dresses and they all had their little jobs. My eldest daughter did a reading for us at the registry office ceremony and my twin daughters were responsible for taking round the guest book that we had at the reception and making sure everyone signed it...So they had a huge part in it and they were so excited. (Mandy)

Reflecting Mandy's experiences, other interviewees spoke of ceremonies as a chance for a good party, where political allegiances and personal problems could be put to one side for the sake of celebration. Although Edward was not considering a civil partnership for himself, he enjoyed the romances and celebrations of others nonetheless. Sandra spoke of bringing people from 'all over the world' to celebrate together, bringing

in brass bands and seeking to make a statement, given the 'long-awaited'
nature of things:

> Yeah, it was brilliant! Fantastic! We had people, we thought it'd be
> quite a low-key small event but it ended up being over 100 people
> and people travelling from all over the world to come. It was quite
> amazing. Egypt and Spain and yes, all over the place... The ceremony
> itself was just us and two witnesses who are our two best male friends
> and we had afternoon tea and a brass band and a jazz band and stuff
> like that, actually in our local very smart church hall. And lots of
> cake. (Sandra)

As Sandra's account of world connectedness suggests, much planning
and financing often went into ceremonies and for some this represented another limitation and impossibility; sometimes there could be
no big party even if partnerships were indeed done in the more everyday moments. The celebration of civil partnerships as one-off special
days perhaps reinforces this moment of celebration/acceptance, against
everyday, ongoing struggles. Beth simply didn't believe in 'spending lots
of money on a wedding or a civil partnership' where it would have
to be 'done on a budget sort of thing or you know not silly amounts
of money'. Kathy speaks of the draw of big parties, where roles can
be played with if not defined, and potential gift lists imagined if not
received:

> Every now and again I'll say, 'Well, if we did, we could get the house
> tidied... Think of all the gifts we could get, we could actually get a
> toaster that pops up on both sides at the same time. But no, it's a
> bit of a joke and we're not thinking about it. But they have been
> to a few civil ceremonies and so they're quite like, 'Oh.' Both of
> them, they've been to a fancy dress one, so it's not a good exam-
> ple of people taking things very seriously. They know about it and
> they ask about it, Harry's very much, 'Well you could do, you know,
> you really, really could', and they've chosen what role they want to
> play. Celia doesn't want to do bridesmaid because she doesn't want to
> wear a dress but she'll happily show people to their seats and throw
> petals... no doubt it will be on and off the agenda for many years,
> but I can't see it happening, unless we have to, for the kids. If it was
> a case we had to, we might do it, but it's not something either of
> us either seriously mentioned or contemplated at all. But we're look-
> ing at the colour co-ordinated kitchen stuff at Fenwick's and we're

thinking, 'Just think, if we could tie in the new house with a civil ceremony and get things!' (Kathy)

Kathy's tale moves from the humorous to the serious, bringing in a sense of solidarity and refusal in considerations of what her closest friends are doing – against that which others want. Like Kathy's sense of doing things differently, Kevin speaks of celebrating family outside of the models on offer, again negotiating points of sameness and difference. Families, it would seem, have always celebrated as well as argued:

> I mean, we did have, after Jo was born, about, it must have been about eight or nine months afterwards we had a kind of celebratory party and we invited all the families and lots, hundreds of people, at a big community centre in Cardiff, and that was very much about that kind of 'Let's acknowledge these things are done in different way'. And I like the idea of that. So the Civil Partnership is about that really. (Kevin)

Cause for celebration was in the welcoming, supportive responses received by interviewees' families, even as this was cause for surprise: 'I was surprised at how pleased everyone was for us, and how chuffed Gwynn's family in particular were...' (Mel). Susan had reached an inclusive compromise where her parents would attend and things would not be 'rubbed in their face'. Others reported more ambivalent family reactions, expressed as a sighing 'hmmm' ('They would accept it but there would be an element of "Hmm"', Nigel). Scaling things up, from a non-committal 'hmm', was Nigel's son for whom the thought of his dad having a civil partnership was a bit too much. Nigel tells of a soap character having a civil partnership, provoking an adverse reaction from his son – a reaction that he has kept from his partner, seeking to mediate both their needs:

> Alistair said, 'Dad, you're never going to do that are you?' and I actually tried to explore it a bit and I said 'Well, why?' and he said he'd be too embarrassed. So I took, as a joke, Gilbert gave me this ring and I took it off and put it on that finger and he said 'Dad don't do that! Don't be silly!' and he was quite definite... And I think if I did do it, I would have to, I wouldn't say I'd have to have his blessing but I'd do it when he was older... I think he just sees me being gay as being kind of acceptable, if that's the right word, but I think Civil Partnership is one step too far for him... If Gilbert knew that, he would do

a wobbly because it should be my decision but I'd have to bring him into it as well because I want him as part of that ceremony, and that's why I will probably do it when he is older. But I don't know what it does for the family unit. I think it's more for the people involved than for the family to be honest. (Nigel)

A consequential deciding factor was the 'best interests of children', where it might offer children more security, which for Kathy would be the only reason to ever consider a civil partnership. Paula relates this parental relevance backwards to those considering having children in the context of an openly lesbian relationship, where there may now be a legally legitimised 'very different context'. The sense of material security was emphasised alongside an emotional security in being part of a legitimate, socially and legally recognised unit – a 'force to be reckoned with', as Mandy expressed. Karen also tells of the importance in feeling similar to peers, where children can use family terms, which are shared and understood. Again the force of language comes into play with a civil partnership allowing access to many well-rehearsed and therefore easily understood ways of expressing and being expressed:

> I would like to show commitment to whatever partner was mine at that time when I do decide to do it. I would like Erin to feel that she was part of a family, not separated 'cause that's a thing a lot of children, before civil partnerships, may have felt a bit isolated because their parents weren't married and, you know, they didn't have the family life or whatever. I think now that that's been introduced as a legal thing it's definitely something I would do. (Karen)

The consolidation of family, for Mandy, is an external and internal process, where everyone can witness commitment and stability in a context where marriage just is promoted as a 'much more stable and appreciated institution than kind of just going through life just living with someone'. Susan stated that a major reason for delaying her anticipated civil partnership was to wait for a time when the children could be properly included. She speaks of taking her family 'with her' both physically and emotionally, where a bit of paper does not easily solve family tensions, serving to query the easy assignment and alignment of 'homonormative' lives:

> ...we've actually postponed it and the other thing was we'd decided not to have the children there because we thought it was too much

for the children to deal with. So we want to wait 'til we feel the children are ready to be there so we decided to cancel. And it caused, well I just wanted to go with a couple of friends and sort of disappear and do it, more for the legal reasons really and the legal grounding it gives you as a partnership, that's why I wanted to do it then. Emma sort of spoke to her father and he said 'Well, I want to be there and I'll pay for it' and it all went a bit haywire, with guests and all that and that's not I want. I thought I'd be too much for my mum and dad to deal with as well really. So, we decided mutually in the end to postpone it so that we could do it when the children were old enough to be there and understand. We can put photos up around the house instead of just brushing it under the carpet really … I'm not entirely sure of all the legalities and what it entitles us to do and things like that. But also to be able to tell the children in the future 'Look me and Emma are for life, this is a relationship, we've got married and this is for life, Emma's not going to disappear out your lives in a few weeks or months or whatever'. (Susan)

The sense of the 'right time' and 'right way' to do things was apparent in Stephen's view, echoing a more traditional, even conservative view of family. A kind of family-by-numbers where two is always better than one:

Yes of course, of course I think it's better to have two people who love each other bringing up children than have it made harder, this is really sounding bad now we, my wife is on her own with these three children, one of them is eighteen and he's obviously old enough to look after himself but the other two they have to have that support. I'm really hoping that she finds somebody that she can feel would be a good role model for my children and would look after them as well as I possibly could when I was living at home. So yes if there's two people living together and whether they're lesbians or homosexuals or heterosexuals then they've got children the positivity for having two people in the house is very strong. (Stephen)

This really is an interesting return to family values, albeit in a topsy turvey manner. James and Steve endorse a sense of really working things through, becoming a strong unit with the passage of time, as opposed to being able to easily get out of pledges and commitments:

Steve: It's a world apart, it's completely different living with someone than being married to

> *James*: You always know if it doesn't work out you can just move, there's still a consequence of that but you can still go. I think the psychological, the change, you've altered completely.
>
> *Steve*: You've got to have a bloody good reason to go. It's not just on a whim.

The sense of becoming 'altered', whether financially or emotionally, was exactly what was unwelcomed by other respondents, many of whom had been married in heterosexual ex-relationships. Some respondents' hesitancies were related to previous relationships and the sense of profoundly losing out in these, being left with nothing and having to 'start again'.

Once bitten, twice shy

While stories of 'long awaited' 'revolutions' were apparent, such stories of struggle and triumph often eclipsed more complicated journeys, where choices were made with and against the financial and emotional weight of the 'past'. Understanding lesbian and gay parents as embodying classed and (variously) sexualised positions potentially casts light upon sameness/difference debates and the fracturing of points of 'sameness' across the life course. The sense of loss in moments of apparent gain partially mirrors the successes in areas of reproductive technologies and legislative approvals, where 'advancements' are rendered more complex in the everyday negotiation, refusal and enactment of parental and relational possibilities. Just as access to – and approval through – various medical and social providers is more than an economic barrier, so too is the uptake of civil partnerships where material and subjective factors, both finances and feelings, intersect to construct opportunities, choices and constraints. Where the medical and social progressions make visible increasing family possibilities, it seems important to remember that interviewees do not arrive at such a place equally, as witnessed in the ongoing (de)sexualisation of (im)proper parents, pathways and prospects. Many are misplaced in the stories of choice and difference, effacing the connections between 'then' and 'now', retold in interviewees' routes to parenting and in reactions to the Civil Partnership Act.

While Ann desired a security for her child, possibly attained through legal partnership, her divorce experience has left her doubting whether this is really achievable, where 'marriage for life' just does not have an emotional currency anymore. Steph expressed a feeling that she would not make the same mistake twice; her reality had been altered in ending her heterosexual marriage, offering her a critical stance from which to comment. Yet such a critical (emotional) distance also comes at a high price, where financial ties, or lack thereof, are still resented and regretted. Others repeated the common adage of 'once bitten, twice shy' (Harriet), where they would seek to protect themselves against both the financial and emotional costs of same-sex marriage, comparing this with what had gone wrong in the past and conveying a similarity rather than a profound difference:

> ... I would do it, yes, I would but with a pre-nup... I got tore to ribbons in my marriage to my son's Mum, financially, and I wouldn't want to go through that again, I wouldn't do it. And so I would want to protect myself from doing that. (Nigel)

As has been seen previously, break-ups are break-ups whether gay or straight and the power they have over other relationships is great. It would seem that a change in the gender construction of the relationship is often not a significant enough change to counteract the similarities to other 'failed' marriages or relationships. Dana conveyed a reluctance to 'start again from scratch', feeling that she would want to do things profoundly differently and more equally. She feels that such differences are not necessarily gained in traditional partnership consolidations, even if officially approved:

> When me and Josie split up and civil partnerships weren't in then they weren't around but I think it would depend. I felt as if I've had to start from scratch again and that was fair enough because Josie brought Billy up although she didn't contribute financially. You know, she was there and so I did owe her you know that money. But it's took me until now and even then you know to kind of start from scratch again and I have been in relationships, I had a relationship since where the woman has got nothing you know and it just bothers me (laughs). If I was to go into a civil partnership again and that woman could take half of what I've worked for all my life and then I would be left with not being able to purchase a house again at my age. Now I'm looking for a relationship where it's more of an equal partnership and somebody more... I can't explain what I mean but who's more my type of personality who's kind of pushed the boundaries in their life and got out, you know, decided to do something and gone out and got it kind of thing. Not somebody who's just sat back and thought the world owed them a favour sort of thing. (Dana)

While Dana talks of the desire in pushing boundaries where her past is not erased but is used to propel her to a better future, Janice's tone is almost self-deprecating, asking who would want the 'package' that is her, comparing her circumstances to disparate pieces, which legal consolidations would fail to join. In detailing a less than appealing 'package' Janice conveys the complexity of her life as a 'jig-saw' rather than a complete and obvious picture. Such 'messiness' was also expressed by other respondents who spoke of the difficult and binding implications of the civil partnerships, bringing a weight which would carry across time, tiring and draining emotional and material resources:

> I mean I spent 5 years trying to get out of my marriage and so it's not something I would enter into lightly 'cause of that I don't know how hard it is to get out of and I've said I don't think people necessarily think that it is as difficult or as binding as it is. (Kate)

Such binds seemingly work with and against mainstreamed inclusions, troubled by prior inclusion on the basis of heterosexual coupledom now ended but ever present, whether in responsibilities, affections and/or regrets. Where heterosexual status may have once signified inclusion, the narrative of 'once bitten, twice shy' cements interviewees' chosen exclusion from same-sex 'marriages', set within the context of stemming losses. It would seem then that for some the partnership party is long over. For others the conflicting emotions and responses to civil partnerships are something which will be worked out over time and experience; once the dust has settled and the cake has been eaten, the value and meaning of this new institution can be assessed. It is clear that while it is in many ways novel and exciting, it does draw heavily on traditional ideas of marriage and commitment, reflected in the sometimes wholesale appropriation of ways of enacting and celebrating. It is, of course, hard to reinvent the wheel and this appropriation is seen by many as reclaiming a right and a rite of passage that has been for so long denied to gays and lesbians. The extent to which these changes will normalise gay and lesbian relationships in the eyes of the wider community, for example, in terms of schools, is yet to be seen. The stances taken towards civil partnerships are numerous, and as ever economics and class cannot be written out of the equation. Nothing comes without cost, be that in terms of the cost of the actual ceremony, the effect on benefits or the lack of a degree of uniqueness, but only time will tell who the real winners and losers are.

Measuring the 'costs' of civic acceptance is no easy matter, where these may constitute a rightful entitlement for some, while acting as a severe impediment to others. The desire for a 'normal', 'ordinary' status operates as a powerful claim, if not antidote, against prior discriminations. Yet there are varied abilities to claim – and materially resource – such an 'ordinariness'; not everyone is positioned as 'legal and above board', least of all benefit claimants whose families may face or fear dissolution. Finances, of course, amount in the everyday practices of parenting, as well as in the one-off celebrations and ceremonies, where rituals themselves endorse – or erode – family formations. Not everyone is at the party, not everyone wants to be. However, there are consequential classed dynamics behind such a negotiation where parents and families are variously materialised, endorsed or disappeared.

Concluding Thoughts

This book has sought to detail the intersections between class and sexuality in lesbians' and gay men's experiences of parenting, from initial routes into parenting and household divisions of labour, to location preferences, schooling choice and community supports. Exploring such an intersection has involved grappling with often unconnected and competing literatures. Such a (dis)connection is evident in research which details the classed constructions and experiences of parenting, focusing mostly on heterosexual families, against quite different research detailing the specificities of lesbian and gay parented families, while frequently negating the 'difference' of class. In utilising both bodies of research, this book has sought to connect and combine. It sought to understand points of 'sameness' and 'difference' across the literature and, importantly, within interviewees' own situation, understandings and experiences as classed and sexual subjects. In doing so it is hoped that the gap in understanding and detailing lesbian and gay parental experiences is somewhat bridged if not yet filled.

Many studies have identified such a continued gap, where empirical research upon lesbians and gay men is still frequently based on those from white backgrounds occupying certain socio-economic positions and geographical locations. Throughout this book the task has been to tentatively bridge theoretical approaches and empirical accounts: undoubtedly, there are gaps in my own approach; notably, a significant absence is the way that ethnicity also structures the participants' classed experiences. Such an absence is not only in terms of the research cohort but rather in the place of ethnicity in the study as a whole. This is intended as (limited) acknowledgement of the ways that whiteness, for respondents, is a valued form of ethnicity, where whiteness can also be seen to be lived differently through the modalities of class.

190

This was witnessed in Chapters 5 and 6 where race, with sexuality and class, mutually constituted notions of a 'good' mix as opposed to an 'excessive' 'mess'. The concept of 'intersectionality' was utilised to bring together the missed out and forgotten. While I still believe that the concept of intersectionality should be expanded to include sexuality there are problems in extracting this term when this expansion of intersectionality departs from or negates race, also effacing the specific legacies and endurances of the term emerging from Black feminist thought.

Continuations and transformations were grappled with in attempting to situate contemporary classed experiences, inequalities and divisions *beyond*, and *including*, the economic. Unpacking the complexity and relevance of class can be difficult when 'absence' or 'irrelevance' discredits attempts. Yet such a situation is made easier by longstanding feminist accounts which succeed in doing just that, in highlighting classed reproductions and intersections amidst complications *and* certainties. Across the empirical chapters, class featured in the construction of choices and chances, from routes into parenting to routes through education. It complexly combined with sexual status, at times ensuring an 'ordinary' respectability, at other times serving to reinforce exclusion and marginalisation. Such a tense positioning intersects expectations, entitlements, confidences and resources – ever threatened and rendered insecure by sexual discrimination, even as these are re-mobilised and re-circulated. This was witnessed across the range of fields presented here, including routes to parenthood, geographies of inclusion and exclusion and the educational system.

The 'families of choice' literature provides a corrective to 'straight and narrow' definitions of families, friendship and parenting. Yet it does so often without rigorous attention to the relevance of class, as facilitating and constraining 'choice'. Possible points of intersection between the social capital evidenced by Weeks et al. (2001) and the specifically classed form highlighted by Bourdieu (1984) are relevant in this theoretical re-framing. Broader social and legal changes are of course also important here, where debates on sexual citizenship oscillate between notions of assimilation/transformation, challenged by attention to the difference that class makes in accessing, claiming and gaining a respectable 'ordinary' status. The desire to be the 'same' in accessing a range of social spheres – as well as the (im)possibility of being so – may be understood as classed and sexualised in its constant (de)legitimisation.

Gay and lesbian parented families do indeed continue to face inequality and discrimination, where one of the ways that middle-class parents compensate for, or resist, this stigma is to reframe themselves as more responsible and thoughtful than their working-class counterparts. In relation to routes into parenting, this claim is based on their experiences as 'family planners' who carefully choose whether and how they wish to be parents, sometimes setting out on time-consuming projects of trying to conceive (typically by means of expensive reproductive technologies). Working-class parents, according to this narrative, often become parents accidentally, or without the same level of thought and agency. Such a middle-class narrative has, in many contexts, become the dominant one and has accordingly eclipsed the experience of working-class lesbian and gay parents. Most working-class interviewees had children from previous heterosexual relationships and/or did not have the financial resources to seek out 'responsible' reproductive technologies. Hence, the dominant academic narrative in 'reflexive', choice-based accounts, and in middle-class parents' own accounts, negates working-class 'queerness', calling into question the quality and *legitimacy* of their parenting. Such processes lead some working-class parents to avoid gay parenting groups and other sites on which the narrative of choice and responsibility has a strong framing presence. Academic literature on lesbian and gay parenting has positively asserted political and personal worth in confronting heteronormative understandings of family but what they have neglected is the classing of parental possibilities where 'choice' may only be mobilised by the chosen few. Throughout everyday parental spaces, choices were often framed by both implicit and explicit classed 'costs' where parents negotiated material and moral assessments. In seeking to make a contribution to the complexities of and displacement of agency and constraint set against the backdrop of particular family changes, this book offers a contribution towards understanding the intersection of class, sexuality and parenthood evidenced in respondents' complex struggles, strategies and successes.

Appendix

1. ABI, 36, identified as middle-class, with a lower middle-class upbringing. She co-parents her daughter (5 years), who she conceived using AI, with her partner.
2. ANDREW, 32, identified as middle-class; he donated sperm to a lesbian couple and maintained a limited relationship with his son.
3. ANGIE, 46, identified as middle-class. She has a 3-year-old son (Thomas) who she adopted with her female partner.
4. ANN, 38, identified as lower middle-class. She is a single-mother with a 5-year-old daughter from a previous heterosexual relationship. Ann has a partner who she doesn't live with.
5. BETH, 35, identified as working-class and was living on benefits and undertaking voluntary work. She has an 11-year-old daughter and a 14-year-old son, from a previous heterosexual relationship. Beth had aspirations to become a counsellor.
6. CAROL, 53, stated that she came from a working-class background but now identified as middle-class because of her employment position as a counsellor. She has two daughters (36, 15 years), one conceived in a previous heterosexual relationship. Her youngest daughter, Abby, was conceived using a donor and Carol is her birth mother. Carol lives with partner who co-parents Abby.
7. CARRIE, 44, identified as working-class. She has two sons (17, 20 years) from a previous heterosexual relationship. Carrie returned to education as a mature student, and now works for the council having previously involved in voluntary youth work/sexual health services.
8. CATHRINE, 28, identified as middle-class. She lives with her partner (Emma, 29) and 2-year-old son, Wayne, who she conceived through AI.
9. CLARE, 32, identified as middle-class. Clare is Lisa's partner and currently they have 1 daughter, Amy (3 years), conceived using a known donor with Lisa as the birth mother. At the time of the interview Clare was pregnant from the same known donor.
10. DANA, 51, is from working-class background and self-defines as working-class although now in a middle-class occupation. Dana recently split with her long-term partner, Josie, and is now single. Dana conceived her son Billy (19 years) through AI and continues to co-parent with her ex-partner. Attempted adoption of a child, before the birth of Billy, ended in failure.
11. DAVID, 52, identified as middle-class and was employed as a solicitor. He has a son (14 years) from a previous heterosexual relationship.
12. DEREK, 48, identified as middle-class and used to own his own business. He has two adult children (one daughter, 23 years, one son, 20 years) from a previous heterosexual relationship. He is estranged from his children and ex-wife.

13. DIANE, 37, identified as working-class. She returned to education as a mature student and was now unemployed. She has a 13-year-old son and a 14-year-old daughter from a previous heterosexual relationship.
14. EDWARD, 63, identified as middle-class. Edward co-parented his son, 21 years, with his ex-wife. He was not legally or biologically related to his son.
15. ELIZABETH, 52, identified as middle-class. She has two sons (19, 23 years) from a previous heterosexual relationship, though she brought her children up mostly in a lesbian-parented household. She has now spilt up with her female partner who does not keep in touch with her sons.
16. GARITH, 59, identified as middle-class. He has two daughters (21, 24 years) from a previous heterosexual relationship.
17. GEMMA, 50, identified as middle-class and is a local government manager. She has twin daughters (15 years) who she co-parented with her lesbian partner, who she has now split-up with.
18. GEOFF, 44, identified as middle-class and has two sons from an ex-heterosexual relationship. He recently divorced his wife and currently had no contact with his sons, following a period of homelessness and emotional breakdown.
19. HARRIET, 38, identified as middle-class. She is a librarian having previously been in the army. She has one daughter from a previous heterosexual relationship.
20. JACQUI, 43, self-defined as working-class but is employed in a middle-class occupation as support worker. She has one daughter and continues to care for her ex-female partner's son.
21. JAMES, 42, identified as middle-class and has a 14-year-old son from a previous heterosexual relationship.
22. JANICE, 45, identified as middle-class and is a lecturer. She has three children from a previous heterosexual relationship (9, 11, 14 years). Janice 'came out' 1 year ago and is a single-parent.
23. JENNY, 29, identified as working-class but is from a middle-class background. She is a single-parent with a 4-year-old daughter conceived in a previous heterosexual relationship.
24. JESS, 42, identified as middle-class. She has three children from a previous heterosexual relationship, which she co-parents with her partner and her two children.
25. JOC, 37, identified as middle-class and is employed in a senior management role. She has one daughter (Emma), and is Sandra's partner.
26. JODY, 40, identified as working-class and is employed as a fork lifter. She has one son and one daughter from a previous heterosexual relationship.
27. KAREN, 22, identified as working-class and was currently unemployed. She had previously worked nightshifts as carer and wants to pursue education when her 3-year-old daughter goes to nursery. Her daughter was conceived in a previous heterosexual relationship.
28. KATE, 39, identified as working-class and works in retail. She has three children from a previous heterosexual relationship (two daughters, 12 and 14 years, one son, 17 years). Her female partner, who she does not live with, also has two children.

29. KATERINA, 52, identified as working-class. She has three children, two daughters (17, 19 years) and one boy (28 years).

30. KATHY, 42, came from a working-class background although now had middle-class employment as a manager of voluntary sector organisation. She has two children (one girl and one boy, 11-year-old twins) who were conceived with AI. Her partner, who gave birth to the twins, works in a mental health organisation as a senior manager.

31. KEVIN, 36, identified as middle-class and has one daughter (Jo, 14 years) from a heterosexual relationship and feels that Daniel (10 years), Jo's brother, is also his son.

32. LISA, 34, identified as middle-class. Clare is Lisa's partner and currently they have one daughter, Amy (3 years), conceived using a known donor with Lisa as the birth mother. At the time of the interview Clare was pregnant from the same known donor.

33. LORNA, 42, identified as middle-class. She had her 10-year-old daughter conceived using a donor with her female ex-partner.

34. LYNN, 39, came from a working-class background and is now employed in a middle-class occupation (social work). Lynn is single-parent, with two children (9-year daughter, 14-year son) from a previous heterosexual relationship.

35. MANDY, 44, identified as middle-class but noted that she was from a working-class background. She was employed as a lecturer and had worked as a youth worker. She has three children conceived in a previous heterosexual relationship; 9-year-old twins and an 11-year-old daughter.

36. MARGARET, 42, identified as middle-class. She has one daughter, conceived using a donor.

37. MARTIN, 59, identified as middle-class and is employed as a librarian having previously worked as a lecturer, returned to home/care for 20 years. He has two daughters (18, 21 years) and two sons (22, 25 years) all adopted in the context of a heterosexual family unit. Martin continues to live with his wife, who has disabilities and is on benefits, while 'out' as a gay man.

38. Maureen, 31, identified as working-class and is unemployed although in a New Deal programme training to be a postal assistant. She previously worked in retail but left due to an injury. Her partner lost her job as a result of homophobic bullying. Maureen has a son (15 years) and a daughter (11 years) conceived in a previous heterosexual relationship. She lives with her partner who has three sons (10, 8, 12 years).

39. MEL, 42, identified as middle-class. Mel was going through the adoption process with her partner of 14 years.

40. MICHELLE, 45, identified as working-class to middle-class. She is a single-parent to her 8-year-old son, conceived using AI when she was with a female ex-partner.

41. NIGEL, 43, identified as middle-class and previously worked in banking, although was retraining as a journalist and was a student. He has a 12-year-old son, Alistair, from a previous heterosexual relationship. His partner Gilbert had a 23-year-old son from a previous heterosexual relationship and lost an 11-year-old daughter to illness.

42. NINA, 35, identified as working-class and works in a charitable organisation. She is a single-parent to two sons (11, 15 years) conceived in a previous heterosexual relationship.
43. PAUL, 55, identified as middle-class. Paul was currently living in a heterosexual family unit and has one son (14 years) and two daughters (21, 25 years) who were all adopted.
44. PAULA, 48, identified as middle-class and is employed as a teacher. Paula left school at 16 years and was once on benefits as a single-parent. Her daughter (28 years) was conceived in a previous heterosexual relationship.
45. PETER, 43, identified as middle-class and is from a working-class background. He has one daughter, Cassie, who is 17 years old.
46. RACHEL, 40, identified as middle-class. She has one daughter (11 years) and one son (14 years) from a previous heterosexual relationship. Rachel left school at 16 years and went into police force. She left the police when she became pregnant, and retrained in youth work and teaching. She is now a trained counsellor and wants to pursue social work.
47. SALLY, 42, identified as middle-class. She has adult children (25, 28 years) with a female ex-partner (partner was birth mother) and a 3-year-old boy conceived through donor insemination with her now deceased female partner. Sally previously worked in the building trade and was working towards establishing her own business. After her partner died Sally took up a degree; she previously completed a diploma in youth and community work and was employed in a management role in a children's home.
48. SAM, 35, identified as middle-class, working as a supply teacher and a waiter. He has a daughter (13 years) and a son (11 years) from a previous heterosexual relationship.
49. SANDRA, 50, identified as middle-class. She has one daughter Emma with Joc.
50. SARAH, 42, identified as middle-class and is employed as a social worker in young people's services. Sarah has two children (6-year son, 8-year daughter) conceived using AI. She has recently split up with her female partner and co-parent, (Jackie) who was employed as a manager for a local authority. Sarah returned to education after leaving school at 16 years.
51. SHARON, 34, identified as middle-class and had just adopted a child with Shirley.
52. SHIRLEY, 35, identified as middle-class and had adopted a child with Sharon.
53. SOPHIE, 45, defines as working-class while feeling that she has a middle-class occupation, working in residential care. She has two children (8, 11 years) and a female partner.
54. STACY, 33, identified as middle-class, employed as a part-time youth worker. She is a single-parent with two sons (5, 3 years), conceived through AI. She recently spilt up with her female partner who is still involved in childcare.
55. STEPH, 54, identified as middle-class and previously worked as a teacher and youth worker. She has three children, two daughters (17, 20 years) and one son (28 years) from a previous heterosexual relationship. Her female partner also has two sons (29, 27 years). Steph does not live with her partner.

56. STEPHEN, 48, has two sons (8, 18 years) and one daughter (10 years) from a previous heterosexual relationship. He continues to care for his two youngest children.
57. STEVE, 46, identified as middle-class and has one daughter (20 years) and one son (18 years) from a previous heterosexual relationship.
58. SUSAN, 50, identified as working-class and has one son and one daughter from a previous heterosexual relationship. She has a female partner, who is an accounts manager in a shop.
59. TRACY, 41, identified as middle-class and owned her own business with her now ex-partner though stated that she came from a working-class background. Tracy previously worked as a midwife. She had her child through AI.
60. VICKY, 42, identified as middle-class but said that she came from a working-class background. Vicky was a teacher, who returned to university, aged 25 years. She has a daughter, 20 years, and her son died at 15 years. Both children were conceived in a previous heterosexual relationship. Vicky now lives with her partner Wendy and they are foster parents.

Notes

1 The straight and narrow?

1. Section 2a (Local Government Act, Scotland, 1986) also known as Section 28 (Local Government Act, 1988) stated that local authorities should not intentionally promote homosexuality, publish material with the intention of promoting homosexuality or promote the teaching in any maintained school of the acceptability of homosexuality as a 'pretended family' relationship. Section 2a was finally repealed by the Scottish Parliament on the 21 June 2000 while the UK parliament took another three years to repeal Section 28.
2. The first national recognition of same sex partnerships came in Denmark in 1989. Naples (2007) outlines the different types of relationship policies that can be utilised by same-sex couples, ranging from registered partnerships or civil unions, including substantively similar – or the same – rights as marriage. The United States stands apart from Canada and European countries on same-sex 'marriage', passing the Defence of Marriage Act in 1996, upholding and 'defending' marriage for heterosexuals only.

2 Gay parents, games lessons and gambling with the future

1. The term 'intersectionality' was introduced by Crenshaw (1993) in 'mapping the margins' of black women's employment experiences in the United States, noting the ways that identity politics frequently conflated and dismissed differences between and within groups (McCall, 2005). The inadequacy of simple additions, through 'and'/'or', is set against a model of structural and political intersectionality, rather than attempting to produce a 'totalising theory of identity', where every identity category is finally and completely known and achieved.
2. The classed aspects to lesbian and gay friendships have received some attention (Blumstein and Schwartz, 1983; Vicinus, 1985; Davis and Kennedy, 1993; Taylor, 2007). In considering the 'complexities of friendship' notions of choice still have to be situated within a frame of selection and distinction; just who counts as friends? Friendships are structured and patterned by social class, mobility, occupational status, leisure interests, gender, ethnic and racial categorisation and age (Jamieson, 1998). While demonstrating that lesbian and gay friendships need to be 'worked at', Weeks et al. (2001) underemphasises the structuring of these sometimes not so 'fluid' choices (Gillies, 2006).
3. Putman (1993, 1995) has generated the most commonly referenced definition of social capital, taken up in UK and US social policies, focusing

on trust and networks and explicitly linking their measurement to economic growth and health. Focusing upon the function of norms and networks, Putman identifies family as a crucial foundation for social capital, which Gillies (2003) criticises as remaining a rather vague and generalised idealisation.

Bibliography

Acker, J. (2008) 'Feminist theory's unfinished business', *Gender and Society* 22(1): 104–108.

Acosta, L. K. (2007) 'Everything would be solved if only we could marry: Queer marriages and U.S immigration policy', in N. Rumens and A. Cervantes-Carson (eds), *Sexual Politics of Desire and Belonging*. Amsterdam: Rodopi.

Adam, B. (1996) 'Detraditionalization and the certainty of uncertain futures', in P. Heelas, S. Lash and P. Morris (eds), *Detraditionalization: Critical Reflections on Authority and Identity*. Oxford: Blackwell.

Adam, B. D. (2006) 'Relationship innovation in male couples', *Sexualities* 9(1): 5–26.

Adkins, L. (2002) *Revisions: Gender and Sexuality in Late Modernity*. Buckingham: Open University Press.

Adkins, L. and Skeggs, S. (2004) (eds) *Feminism After Bourdieu*. Oxford: Blackwell.

Agigian, A. (2004) *Baby Steps: How Lesbian Alternative Insemination Is Changing the World*. Connecticut: Wesleyan University Press.

Ahmed, S. (2004) *The Cultural Politics of Emotion*. Edinburgh: Edinburgh University Press.

Almack, K. (2007) 'Out and about: Negotiating the processes of disclosure of lesbian parenthood', *Sociological Research Online* 12(1), available at http://www.socresonline.org.uk/12/1/almack.html [accessed January 2008].

Anthias, F. (2001) 'New hybridities, old concepts: The limits of "culture" ', *Ethnic and Racial Studies* 24(4): 619–641.

——— (2002) 'Beyond feminism and multiculturalism: Locating difference and the politics of location', *Women's Studies International Forum* 25(3): 275–286.

Anthias, F. and Yuval-Davis, N. (1983) 'Contextualizing feminism: Gender, ethnic and class divisions', *Feminist Review* 15: 62–75.

Armstrong, J. (2006) 'Beyond "juggling" and "flexibility": Classed and gendered experiences of combining employment and motherhood', *Sociological Research Online* 11(2).

Bagnell, G., Longhurst, B. and Savage, M. (2003) 'Children, belonging and social capital: The PTA and the middle class narrative of social involvement in the North-West of England', *Sociological Research Online* 8(4): 1–24, available at http://www.socresonline.org.uk/8/4/bagnell.htm [accessed 10th June 2006].

Ball, S. (2003) *Class Strategies and the Education Market: The Middle-Class and Social Advantage*. London: Routledge/Falmer.

Barney, S. (2005) 'Accessing medicalized donor sperm in the US and Britain: An historical narrative'. *Sexualities* 8(2): 205–220.

Barrett, M. and McIntosh, M. (1982) *The Anti-Social Family*. London: Verso Books.

Bauman, Z. (2003) *Liquid Love: On the Frailty of Human Bonds*. Cambridge: Polity Press.

Bech, H. (1992) 'Report from a rotten state: ' "Marriage" and "Homosexuality" in Denmark', in K. Plummer (ed.), *Modern Homosexualities: Fragments of Lesbian and Gay Experience*. London: Routledge, pp. 134–146.

————— (1997) 'Citysex: Representing lust in public', *Theory Culture Society* 15: 215–241.

Beck, U. (1992) *Risk Society*. London: Sage.

————— (2000) *What Is Globalization?* Oxford: Blackwell.

Beck, U. and Beck-Gernsheim, E. (1995) *The Normal Chaos of Love*. Cambridge: Polity Press/Blackwells.

————— (2002) *Individualization: Institutionalized Individualism and Its Social and Political Consequences*. London: Sage.

Beck-Gernsheim, E. (1998) 'On the way to a post-familiar family: From a community of need to elective affinities', *Theory, Culture and Society* 15: 3–4, 53–70.

————— (2002) *Reinventing the Family: In Search of New Lifestyles*. Cambridge: Polity Press.

Bell, D. and Valentine, G. (eds) (1995) *Mapping Desire*. London: Routledge.

Benkov, L. (1994) *Reinventing the Family: The Emerging Story of Lesbian and Gay Families*. New York: Crown Publishing.

Berger, M. T. (2004) *Workable Sisterhood: The Political Journey of Stigmatized Womanhood with HIV/AIDS*. Princeton, NJ: Princeton University Press.

Berlant, L. (1997) *The Queen of America Goes to Washington City: Essays on Sex and Citizenship*. Duke University Press.

Bernstein, M. and Reimann, R. (eds) (2001) *Queer Families, Queer Politics: Challenging Culture and the State*. Columbia: Columbia University Press.

Bernstien, R. (2005) *Families of Value: Personal Profiles of Pioneering Lesbian and Gay Parents*. New York: Marlowe and Co.

Bettie, J. (2003) *Women without Class: Girls, Race, and Identity*. University of California Press.

Binnie, J. (2004) *The Globalization of Sexuality*. London: Sage.

Binnie, J. and Valentine, G. (1999) 'Geographies of sexuality – Review of progress', *Progress in Human Geography* 23(2): 175–187.

Blumstein, P. and Schwartz, P. (1983) *American Couples: Money, Work, Sex*. New York: William Morrow.

Bock, D. J. (2000) 'Doing the right thing? Single mothers by choice and the struggle for legitimacy', *Gender and Society* 14(1): 62–86.

Boggis, T. (2000) 'First class: Economics and queer families', in J. Wells (ed.), *Home Fronts: Controversies in Non-Traditional Parenting*. Los Angeles: Alyson Books.

————— (2001) 'Affording our families: Class issues in family formation', in M. Bernstein and R. Reimann (eds), *Queer Families, Queer Politics: Challenging Culture and the State*. Columbia: Columbia University Press.

Bourdieu, P. (1977) *Outline of a Theory of Practice*. Cambridge: Cambridge University Press.

————— (1984) *Distinction: A Social Critique of the Judgement of Taste*. London: Routledge.

————— (1985) 'The social space and the genesis of groups', *Theory and Society* 14: 723–744.

————— (1987) 'What makes a social class? On the theoretical and practical existence of groups', *Berkeley Journal of Sociology* 32: 1–18.

————— (1990) *In Other Worlds: Essays Toward a Reflexive Sociology*. Stanford: Stanford University Press.

Brah, A. and Phoenix, A. (2004) 'Ain't I a woman? Revisiting intersectionality', *Journal of International Women's Studies* 5(3): 75–86.

Brannen, J. and Nilsen, A. (2006) 'From fatherhood to fathering: Transmission and change among British fathers in four-generation families', *Sociology* 40(2): 335–352.

Brekhaus, W. H. (2003) *Peacock, Chameleons and Centaurs: Gay Suburbia and the Grammar of Social Identity*. Chicago: University of Chicago Press.

Browne, K., Lim, J. and Brown, G. (2007) *Geographies of Sexualities: Theories, Practices and Politics*. London: Ashgate.

Butler, J. (1990) *Gender Trouble*. New York: Routledge.

—— (2002) 'Is kinship always already heterosexual?', *A Journal of Feminist Cultural Studies* 13(1): 14–44.

Byrne, B. (2006) *White Lives: The Interplay of 'Race', Class and Gender in Everyday Life*. London, New York: Routledge.

Cahill, S. (2005) 'Welfare moms and the two grooms: The concurrent promotion and restriction of marriage in US public policy', *Sexualities* 8: 239–254.

Carrington, C. (1999) *No Place Like Home: Relationships and Family Life Among Lesbians and Gay Men*. Chicago: University of Chicago Press.

Castells, M. (1996) *The Information Age: The Rise of the Network Society. Volume 1*. Oxford: Blackwell.

—— (1997) *The Information Age: The Power of Identity. Volume 2*. Oxford: Blackwell.

—— (1998) *The Information Age: Economy, Society and Culture End of Millennium. Volume III*: Oxford: Blackwell.

Chambers, D. (2001) ' "What if?" The legal consequences of marriage and the legal needs of lesbian and gay male couples', in M. Bernstein and R. Reimann (eds), *Queer Families, Queer Politics: Challenging Culture and the State*. New York: Columbia University Press.

Chambers, D., Tincknell, E. and Van Loon, J. (2004) 'Peer regulation of teenage sexual identities', *Gender and Education* 16(3): 397–415.

Charlesworth, S. (2000) *A Phenomenology of Working Class Experience*. Cambridge: Cambridge University Press.

Chasin, A. (2000) *Selling Out. The Gay and Lesbian Movement Goes to Market*. Basingstoke: Palgrave.

Christensen, P., James, A. and Jenks, C. (2000) 'Home and movement: Children constructing "family time" ', in S. Holloway and G. Valentine (eds), *Children's Geographies*. London: Routledge, pp. 230–243.

Clarke, V. (2000) 'Lesbian mothers: Sameness and difference', *Feminism and Psychology* 10(2): 273–278.

—— (2001a) 'Lesbian and gay parenting: Resistance and normalisation', *Lesbian and Gay Psychology Review* 2(1): 3–8.

—— (2001b) 'The psychology and politics of lesbian and gay parenting: Having our cake and eating it?', *Lesbian and Gay Psychology Review* 2(2): 36–42.

—— (2002) 'Sameness and difference in research on lesbian parenting', *Journal of Community and Applied Social Psychology* 12: 210–222.

—— (2003) 'Lesbian and gay marriage: Transformation or normalization', *Feminism and Psychology* 13(4): 519–529.

—— (2006) 'Focus on activism: Challenging preconceptions of lesbian parenting', *Lesbian and Gay Psychology Review* 7(1): 78–84.

Clarke, V. and Finlay, S. J. (2004) 'For better or worse? Lesbian and gay marriage', *Feminism and Psychology* 14(1): 17–23.
Clarke, V. and Kitzinger, C. (2005) ' "We're not living on planet lesbian": Constructions of male role models in debates about lesbian families', *Sexualities* 8(2): 137–152.
Clarke, V., Burgoyne, C. and Burns, M. (2006) 'Just a piece of paper? A qualitative exploration of same-sex couples' multiple conceptions of civil partnerships and marriage', *Lesbian and Gay Psychology Review* 7(2): 141–161.
Cooper, D. and Herman, D. (1995) 'Getting "the Family Right": Legislating heterosexuality in Britain, 1986–91', in D. Herman and C. Stychin (eds), *Legal Inversions; Lesbians, Gay Men, and the Politics of Law*. Philadelphia, PA: Temple University Press.
Crenshaw, K. W. (1993) 'Mapping the margins: Intersectionality, identity politics and violence against women of color', in A. Albertson Fineman and R. Mykitiuk (eds), *The Public Nature of Private Violence*. New York: Routledge.
Cussins, C. (1998) 'Quit snivelling, cyro-baby. We'll work out which one's your mama', in R. Davis-Floyd and J. Dumit (eds), *Cyborg Babies from Techno-Sex to Techno-Tots*. London: Routledge.
Dalton, S. (2001) 'Protecting our parent-child relationships: Understanding the strengths and weaknesses of second-parent adoption', in M. Bernstein and R. Reimann (eds), *Queer Families, Queer Politics: Challenging Culture and the State*. New York: Columbia University Press.
Dalton, S. and Bielby, D. (2000) 'That's our kind of constellation: Lesbian mothers negotiate institutionalized understandings of gender within the family', *Gender and Society* 14: 36–61.
Davis, K. (2008) 'Intersectionality as buzzword: A sociology of science perspective on what makes a feminist theory successful', *Feminist Theory* 9(1): 67–85.
Davis, M. D. and Kennedy, E. L. (1993) *Boots of Leather, Slippers of Gold*. London: Routledge.
Devine, F. (2004) *Class Practices, How Parents Help Their Children Get Good Jobs*. Cambridge: Cambridge University Press.
Donovan, C. (2000) 'Who needs a father? Negotiating biological fatherhood in British lesbian families using self-insemination', *Sexualities* 3(2): 149–164.
Duggan, L. (2002). 'The new homonormativity: The sexual politics of neoliberalism', in R. Castronova and D. D. Nelson (eds), *Materializing Democracy: Toward a Revitalized Cultural Politics*. Durham, NC: Duke University Press.
Duncan, S. (1995) 'Mothering, class and rationality', *Sociological Review* 53(2): 49–76.
Dunne, G. A. (1997). *Lesbian Lifestyles: Women's Work and the Politics of Sexuality*. London: Macmillan.
——— (ed.) (1998) *Living 'Difference': Lesbian Perspectives on Work and Family Life*. Binghamton, NY: The Haworth Press.
——— (1999) *The Different Dimensions of Gay Fatherhood*. Report to the Economic and Social Research Council. The Gender Institute, London School of Economics.
——— (2000) 'Opting into motherhood: Lesbians blurring the boundaries and transforming the meaning of parenthood and kinship', *Gender and Society* 14(1): 11–35.

Durham, M. (2000) *The Christian Right, the Far Right and the Boundaries of American Conservatism.* Manchester: Manchester University Press.

Edwards, R. and Gillies, V. (2004) 'Support in parenting: Values and consensus concerning who to turn to', *Journal of Social Policy* 33(4): 627–647.

—— (2005) *Resources in Parenting: Access to Capitals Project Report.* London: South Bank University.

Edwards, R., Hadfield, L., Lucey, H. and Mauthner, M. (2006) *Sibling Identity and Relationships: Sisters and Brothers.* London: Routledge.

Epstein, D. (1994) *Challenging Lesbian and Gay Inequalities in Education.* Buckingham: Open University Press.

Ertman, M. (2003) 'What's wrong with a parenthood market? A new and improved theory of commodification', *North Carolina Law Review* 82(December): 1–59.

Evans, G. (2006) *Educational Failure and Working Class White Children in Britain.* Houndsmill, Basingstoke, Hampshire: Palgrave Macmillan.

Fielding, S. (2000) 'Walk on the left! Children's geographies and the primary school', in S. Holloway and G. Valentine (eds), *Children's Geographies.* London: Routledge.

Finch, J. and Mason, J. (1993) *Negotiating Family Responsibilities.* London: Routledge.

Foucault, M. (1978) *The History of Sexuality: An Introduction*, trans. R. Hurley. Harmondsworth: Penguin.

Franklin, S. and McKinnon, S. (eds) (2001) *Relative Values: Reconfiguring Kinship Studies.* Durham, NC: Duke University Press.

Fraser, M. (1999) 'Classing queer politics in competition', *Theory, Culture & Society* 1(2): 107–131.

Furedi, F. (2002) *Paranoid Parenting: Why Ignoring the Experts May Be Best for Your Child.* Chicago: Chicago Review Press.

Gabb, J. (1999) 'Imag(in)ing the queer lesbian family', *Journal of the Association for Research on Mothering* 1(2): 9–20.

—— (2001) 'Desirous subjects and parental identities: Toward a radical theory on (Lesbian) family sexuality', *Sexualities* 4(3): 333–352.

—— (2004) 'Critical differentials: Querying the incongruities within research on lesbian parent families', *Sexualities* 7(2): 167–182.

—— (2005) 'Locating lesbian parent families: Everyday negotiations of lesbian motherhood in Britain', *Gender, Place and Culture* 12(4): 419–432.

Gamson, J. (1998) *Freaks Talk Back: Tabloid Talk Shows and Sexual Nonconformity.* Chicago, IL: University of Chicago Press.

Giddens, A. (1992) *The Transformation of Intimacy: Sexuality, Love and Eroticism in Modern Societies.* Cambridge: Polity.

Gillies, V. (2003) *Family and Intimate Relationships: A Review of the Sociological Research.* London: South Bank University.

—— (2005) ' "Meeting parents" needs? Discourses of "support" and "inclusion" in family policy', *Critical Social Policy* 25(1): 70–90.

—— (2006) 'Working class mothers and school life: Exploring the role of emotional capital', *Gender and Education* 18(3): 281–293.

—— (2007) *Marginalised Mothers: Exploring Working-Class Experiences of Parenting.* London, New York: Routledge.

Gluckman, A. and Reed, B. (1997) 'The Gay Marketing Moment', in A. Gluckman and B. Reed (eds), *Homo Economics: Capitalism, Community and Lesbian and Gay Life*. New York: Routledge.

Goffman, E. (1973) *Stigma: Notes on the Management of Spoiled Identity*. Harmondsworth: Penguin.

Golombok, S. (2001) *Parenting. What Really Counts?* London: Routledge.

Gosling, V. K. (2008) ' "I've always managed, that's what we do": Social Capital and women's experiences of social exclusion', *Sociological Research Online* 13(1): 1–19.

Haimes, E. (2003) 'Embodied spaces, social places and Bourdieu: Locating and dislocating the child in family relationships', *Body and Society* 9(1): 11–33.

Haimes, E. and Weiner, K. (2000) ' "Everybody's got a dad ..." Issues for lesbian families in the management of donor insemination', *Sociology of Health and Illness* 22(4): 477–499.

Hanafin, J. and Lynch, A. (2002) 'Peripheral voices: Parental involvement, social class, and educational disadvantage', *British Journal of Sociology of Education* 23(1): 35–49.

Hare, J. and Richards, L. (1993) 'Children raised by lesbian couples. Does context of birth affect father and partner involvement?', *Family Relations* 42: 249–262.

Head, E. (2005) 'The captive mother? The place of home in the lives of lone mother', *Sociological Research Online* 10(3), available at http://www.socresonline.org.uk /10/3/ head.html [accessed 4th August 2008].

Hennessy, R. (2000) *Profit and Pleasure: Sexual Identities in Late Capitalism*. London: Taylor and Francis Group.

Hequembourg, A. (2004). 'Unscripted motherhood: Lesbian mothers negotiating incompletely institutionalized family relationships', *Journal of Social and Personal Relationships* 21(6): 739–762.

Hequembourg, A. and Farrell, P. (1999) 'Lesbian motherhood: Negotiating marginal-Mainsteam Identities', *Gender and Society* 13(4): 540–557.

Herman, D. (1997) *The Antigay Agenda: Orthodox Vision and the Christian Right*. Chicago, IL: University of Chicago Press.

Hicks, S. (2005) 'Is gay parenting bad for kids? Responding to the "very idea of difference" in research on lesbian and gay parents', *Sexualities* 8(2): 153–168.

Hicks, S. and McDermott, J. (eds) (1999) *Lesbian and Gay Fostering and Adoption: Extraordinary yet Ordinary*. London: Jessica Kingsley Publishers.

Hockey, J., Meah, A. and Robinson, V. (2007) *Mundane Heterosexualities: From Theory to Practices*. London: Palgrave Macmillan.

Hogben, S. and Coupland, J. (2000) 'Egg seeks sperm: End of Story ...? Articulating gay parenting in small ads for reproductive partners', *Discourse and Society* 11(4): 459–485.

Hostetler, A. J. and Cohler, B. J. (1997) 'Partnership, singlehood, and the lesbian and gay life course: A research agenda', *Journal of Gay, Lesbian and Bisexual Identity* 2(3/4): 199–230.

Hull, K. (2006) *Same-Sex Marriage: The Cultural Politics of Love and Law*. Cambridge: Cambridge University Press.

Jackson, S. (2001) 'Why a materialist feminism is (still) possible – and necessary', *Women's Studies International Forum* 24(3/4): 283–293.

—— (2007) 'Families, domesticity and intimacy: Changing relationships in changing times', in D. Richardson and V. Robinson (eds), *Introducing Gender and Women's Studies: Third Edition*. Basingstoke, New York: Palgrave Macmillan.

Jamieson, L. (1998) *Intimacy: Personal Relationships in Modern Societies*. Cambridge: Polity Press.

—— (2004) 'Intimacy, negotiated non-monogamy and the limits of the couple', in Duncombe, J., Harrison, K., Allan, G. and Marsden, D. (eds), *The State of Affairs: Explorations in Infidelity and Commitment*. London: Routledge.

Johnson, P. and Lawler, S. (2005) 'Coming Home to Love and Class', *Sociological Research Online* 10(3): 1–12 [accessed 4th August 2008].

Jones, C. (2005) 'Looking like a family: Negotiating bio-genetic continuity in British lesbian families using licensed donor insemination', *Sexualities* 8(2): 221–237.

Kefalas, M. (2003) *Working-Class Heroes: Protecting Home, Community, and Nation in a Chicago Neighbourhood*. California: University of California Press.

Klesse, C. (2007) 'Gender, sexuality, and race in post/modernisation theories on the intimate', in A. Cervantes-Carson and Rumsfeld N. (eds), *The Sexual Politics of Desire and Belonging. Interdisciplinary Readings on Sex and Sexaulity*. Tijnmuiden: Rodopi, pp. 59–79.

Kosciw, J. and Diaz, E. (2008) *Involved, Invisible, Ignored: The Experiences of Lesbian, Gay, Bisexual and Transgender Parents and Their Children in Our Nation's K-12 Schools*. Washington: The Gay, Lesbian and Straight Education Network.

Lareau, A. (2003) *Unequal Childhoods: Class, Race and Family Life*. London: University of California Press.

Lawler, S. (2000) *Mothering the Self: Mothers Daughters, Subjects*, London: Routledge. www.socresonline.org.uk/10/3/johnson.html.

Lewin, E. (1993) *Lesbian Mother: Accounts of Gender in American Culture*. Ithaca and London: Cornell University Press.

—— (1998) *Recognising Ourselves: Ceremonies of Lesbian and Gay Commitment*. New York: Columbia University Press.

Lewis, J. (2001) *The End of Marriage? Individualism and Intimate Relations*. Cheltenham: Edward Elgar.

Lindsay, J., Perlesz, A., Brown, R., McNair, R., Vaus, D. and Pitts, M. (2006) 'Stigma or respect: Lesbian-parented families negotiating school settings', *Sociology* 40(6): 1059–1077.

Lovell, T. (2000) 'Thinking feminism with and against Bourdieu', *Feminist Theory* 1(1): 11–32.

Mallon, G. P. (2004) *Gay Men Choosing Parenthood*. New York, Chichester, West Sussex: Columbia University Press.

McCall, L. (2005) 'The complexity of intersectionality', *Signs* 30(3): 1771–1800.

McDermott, E. (2004) 'Telling lesbian stories: Interviewing and the class dynamics of "talk"', *Women's Studies International Forum* 27(3): 177–187.

Meeks, C. and Stein, A. (2006) 'Refiguring the family: Towards a post-queer politics of gay and lesbian marriage', in D. Richardson, J. McLaughlin and M. Casey (eds), *Intersections in Feminist and Queer Theory*. Basingstoke: Palgrave Macmillan.

Mercier, L. R. and Harold, R. D. (2003) 'At the interface: Lesbian-parent families and their children's schools', *Children and Schools* 25: 35.

Moran, L. (2000) 'Homophobic violence: The hidden injuries of class', in S. R. Munt (ed.), *Cultural Studies and the Working Class: Subject to Change*. London: Cassell.

Morgan, D. H. J. (1975) *Social Theory and the Family*. London: Routledge.

Morgan Centre for the Study of Relationships and Personal Life (2006) *Gay and Lesbian 'Marriage': An Exploration of the Meanings and Significance of Legitimating Same-sex Relationships*. Economic and Social Research Council.

Murphy, J. S. (2001) 'Should lesbians count as infertile couples? Antilesbian discrimination in assisted reproduction', in M. Bernstein and R. Reimann (eds), *Queer Families, Queer Politics: Challenging Culture and the State*. New York: Columbia University Press.

Murray, C. (1990) *The Underclass Revisited*. American Enterprise Institute Online.

Namaste, K. (1996) 'Genderbashing: Perceived transgressions of normative sex-gender relations in public spaces', *Environment and Planning D – Society and Space* 14(2): 221–240.

Naples, N. (2004) 'Queer parenting in the new millennium', *Gender and Society* 18(6): 679–684.

—— (2007) 'Sexual citizenship in international context: Towards a comparative intersectional analysis of social regulation', in N. Rumens and A. Cervantes-Carson (eds), *Sexual Politics of Desire and Belonging*. Amsterdam: Rodopi.

Nardi, P. (ed) (1992) *Men's Friendships*. Newbury Park: Sage.

Nardi, P. (1999) *Gay Men's Friendships*. Chicago: Chicago University Press.

Nayak, A. and Kehily, M. J. (1996) 'Playing it straight: Masculinities, homophobias and schooling', *Journal of Gender Studies* 5: 211–230.

O'Brien, J. (2007) 'Queer tensions: The cultural politics of belonging and exclusion in same gender marriage debates', in N. Rumens and A. Cervantes-Carson (eds), *Sexual Politics of Desire and Belonging*. New York: Rodopi.

Pahl, R. E. (2002) 'Towards a more significant sociology of friendship', *European Journal of Sociology* 43(3): 410–423.

Parks, C. A. (1998) 'Lesbian parenthood: A review of the literature', *American Journal of Orthopsychiatry* 68: 376–389.

Penelope, J. (ed.) (1994) *Out of the Class Closet: Lesbians Speak*. Freedom, CA: The Crossing Press.

Perlesz, A. and McNair, R. (2004) 'Lesbian parenting: Insiders' voices', *Australian and New Zealand Journal of Family Therapy* 25(3): 129–140.

Perlesz, A., Brown, R., McNair, R., Lindsay, J., Pitts, M. and de Vaus, D. (2006) 'Lesbian family disclosure: Authenticity and safety within private and public domains', *Lesbian and Gay Psychology Review* 7(1): 54–65.

Phelan, S. (2001) *Sexual Strangers: Gays, Lesbians and Dilemmas of Citizenship*. Philadelphia: Temple University Press.

Phoenix, A., Woollett, A. and Lloyd, E. (eds) (1991) *Motherhood: Meanings, Practices and Ideologies*. London: Sage.

Plummer, K. (1995) *Telling Sexual Stories: Power, Change and Social Worlds*. London: Routledge.

—— (2008) 'Studying sexualities for a better world? Ten years of sexualities', *Sexualities* 11(7): 7–22.

Putman, R. D. (1993) 'The prosperous community: Social capital and public life', *American Prospect* 4(13): 35–42.

⸻ (1995) 'Bowling alone: America's declining social capital', *Journal of Democracy* 6(1): 65–78.

Raffo, S. (ed.) (1997) *Queerly Classed: Gay Men and Lesbians Write about Class.* Boston, MA: South End Press.

Rapp, R. (1982) 'Family and class is contemporary America: Notes toward an understanding of Ideology', in B. Thorne and M. Yalom (eds), *Rethinking the Family.* New York: Longman, pp. 168–187.

⸻ (2000) *Testing Women, Testing the Fetus: The Social Impact of Amniocentesis in America.* New York: Routledge.

Reay, D. (1995) 'They employ cleaners to do that: Habitus in the primary classroom', *British Journal of Sociology of Education* 16(3): 353–371.

Reay, D. (2000) 'Children's urban landscapes: Configurations of class and place', in Munt, S. R. (ed.), *Cultural Studies and the Working Class: Subject to Change.* London: Cassell.

⸻ (2004) 'Mostly roughs and toughs': Social class, race and representation in inner city schooling', *Sociology* 38(5): 1005–1023.

Renold, E. (2000) ' "Coming out": Gender (hetero)sexuality and the primary school', *Gender and Education* 12(3): 309–326.

Reese, E. (2005) *Backlash against Welfare Mothers: Past and Present.* Berkeley: University of California Press.

Reynolds, S. (2007) 'Changing marriage? Messing with Mr. In-Between?: Reflections upon media debates on same-sex marriage in Ireland', *Sociological Research Online* 12(1): 1–19.

Richardson, D. (2004) 'Locating sexualities: From here to normality', *Sexualities* 7(4), 391–411.

⸻ (2005) 'Desiring sameness? The rise of a neoliberal politics of normalisation', *Antipode* 37(3): 515–535.

Richardson, D., McLaughlin, J. and Casey, M. (eds) (2006) *Intersections in Feminist and Queer Theory.* Basingstoke: Palgrave Macmillan.

Ryan-Flood, R. (2005) 'Contested heteronormativities: Discourses of fatherhood among lesbian parents in Sweden and Ireland', *Sexualities* 8(2): 239–254.

Savage, M., Bagnall, G. and Longhurst, B. (2005) *Globalisation and Belonging.* London: Sage.

Sayer, A. (2005) *The Moral Significance of Class.* Cambridge: Cambridge University Press.

Schneider, D. M. (1968) *American Kinship: A Cultural Account.* Englewood Cliffs, NJ: Prentice Hall.

Schilt, K. (2008) 'The unfinished business of sexuality: comment on Andersen', *Gender and Society* 22(1): 109–114.

Seidman, S., Meeks, C. and Traschen, F. (2002) 'Beyond the closet? The changing social meaning of homosexuality in the United States', in C. L. William and A. Stein (eds), *Sexuality and Gender.* Oxford: Blackwell.

Sennett, R. and Cobb, J. (1972) *The Hidden Injuries of Class.* New York: Vintage Books.

Shipman, B. and Smart, C. (2007) ' "It's made a huge difference": Recognition, rights and the personal significance of civil partnership', *Sociological Research Online* 12(1): 1–24.

Short, L. (2007) 'Lesbian mothers living well in the context of heterosexism and discrimination: Resources, strategies and legislative change', *Feminism and Psychology* 17(1): 57–74.

Silva, E. B. (ed.) (1996) *Good Enough Mothering? Feminist Perspectives on Lone Motherhood*. New York and London: Routledge.

Skeggs, B. (1997) *Formations of class and gender*. London: Sage.

—— (1999) 'Matter out of place: Visibility and sexualities in leisure spaces', *Leisure Studies* 18(3): 213–232.

—— (2001) 'The toilet paper: Femininity, class and mis-recognition', *Women's Studies International Forum* 24(3/4): 295–307.

—— (2004) *Class, Self, Culture*. London: Routledge.

Skolnick, A. (1992) *The Intimate Environment: Exploring Marriage and the Family*. New York: Harper and Collins.

Smeaton, D. (2006) *Dads and Their Babies: A Household Analysis*. Policy Studies Institute, University of Westminster, Equal Opportunities Commission.

Smith, A. M. (1994) *New Right Discourse on Race and Sexuality: Britain, 1968–1990*. Cambridge: Cambridge University Press.

—— (1997) 'The good homosexual and the dangerous queer: Resisting the "New Homophobia"', in L. Segal (ed.), *New Sexual Agendas*. London: Palgrave Macmillan.

Smith, F. and Barker, J. (2000) 'Out of school, in school: A social geography of out of school care', in S. Holloway and G. Valentine (eds), *Children's Geographies*. London: Routledge, pp. 245–256.

Stacey, J. (1993) 'Good riddance to "the family": A response to David Popenoe', *Journal of Marriage and the Family* 55(3): 545–547.

—— (1996) *In the Name of the Family: Rethinking Family Values in the Postmodern Age*. Boston, Massachusetts: Beacon Press.

—— (2006) 'Gay parenthood and the decline of paternity as we knew it', *Sexualities* 9(1): 27–55.

Stacey, J. and Biblarz, T. J. (2001) '(How) Does the sexual orientation of parents matter?', *American Sociological Review* 66(2): 159–183.

Stein, A. (1997) *Sex and Sensibility: Stories of Lesbian Generation*. Berkely: University of California Press.

—— (2005) 'Make room for daddy: Anxious masculinity and emergent homophobia in neopatriarchal politics', *Gender and Society* 19(5): 601–620.

Sullivan, A. (1995) *Virtually Normal: An Argument About Homosexuality*. New York: Knopf.

—— (2001) 'Alma-mater: Family "Outings" and the making of the modern other mother (MOM)', in M. Bernstein and R. Reimann (eds), *Queer Families, Queer Politics: Challenging Culture and the State*. New York: Columbia University Press.

—— (2004) *The Family of Woman: Lesbian Mothers, Their Children and the Undoing of Gender*. Berkeley, Los Angeles, London: University of California Press.

Tasker, Y. and Golombok, S. (1997) *Growing up in a Lesbian Family*. New York: Guilford Press.

Taylor, Y. (2004) 'Negotiation and navigation: An exploration of the spaces/places of working-class lesbians', *Sociological Research Online* 9(1): 1–24, available at http://www.socresonline.org.uk/9/1/taylor.html [accessed 4th August 2008].

—— (2005) 'Classed in a classless climate', *Feminism and Psychology* 15(4): 491–500.

—— (2007) *Working-Class Lesbian Life: Classed Outsiders*. London: Palgrave Macmillan.

—— (2008) ' "That's not really my scene": Working-class lesbians in (and out of) place', *Sexualities* 11(5): 523–546.

—— (2009) 'Interesting intersections? Researching class, gender and sexuality', in M. Berger and K. Guidroz (eds), *The Intersectional Approach: Transforming Women's and Gender Studies through Race, Class and Gender*. North Carolina: University of Chapel Hill.

Thompson, C. (2001) 'Strategic naturalizing: Kinship on an infertility Clinic', in S. Franklin and S. McKinnon (eds), *Relative Values Reconfiguring Kinship Studies*. Durham, NC: Duke University Press.

Urry, J. (2000) *Sociology Beyond Societies: Mobilities for the Twenty-First Century*. London: Routledge.

Valentine, G. (1993) 'Hetero-sexing space: Lesbian perceptions and experiences of everyday spaces', *Environment and Planning D – Society and Space* 9(3): 395–413.

—— (2007) 'Theorizing and researching intersectionality: A challenge for feminist geography', *The Professional Geographer* 59(1): 10–21.

Valetine, G., Skelton, T. and Butler, R. (2003) 'Coming out and outcomes: Negotiating lesbian and identities with, an in, the family', *Environment and Planning D: Society and Space* 21: 479–499.

Vicinus, M. (1985) *Independent Women: Work and Community for Single Women, 1850–1920*. London: Virago.

Vincent, C. (2000) *Including Parents? Citizenship, Education and Parental Agency*. Buckingham: Open University Press.

—— (ed.) (2002) *Social Justice, Education and Identity*. London: Routledge.

Waites, M. (2005) 'The fixity of sexual identities in the public sphere: Biomedical knowledge, liberalism and the heterosexual/homosexual binary in late modernity', *Sexualities* 8(5): 539–569.

Walby, S. (1997) *Gender Transformations*. London: Routledge.

Walkerdine, V. and Lucey, H. (1989) *Democracy in the Kitchen: Regulating Mothers and Socialising Daughters*. London: Virago.

Walkerdine, V., Lucey, H. and Melody, J. (2001) *Growing Up Girl: Psychosocial Explorations of Gender and Class*. Basingstoke: Palgrave Macmillan.

Wallis, A. and VanEvery, J. (2000) 'Sexuality in the primary school', *Sexualities* 3(4): 409–423.

Wan, M. (1995) *Building Social Capital: Self-help in the 21st Century Welfare State*. London: IPPR.

Weeks, J. (1995) *Invented Moralities: Sexual Value in an Age of Uncertainty*. Oxford: Polity Press.

—— (1996) 'The construction of homosexuality', in S. Seidman (ed.), *Queer Theory/Sociology*. Oxford: Blackwell Publishing.

Weeks, J., Heaphy, B. and Donovan, C. (2001) *Same Sex Intimacies: Families of Choice and Other Life Experiments*. London, New York: Routledge.

Weston, K. (1991). *Families We Choose: Lesbians, Gays, Kinship*. New York: Columbia University Press.

—— (1995) 'Get thee to a big city: Sexual imaginary and the great gay migration', *GLQ* 2: 253–277.

Wilson, R. A. (2007) 'With friends like these: The liberalization of queer family policy', *Critical Social Policy* 27(1): 50–76.

Wright, E. J. (1998). *Lesbian Step Families: An Ethnography of Love*. Binghamton, NY: Harrington Park Press.

Yuval-Davis, N. (2006) 'Intersectionality and feminist politics', *European Journal of Women's Studies* 13(3): 193–209.

Zweig, M. (2000) *The Working-Class Majority: America's Best Kept Secret*. Ithaca: ILR Press.

Index